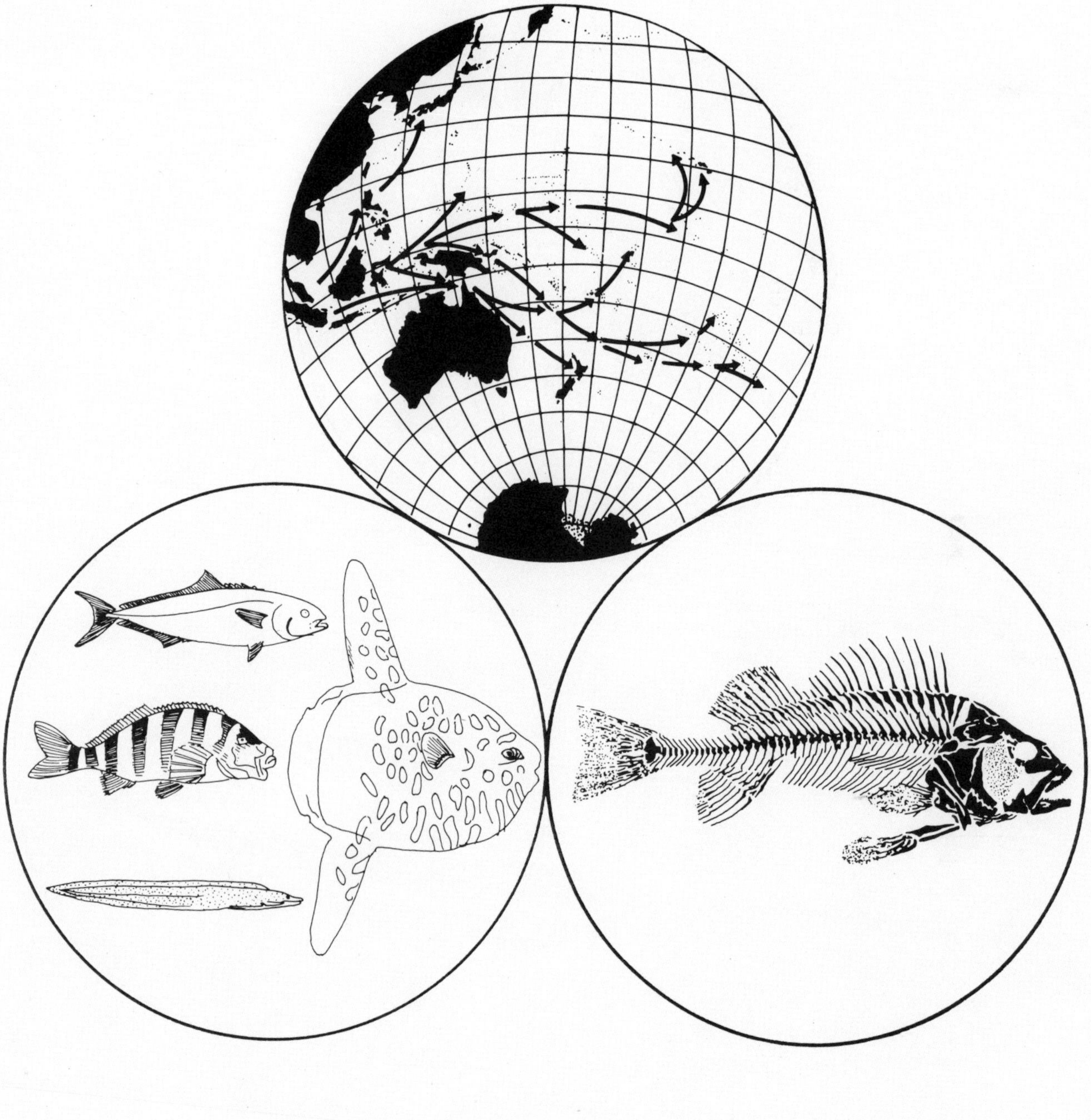

Wade Doak's
WORLD OF
NEW ZEALAND FISHES

WADE DOAK was born in Canterbury in 1940. His first diving experience prompted him to write *The Elingamite and its Treasure* in 1969. Since then he has concentrated on exploring New Zealand waters, observing marine life and recording it in photographs. These activities have resulted in four books, *Beneath New Zealand Seas*, *Fishes of the New Zealand Region*, *The Cliff Dwellers*, and *Wade Doak's World of New Zealand Fishes*.

He has been on three major South Seas underwater and anthropological research expeditions, described in *Sharks and Other Ancestors* and *Islands of Survival*.

Since 1975 Wade and his wife, Jan, have carried out intensive research into the capacities of dolphins and whales in the wild. The excitement and wonder of their encounters are captured in *Dolphin Dolphin* and *Encounters with Whales & Dolphins*.

In 1984 Wade Doak produced his first historical study, *The Burning of the 'Boyd'*, a fascinating saga of culture clash in early New Zealand. His diving autobiography, *Ocean Planet*, was also published in 1984.

During all his diving life the complex social lives of fishes have fascinated him intensely. In 1990 he had the opportunity with Television New Zealand to make two 'Wild South' documentaries complementary to this book.

By the same author

The Elingamite and its Treasure
Beneath New Zealand Seas
Sharks and Other Ancestors
Islands of Survival
Fishes of the New Zealand Region
The Cliff Dwellers
Diving for Treasure
Dolphin Dolphin
The Burning of the 'Boyd'
Ocean Planet
Encounters with Whales & Dolphins

Wade Doak's
WORLD OF
NEW ZEALAND FISHES

Hodder & Stoughton
AUCKLAND LONDON SYDNEY TORONTO

This book is dedicated to the creation of marine reserves
at appropriate intervals around all the coastlines of the world.

Copyright © 1991 Wade Doak
First published 1991
ISBN 0 340 533242

All rights reserved. No part of this publication may be reproduced or transmitted in any form or by any means, electronic or mechanical including photocopy, recording, or any information storage and retrieval system, without permission in writing from the publisher.

Book design by Hal Chapman
Typeset by Typocrafters Ltd, Auckland.
Printed and bound by Kyodo Printing Ltd, Singapore, for
 Hodder & Stoughton Ltd, 46 View Road, Glenfield, Auckland, New Zealand.

Acknowledgements

Over the years that they have helped me I owe a great debt of gratitude to diving scientists A. M. Ayling, D. R. Schiel, J. H. Choat, L. D. Ritchie, B. C. Russell, R. V. Grace, G. R. V. Anderson, G. R. Allen, W. A. Starck, K. Tricklebank and M. P. Francis. Dr W. J. Ballantine of Leigh Marine Laboratory has been a constant source of advice and inspiration.

For assistance with drawings and diagrams I am grateful to A. M. Ayling, Professor John Morton, G. and J. Couchman, and Dr Michael Kingsford. Three of the photographs I have used belong respectively to: Peter Thompson, page 9; Roger Kempthorne, page 183; and Jaan Voot, page 185. To my very dear friend Hal Chapman, who has designed and illustrated so many of my books, special appreciation is due.

Lastly I wish to acknowledge the immense help I have had from my wife Jan, both under the sea and in the preparation of this manuscript.

★ ★ ★

I wish to thank the Natural History Unit of Television New Zealand for assistance in the making of two 'Wild South' documentaries complementary to this book, 'Masters of Inner Space' and 'City Under the Sea'. Readers will find much in those documentaries which parallels and extends the material in this book.

Contents

Prologue: Reef fishes world-wide — 8

PART ONE
Masters of inner space: reef fish form and function

Fish design — 12
Swimming styles — 16
Fin functions — 16
The fish's head — 22
Evolution of fish design — 23
The sensory world of fishes — 28
The functions of colour in reef fishes — 32

PART TWO
City under the sea: portrait of a reef fish community at the Poor Knights Islands

The Poor Knights community — 42
The guilds — 46

Guild of the plankton pickers
  Pink maomao — 50
  Splendid perch — 55
  Butterfly perch — 56
  Demoiselle — 58
  Blue maomao — 64
  Trevally — 66
  Koheru — 67
  Sunfish — 68
  Golden snapper — 70
  Slender roughy — 71
  Big eye — 72

Guild of the open-water hunters
  Kingfish — 74
  Kahawai — 75
  John dory — 76

Guild of the plant grazers and browsers
  Black angelfish — 78
  Parore — 84
  Marblefish — 84
  Silver drummer — 85
  Butterfish — 86

Guild of the invertebrate gleaners
  Red moki — 88
  Painted moki — 91
  Blue moki — 92
  Porae — 92

Guild of the invertebrate grazers
  Leatherjacket — 94
  Sharpnosed pufferfish — 98
  Mado — 100
  Bluefish — 101

Guild of the invertebrate browsers
  Snapper — 102
  Tarakihi — 104
  Lord Howe coralfish — 106
  Long-finned boarfish — 108

Kelpfish	110
Flounder	110
Eagle ray	112
Sting ray	112

Guild of the bottom grubbers

Goatfish	114

Guild of the bottom fossickers

Wrasses	118
Spotty	121
Banded wrasse	124
Scarlet wrasse	126
Orange wrasse	128
Green wrasse	130
Red pigfish	132
Fox fish	134
Elegant wrasse	135
Rainbow fish	136
Sandager's wrasse	138

Guild of the parasite pickers

Combfish	146
Crimson cleanerfish	152

Guild of the bottom stalkers

Morays and congers	158
Grey moray	160
Yellow moray	160
Mottled moray	162
Mosaic moray	162
Speckled moray	162
Conger eel	165
Garden eel	165
Lizard fish	166
Scorpion fish	168
Rock cod	170
Giant stargazer	171
Triplefins and blennies	172
Halfbanded perch	180
Yellowbanded perch	181
Toadstool grouper	183
Goldribbon grouper	183
Spotted black grouper	184
Hapuku	187
Reef fish ecology through time and space	188

PART THREE
Reef fishes of tropical waters

Tropical relatives	194

PART FOUR
The learning capacities of reef fishes

How smart are reef fishes?	212
Appendix A: The families	217
Appendix B: Dayshift and nightshift guilds	219
Further reading	220
Index of common and scientific names	221
Index of scientific names	223

Prologue
Reef fishes world-wide

Having dived in two oceans and both hemispheres I now realise that, while species may differ, the basic pattern of reef fish communities holds true all over the world. Despite local names and variations in families (see Appendix A), there is a cosmopolitan reef fish scene. Whether in the Caribbean, California, Japan, the Mediterranean, southern Africa or Australia, I find myself descending through silvery schools of jacks and scad, bright colonies of anthias and damselfishes, all feeding on planktonic animals. Through them hurtle powerful, streamlined yellowtails on the attack. Near the reef hovers a school of sea bream awaiting the evening hours before descending to feed. Rays skim the sand like undersea birds. A john dory drifts by like a shadow, stalking its mid-water prey; from crevices and holes gape-jawed morays stare. Angelfishes thrust their pouting mouths into encrusting life as colourful as themselves. At the portals of caves and tunnels, solitary groupers and scorpion fishes rest, their jaws visible in the half-light.

Out on the white sand goatfishes dabble their barbels in search of tasty morsels, and lizard fishes lie poised, ready to engulf passing prey with their jack-in-the-box jaws. Everywhere over the reef multi-hued wrasses weave about, snipping at delicacies, while the ubiquitous triggerfishes and puffers nibble at sponges and other organisms too tough for most fishes to stomach. Over the bottom, tiny blennies and triplefins jump and pause, erecting their dorsal fins as signal flags and chasing neighbours from their territories.

In 1972 my book *Fishes of the New Zealand Region* was published, presenting descriptions and colour plates of some 80 different reef fishes. That book had a scientific approach and was favoured with several reprints. Since then several excellent guide books have appeared, which cover this ground exhaustively. There is another way of regarding reef fishes; a more aesthetic, entertaining and philosophical approach that does not regard them as a collection of bones, spines and scales to be preserved in alcohol, sport on a hook, or a tasty meal.

Since I began my studies, the Poor Knights Islands have become a marine reserve. In certain areas their inhabitants are protected from all molestation. Without any keepers, with no walls and no food handouts — just the stroke of a pen on paper — we have discovered how to create the most exciting of all natural zoos. In marine reserves the fishes are much more trusting and approachable than most terrestrial wild animals, and we soon learn to value each individual for the delight it can give countless visitors, rather than for its transient role as a fish dinner.

It may be that in our lifetimes reef fishes will be regarded much as birds are today. We may farm a few species or raise them in large enclosures, like salmon, but the rest we will protect, study and enjoy for their beauty of form and colour, and for their ecological value. Just as it would be unthinkable to bring home a sackful of native birds, one day we may realise that reef fishes are worth more alive than dead. Because they live in the sea and we breathe air, until now we have had a much lower regard for fishes than for birds. This is changing, and in my lifetime the edge of the sea has ceased to be a barrier to our bodies. I hope this will soon extend to our minds and our ethics, and that we will look on the reef fish communities, which are the most vulnerable and most accessible to man, as deserving of extensive protection. We have been destroying our marine libraries and art galleries.

New Zealand's first marine reserve was declared in 1975 at Goat Island near Leigh, an hour's drive from Auckland city. Since then the recovery of reef fish populations there has been dramatic. Local fishermen, once concerned at losing fishing territory, now appreciate the value of the reserve in restocking adjacent waters. The people of Auckland city flock there in such numbers over the summer months that car-parking is a major problem. At the sea's edge, snapper and blue maomao swarm to be hand-fed by unbelieving Japanese tourists. Retired people, who would normally play bowls, come there to snorkel amongst the friendly reef fishes on quiet summer evenings. Hundreds of young people have cut their teeth as divers within this reserve, which was mainly set up as an adjunct to Auckland University's Goat Island Marine Laboratory.

In writing this book I have a dream: if only the intrinsic qualities of reef fishes were widely appreciated, and along all the shores of the world, at reasonable intervals, we could establish more and more such reserves to protect reef fishes and their ecosystems. Just as every city has amenities such as libraries, parks and gardens, art galleries and zoos, an accessible undersea area should be set aside for marine recreation and education. Functioning at the same time as conservation zones, a system of such coastal reserves would be the best way to ensure that the sea could continue to contribute food for a crowded planet. Otherwise the negative trend is all too clear. Like canaries in a coal mine, healthy reef fish populations are a measure of the impact humanity is having on this planet's most vital organ: the ocean.

Reef fishes swarm around Sue Thompson and daughter Hannah at Leigh Marine Reserve — an experience that could be the heritage of every child...
(Peter Thompson)

Deep scene: 'red mullet' or goatfish at Poor Knights Islands Marine Reserve.

Part One

Masters of inner space: Reef fish form and function

Fish design

Finning slowly and sinuously like a fish, I thread my way through a golden jungle of kelp plants. Beyond the glade of rubbery stalks I glimpse a patch of sand and a wall of rock. Where they meet, the cliff is undercut in a deep recess. I peer within. As my eyes become accustomed to the gloom I see it is swarming with reef fishes: a scorpion fish roosts on a small outcrop; a moray gape-jaws from a crevice; eight other kinds of reef fishes hover quietly or weave to and fro in the twilight. Many are touching each other, brushing heads with fins, but there is no hostility. Out over the sunlit coralline sand another ten species swim about at varying speeds and with different swimming styles. Beneath the rock are the plant eaters, who have gorged themselves at first light, and the night hunters. Outside, the day shift is at work.

If we look closely at a community of reef fishes, learning to recognise each species, new insights develop. The immense range of body forms provides a key to understanding how such a complex, closely knit community functions. How can so many species co-exist in one small area? Where do all these different-shaped mouths and bodies find their food? On land we have few chances to get such an intimate view of animal society.

The fish is basically a mobile set of jaws powered through the sea by a muscular body and a flexible array of fins; but the dense waterworld has sculptured its form perfectly to match its lifestyle. As aircraft designers know, the ideal shape to maximise volume and minimise drag is the spindle: fast-moving fishes conserve energy with this shape. But not all fishes need to go fast. Of the 20,000 different kinds in the world, the average is only 15 cm long. Most of these live in coastal reef systems. Each reef fish is precisely adapted to the one particular niche in the reef that supplies it with food and shelter, energy and survival. There are many more opportunities for small fishes than large.

The basic food for animals is plant material. However, if all the fishes on a reef were plant eaters, they would be competing with each other for nutrients. Instead, they have branched out to tap every available energy source in that community. Flowing over the reef day and night, a parade of tiny, floating creatures provides a feast for plankton pickers, who use the reef as refuge and dormitory. Along the cliff face big, open-water predators swoop, ready to snap up any unwary fish, especially in the dim light at dawn and dusk.

Across the reef meadows range the plant-eating fishes. On coral reefs little seaweed is visible, but only because it is constantly grazed to a thin fuzz by vast armies of parrotfishes. In cooler waters tall, tough seaweeds abound, but only because few fishes can digest them. Many more species feed on the myriad, encrusting life forms festooning every inch of rock: a wall of tiny mouths that suck, filter and ensnare the passing parade of plankton. And then there are all the mobile creatures that crawl, wriggle and creep amidst this array, grazing the sea plants or preying upon each other. Each is a potential meal for the fish adapted to eating it.

Plant-eating fishes each have their special preferences and modes of feeding; and so have all the carnivores. One nibbles sponges; another nips off the stinging tentacles of corals; strong jaws crunch limpets; baby sea-urchins are vacuum-cleaned from crevices by kissing mouths; and worms are dabbled for beneath the sand by sensitive feelers.

Only because of all these specialised modes of feeding can such a variety of animals live together in relative harmony, without one outdoing its neighbours and taking all. Instead, over the 370 million years since fishes evolved from some worm-like ancestor, they have exploited every possible energy source. From pole to pole, in ocean, lake and stream, they have found every opportunity not already tapped by others in a crowded world. This radiation of species into so many food niches has led to the immense variation in body plan and the harmony I saw in that rocky recess.

From the spindle form of fast, pelagic (open sea) fishes, to the upright, slow-moving seahorse in its weedy refuge, the demands of lifestyle have wrought miracles in the basic fish design. On the reef there is no need for a high-speed body, either for attack or escape. Handy hiding places abound, and a formidable array of defences for the slow mover has evolved. Furthermore, there are many more opportunities for finding a meal that require stealth, disguise or manoeuvrability, rather than sheer speed. Each of these requirements demanded evolution away from the classic spindle form of the high seas predator.

Some, such as rays, flounders and stargazers, are horizontally compressed for sea-floor fossicking and stalking. Conversely, others have deep, vertically compressed bodies that facilitate mid-water stalking of other fishes, or delicate manoeuvring into cracks and crannies to nip off encrusting life or pry loose the wrigglers and crawlers.

Still other opportunities exist for fishes with tapering cylindrical bodies, able to hunt over the bottom or make rapid lunges at overhead prey. Even more elongate forms muscle into all the galleries, chambers and confines of the reef where crabs and other mobile creatures lurk: fishes such as rock cods, morays and conger eels.

From the perfect spindle form (kingfish, centre right), fishes have adapted their bodies in many extremes to suit lifestyle: from the circular sunfish to the elongate eel and deep-bodied red moki (bottom right).

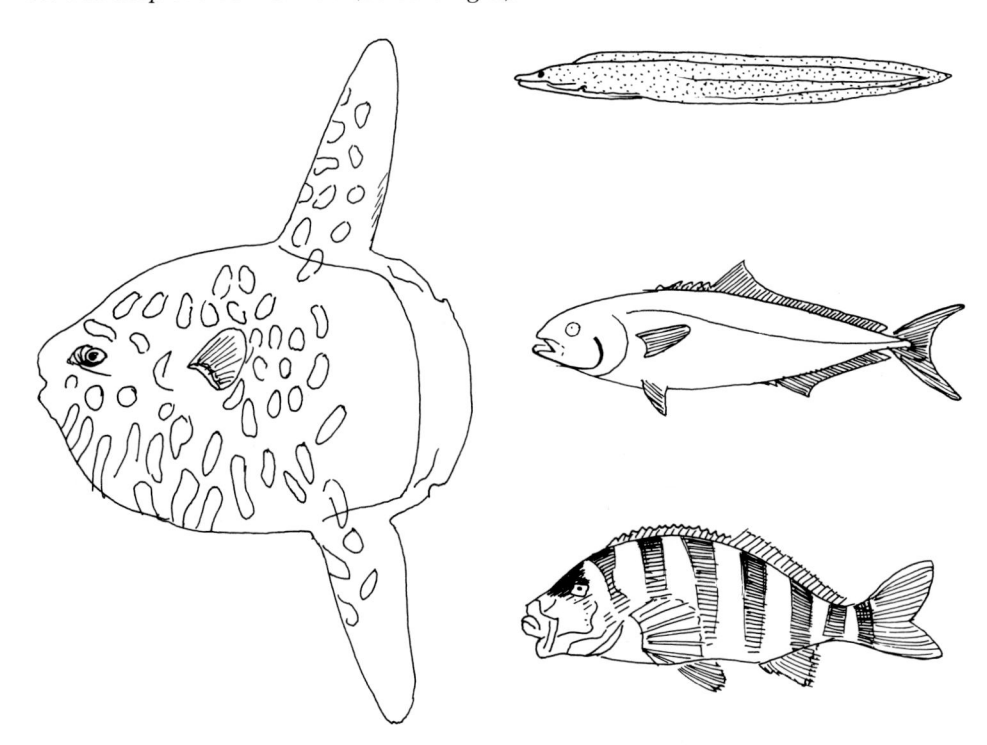

Fish Design
Spindle-shaped for speed: kingfish.

Flattened for bottom feeding: eagle ray.

Wafer thin for mid-water hunting: john dory.
Elongate for stalking in fissures: grey moray.

Swimming styles

Closely related to the effect of lifestyle on fish design are the modes of propulsion reef fishes use. All fishes have three basic sources of power: wave action of the body muscles, fin movement, and the water-jet effect of gill pumps. Depending on their needs, any combination of these may be used and there are four basic swimming methods: trevally-style, wrasse-style, triggerfish-style and eel-style.

As I look around the reef I see fast, spindle-shaped fishes — kingfishes, koheru and trevally — cleaving the water with rapid flexures of the rear third of their silvery bodies and thwacking, vee-shaped tails. Over the rocks slower, deep-bodied fishes like moki mooch about with gentle, muscular undulations from head to tail, braking with pectoral fins, poising on outcrops and turning on the fulcrum of a raised dorsal with the rudder action of a broad tail. If they are alarmed, this same powerful tail can give them a fast start, but they cannot maintain high speed and soon seek refuge.

Close to the bottom, wrasses scull with rhythmically beating pectoral fins. For them the tail is just a rudder — any flexure of the body would be a hindrance as their sharp eyes and needle teeth search sand and rock for minute prey animals.

Triggerfishes and puffers have rigid bodies for defence and make little use of body flexure. Tails folded like fans, they waft to and fro or glide close to the rocks, powered by their rear-angled dorsal and anal fins. Looking closely, I see waves of movement rippling along their fins, pushing the water backwards. Such fishes can hover very efficiently and even move in reverse as they feed head down over a rocky bottom or reverse into a refuge. Seahorses and john dory also use this swimming style.

Lurking predators like scorpion fishes rest on the bottom, ready to spring into action with a jet-propelled boost from their large gill flaps. Over the sand a moray writhes, to vanish into a crevice. With eels, the body flexures are extreme to compensate for the friction such length creates. At each bend in its body circular eddies develop, so that the eel literally rolls through the water between liquid roller bearings. Since river eels have to travel vast distances to reach remote breeding grounds in mid-ocean, this swimming mode must be efficient. Rock cod and oblique-swimming triplefins also use this swimming style.

Fin functions

It was once thought that fins had a major role in fish propulsion, but, except for the pectoral scullers and fin undulators, fins are mainly used for the delicate, precise manoeuvring that life on the reef demands. Although fishes live in a world of much diminished gravity, a 20 kg fish still weighs 1 kg in the sea. Buoyancy from the swim bladder would compensate for much of this weight, but it is still slightly negative and a small amount of lift is needed. This the pectoral fins provide, enabling the fish to hover. The fins also serve as brakes. Like an oar, one pectoral thrusts out and the fish veers aside; for sudden braking both fins are thrust out. From the keel, pelvic (or ventral) fins do likewise, besides stabilising the fish against any excess lift the pectorals may create. Also, respired water from the gills may drive the fish forward slightly, so sinuous back-paddling of the pectorals counteracts this, keeping the fish on station. Anybody who has tried to design a small submarine would appreciate the elegant control of a reef fish; especially the plankton feeders, the 'swallows of the sea', with their countless delicate fin movements — a flick of the scissor tail, a hover, a glide — keeping the nimble fishes on course, rising or descending in pursuit of their fast-moving prey. Other fishes with small pectorals lack this dexterity and swerve aside from obstacles rather than stop and hover.

Rays fly through the sea with rhythmic undulations of their enlarged pectoral fins; the tail provides no propulsion at all. With its wing-like pectorals, the flying fish can leap out and glide above the surface for up to 10 seconds at 32 km per hour.

Pelvic fins (also called 'ventrals', depending on their position) may be just in front or behind the pectorals, according to body form. Some fishes have none. These fins provide balance and prevent fore and aft pitching. They also serve as undercarriage for bottom-lurking species, such as lizard-fishes. With deep-bodied fishes, pectorals are often high on the sides, and there are no pelvic fins. As they swim, the tail is often folded like a fan.

Dorsal and anal fins keep the fish on an even keel, correcting any tendency to roll, and help them maintain a true course. Their importance is obvious with deep-bodied fishes like the john dory and long-finned boarfish, which have high dorsals to provide stability. With eels, the dorsal and anal fins are continuous with the tail. They act as stabilisers to prevent rolling and assist in turns. Congers and morays have no pelvic fins, and the morays dispense with pectorals as well. For many reef fishes, the dorsal and anal fins also serve to maximise body size in aggressive and sexual displays. For signalling purposes they often bear special markings, such as dots or tiny coloured flags, as does the tail. Sharp dorsal spines provide defence for some fishes.

While many fishes, such as the trevally (top left), are propelled by the tail and tail fin, some like the spotty (top right) use a sculling action of the pectorals. With eels power comes from travelling waves of curvature along their entire length. Stiff-bodied leatherjackets just ripple dorsal and anal fins.
(Sue Thompson, 'Fish of the Marine Reserve', Leigh Laboratory, 1981)

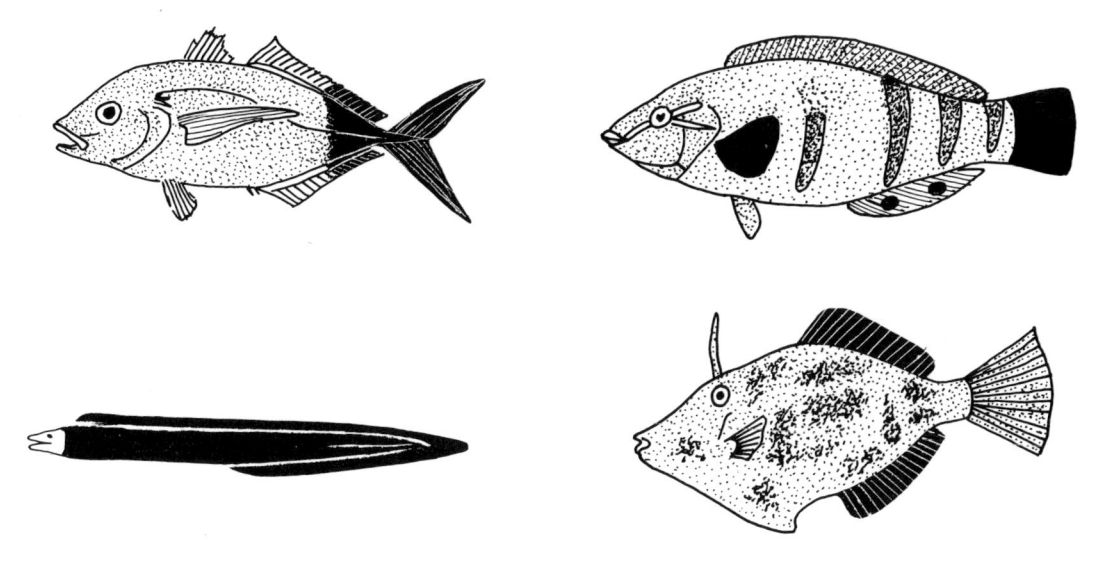

Tail fins (caudals) vary widely in shape and function. With high-speed, pelagic fishes, the tail is vee-shaped to minimise friction, as with a jet plane. For deeper-bodied fishes, only a moderate tail vee is needed, the broader surface providing rapid acceleration for attack or escape.

Fishes that live in shallow, turbulent waters often have a vee-less, rudder-shaped tail to counter violent eddies and swirls. Weed-eating fishes, such as the drummer, show this trait. Groupers that lurk on the bottom and lunge rapidly at prey also have broad tails for sprint starts. Wrasses use their tails as a rudder for flight reactions and for sexual display, but not as a main source of propulsion. For the bizarre sunfish the tail is just a vertical steering flap, with so little propulsive function the fish cannot react quickly to escape, and divers can easily overcome the mighty creature to observe or photograph it. Dolphins treat the sunfish as a toy. But once the tall dorsal and anal fins overcome its inertia, sculling from side to side in unison, the sunfish can leap from the sea several times in succession, flopping on its side with resounding splashes.

Leatherjackets attain manoevrability by reversing the ripple movements of anal and dorsal fins.
(Heinrich Hertel, Structure, Form and Movement. Reinhold, New York, 1966)

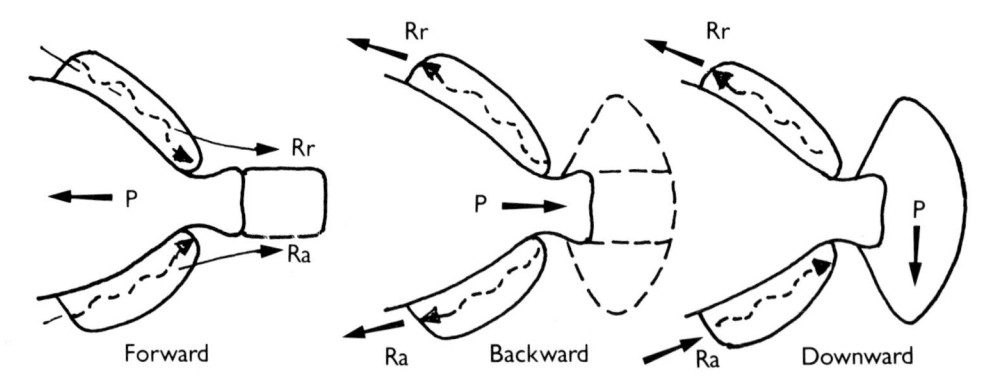

P = resultant thrust
Rr = fin flow induced by undulation of dorsal fin
Ra = flow induced by undulation of anal fin

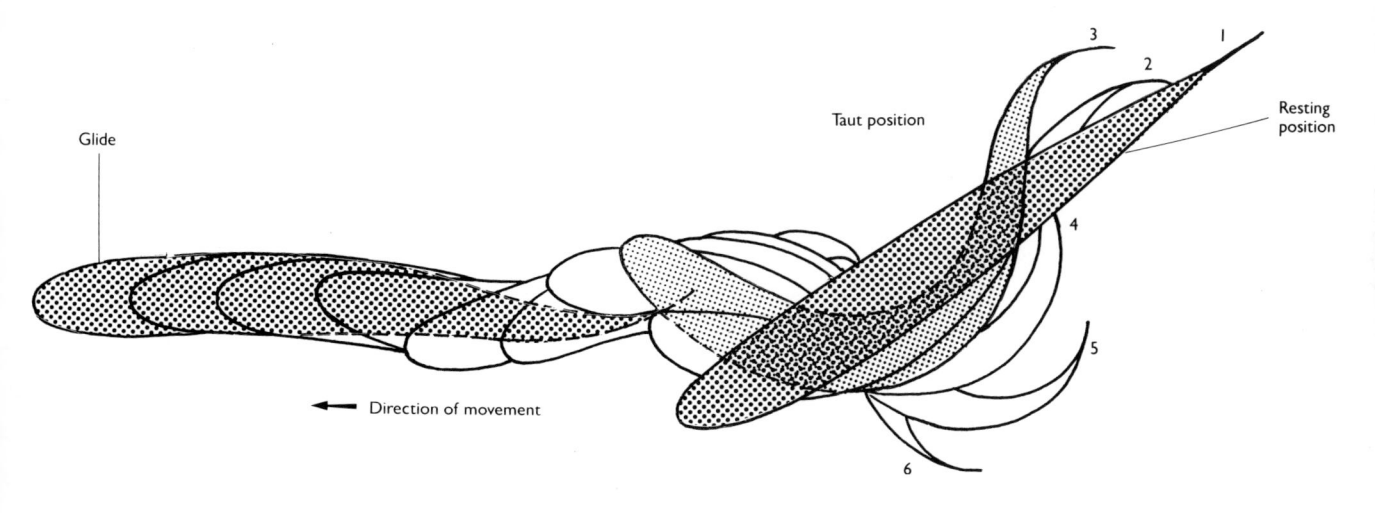

Fishes with fast start tails achieve rapid acceleration from rest by a process of bending and twisting.
(Heinrich Hertel, *Structure, Form and Movement*. Reinhold, New York, 1966)

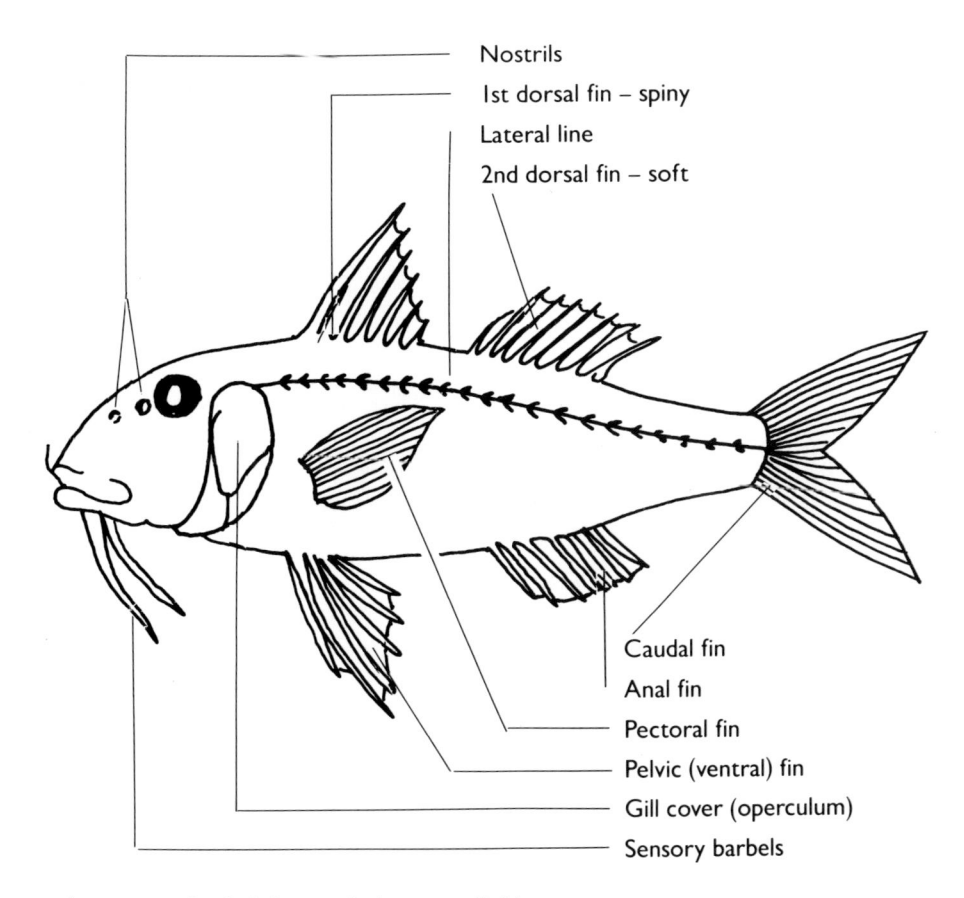

Anatomy of a fish (example is a goatfish).

19

Fin Functions
Pectoral sculler: red pigfish.

Tail swimmer: golden snapper. *Ripple-fin swimmer: leatherjacket.*

Fast start tail: green wrasse.

Grasping pectoral fins: kelpfish. *Pectoral fins as brakes: butterfly perch.*

The fish's head

A major factor in determining the form of a fish is the relationship between its lifestyle and the shape of its head; breathing and feeding requirements have tailored the head in a great variety of ways. Fishes can move faster than most sea creatures because of their efficient gills. Only one fifth of the air we breathe contains the vital oxygen that combines with food to energise our muscles; but in water there is 10 times less oxygen available. Fast-moving fishes, which swim perpetually, have superbly shaped heads to match the streamlining of their bodies; they must rely on high speed to increase water flow over their relatively small gills. Fishes that lurk on the bottom, like the scorpion fish, stargazer and grouper, need large heads and capacious gills to pump an adequate supply.

With its slim head for muscling into crevices, the moray eel must keep its mouth open all the time to maintain a good flow — it isn't slavering to bite you. It has no gill plates, as they would get caught when it withdrew into its lair, just small slits and a system of valves, linked with the mouth.

Feeding requirements also exert a major influence on head shape. The john dory has such telescopic jaws it can stalk prey in mid-water and then, in a sudden thrust, its mouth extends into a long tube and snatches its dinner. Coralfishes and long-finned boarfishes have delicate tube mouths, fitted with tiny teeth for nipping off encrusting animals in nooks and crannies. The grouper has a powerful, prey-engulfing maw, while the mouths of plankton-feeders are small, upturned and close to the eyes for nimble, accurate selective feeding.

Like a tiny fighter plane propped on its sturdy, ventral fins, the lizard fish lurks in wait for passing prey. Stubby pectorals extend in readiness for a rapid take-off. In a sudden lunge its double-hinged jaws expand, rather like those of a snake, or the frame of a purse, to swallow a fish virtually as large as its own pointed head.

Fish's Head
Head shape influenced by feeding style:
crevice-probing red pigfish, and weed-browsing black angelfish.

Evolution of fish design

Ultimately, any physical trait that improves a fish's survival chances will be incorporated in its design. Natural selection favours such a trait, with increased reproductive success; it may increase the energy the fish gets from its food or the number of young it can produce. One fish may escape predators through traits that enhance speed by reducing drag. Another may cheat death by becoming less conspicuous, or developing special defences such as poisonous spines, toxic mucus or rigid armour.

Any trait that enables the fish to get more food or decreases energy use tends to increase the number of eggs laid by females and so this useful gene is transmitted.

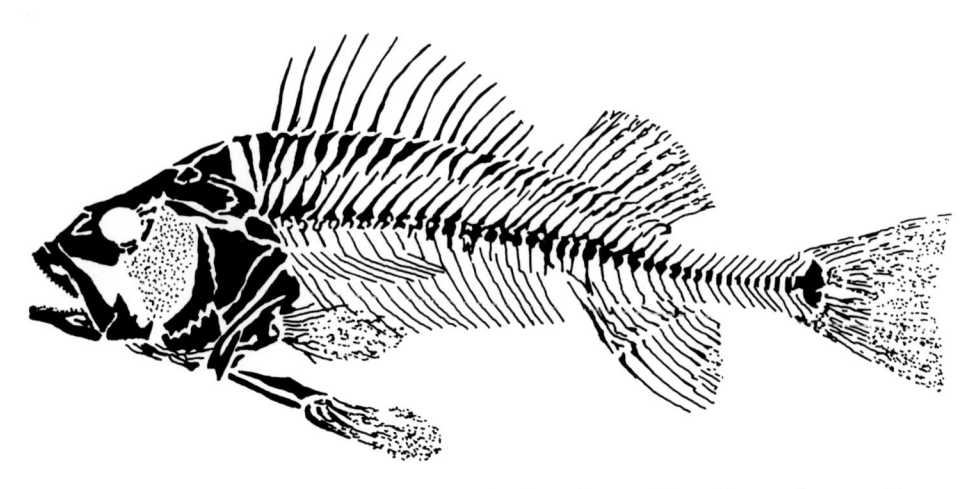

The skeleton of a fish resembles an arrow designed to guide and propel a set of jaws.
(N.B. Marshall, *The Life of Fishes.* Weidenfeld and Nicholson, London, 1965)

In a mature female fish, the eggs may comprise a fifth of its weight. As in aircraft, space is at a premium inside the fish body, and carrying a lot of eggs would reduce speed. Accordingly, some fishes produce large quantities of very tiny eggs, but this strategy handicaps the newly hatched juveniles, which have to compete with those hatched from larger eggs. Some fishes use the strategy of laying a small number of eggs in nests on the reef and guarding them until they hatch. Others spawn in great numbers in open water, at the mercy of the elements and the plankton feeders.

It has been calculated that if a fish obtains one per cent more food than another, it can produce about seven per cent more eggs; and if it uses one per cent less energy, it produces about three per cent more eggs.

Just like the modern car, any design improvement that minimises energy use but enhances acceleration, speed and manoeuvrability will be selected in the evolution of the fish. Energy saved will be available for growth and so increase egg production. In the same way, any changes in form that reduce predation and enable it to get more food also favour reproductive success. Every fish on the reef is the result of a complex interplay of these factors. I find it fascinating to watch each one and consider the strategies that have shaped it.

Jaws of Predators
Mosaic moray.

Lizard fish.

Scorpionfish.

John dory.

Refined, crevice-probing mouth: longfinned boarfish.

Bottom-grubbing mouth: goatfish.

Plankton-feeding mouth; eye close by: demoiselle.

Bottom-kissing lips: porae.

Fossicking canines: Sandager's wrasse.

Beak-like, nibbling jaws: leatherjacket. ▶

Powerful crushing jaws: green wrasse.

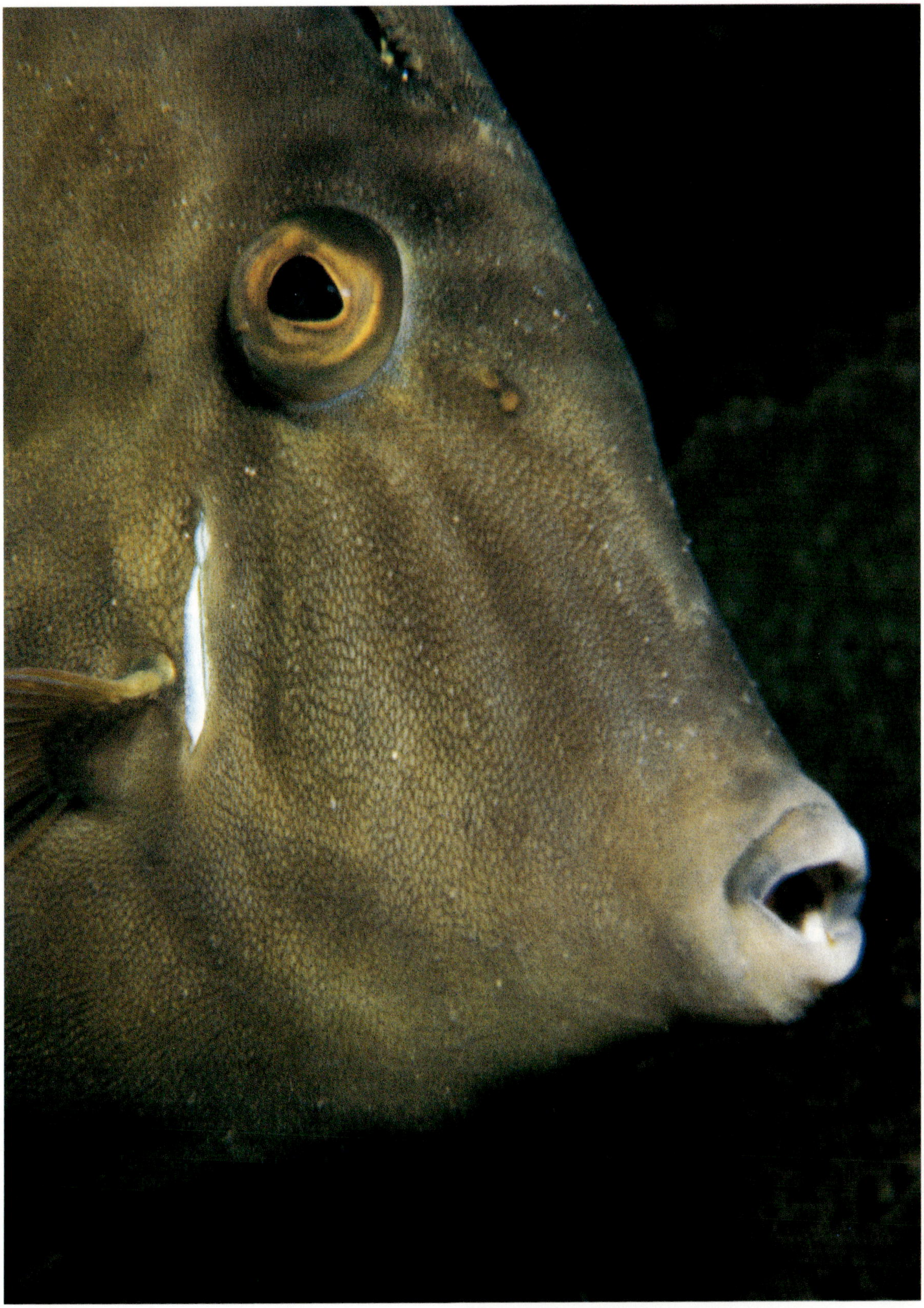

The sensory world of fishes

Life within the dense hydrosphere of a water planet offers a rich array of sensation. Much better than air, water transports energy disturbances in the form of vibrations. Of all creatures, the fish is best equipped to receive such information, in areas of experience of which humans know little. Only to man is the ocean a silent world!

Besides their unique distance-touch capacity, reef fishes have excellent colour vision and hearing; they are receptive to taste, smell and touch, and to tiny changes in temperature and salinity. Much like the needle of a record-player, hairlike sensors project into the mucus-filled canals along both sides of a fish's body and may extend, as with the moray, in three rows on the head. Bathed in fluid, these hairs pick up incoming vibrations and transmit them as messages to the brain. Any local disturbances can be detected by this lateral line system and the fish can also feel the bounce-back of vibrations from its own movements, reflected by surrounding rocks and kelp plants. With such a distance-touch radar system the fish is aware

Twin nostril apertures in front of eye: snapper.

The nasal organs of eels are 100 times more efficient than those of humans. As with most fishes, water is drawn through the front nostril, over a set of odour receptors, to exit by the rear aperture.
(N.B. Marshall, *The Life of Fishes.* Weidenfeld and Nicholson, London, 1965)

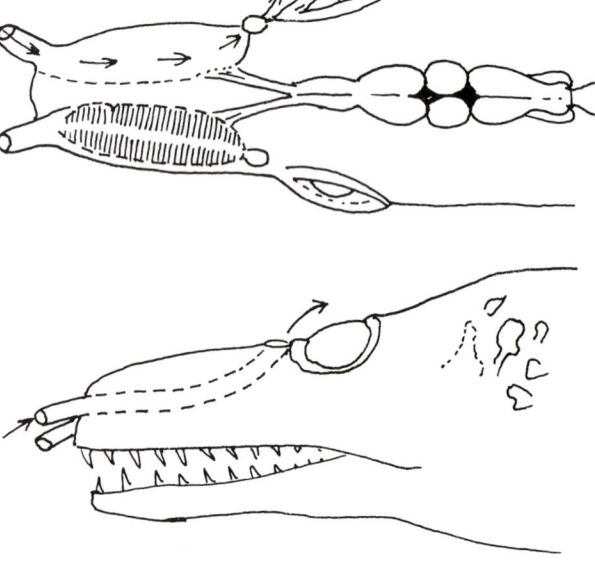

of its position, as well as of anything moving in its vicinity, and can readily avoid obstacles in the dark.

Sound waves travel five times faster through water than through air, so they spread much further and with less delay. The fish has no external ears, yet it is extraordinarily sensitive to sound; its whole body acts as a sound receiver, and in many cases an air-filled bladder acts as an amplifier. However, the fish does have internal ears, housed in capsules within the skull, just behind the eyes. These receive sound stimuli and also act as balance organs, keeping it in a state of instant alertness. The fish can hear lower frequencies than the submerged human ear, but does not respond to higher frequencies, as do dolphins.

Odours spread more rapidly in air than water, but in a world where vision is often limited, taste-smell, or 'chemoreception', is a highly developed sense. With Pacific salmon it has been well proven that in order to reproduce they find their way back to the stream where they themselves were spawned, by detecting its characteristic odour at the mouth and following this to the source.

Most fishes have nostrils on either side of the snout, just in front of the eye. Each consists of an inlet pore and an outlet. As food odours, wafted by a current, reach its nostrils, the fish may track from side to side to detect the direction of the source. The greater the distance between the nostrils, the better the tracking powers. The nostrils of the moray eel gain sensitivity by extending as flexible tubes. With hammerhead sharks the nostrils are set out on bizarre extensions of the head; fishes that rely more on vision than smell-taste, such as flying fishes and damselfishes, may have only a single pore for each nostril.

Fishes also have taste buds all over their bodies. With some, like goatfishes, rock cod and cat fishes, they are concentrated on sensory barbels, like long whiskers, that they dabble in mud and sand, probing for morsels.

Some people like to believe fishes are insensitive to pain, so they cut them up for bait while still alive, but the skin of a fish is covered with myriad nerve-endings, ultra-sensitive to touch and minute changes in temperature, salinity and pressure.

A fish has no neck, yet vision is very important in the reef community. The lens of its eye bulges beyond the surface of its head to provide all-round viewing — like the fish-eye lens used in photography. Such an eye can discern distant objects and detect movement to the side, but gets the clearest images directly ahead. So a fish has its most effective vision where most needed — stalking prey, food foraging, avoiding enemies or courting a mate. Its eye has a further adaptation for ocean dwelling: it enhances the contrast of images in murk or at twilight, better than our own vision.

Those reef fishes that rely on sight for food capture or for recognising signal patterns have the finest vision. Experiments show their colour vision is much like our own. Some can distinguish 24 spectral hues and may exceed our capacity at the violet end of the spectrum, with keen discrimination of varied shades of grey.

Sight-feeding fishes often have binocular vision like humans. Owing to the position of their eyes, or the protruding sockets, both eyes can be focused on the prey, enabling them to judge distance precisely. Predators like the scorpion fish, john dory and flounder have bulging eye sockets — with plankton feeders they are close to the mouth.

Fish Senses
Barbel clad with taste buds: rock cod.

Wide-spaced directional nostril tubes: grey moray.

Wide-angle protruberant eyes: red pigfish.

Binocular vision; nocturnal hunter: toadstool grouper.

The functions of colour in reef fishes

Why is it that some fishes on the reef grab our attention with their brilliant rainbow hues, while others blend in so well with their surroundings it is hard to know they are there? For creatures with such excellent vision, colour is no accident. Over millions of years, patterns have evolved that contribute to survival. An understanding of the functions of colour in the reef fish community leads to an appreciation of their varying lifestyles.

In the fish world, colour serves purposes similar to those in human society: it is used to conceal, disguise or advertise. For fishes that feed on seaweed or browse on encrusting animals, concealment from predators may be more important. Fishes with cryptic coloration resemble the patterns and tones of their surroundings, melting into the fronds of seaweed glades or blending with scattered pebbles on the bottom. Lurking predators, like the scorpion fish, use camouflage to deceive their prey.

Some have the chameleon-like ability to change colour rapidly as they move over the reef. When the eye perceives that the background is light-coloured sand, a message to colour cells beneath the skin causes pigment to contract so the fish becomes pale, with perhaps a pattern of markings that disrupt its outline. Over weed and rock the pigment cells expand and the fish flushes with colour.

Many fishes make use of the optical principle called 'countershading' to reduce their visibility to predator or prey. The back, directed towards the light, is a dark colour, grading through to the underside, which is pale. From above or below, to predator or prey, this reduces the fish to a shadow. With some nocturnal species that spend the day in caves, the effect may be reversed; as most light strikes them after bouncing off the cave floor, their undersides are dark and their backs pale.

Silvery fishes, which range widely, have skin that acts like a mirror to reflect all backgrounds, including the under surface of the sea, making it difficult to distinguish the fish itself. If fishes are too well disguised or too uniform it may be hard for them to stay in a schooling formation, so we see subtle markings such as white or black dots near the tail, a saddle on the neck or blue spots on the sides, which enable the school to keep together without being too conspicuous.

Disruptive colour patterns use another optical principle to disguise the fish's outline. Such patterns break the outline up into vertical or horizontal stripes, oblique bands or contrasting patches of colour. Mottling, polka dots and scribbled patterns also break up the body outline, merging it with variegated surroundings. A false eye spot (ocellus) directs attention away from the real eye, which may also be made less conspicuous by an eye stripe. Each pattern seems to have its appropriate strategy. I have noticed that vertical bands appear on the more slow-moving, deep-bodied, solitary or sedentary species, while horizontal bands or lines are used by faster moving, sleeker fishes that form loose schools.

On the other hand, many reef fishes proclaim their presence with vivid colour patterns. Such fishes often have long, sharp, dorsal spines, and deep inflexible bodies that make it impossible for a predator to swallow them, so they can afford to display their fine colours. For others, refuges in the reef abound.

Just as birds use song and mammals use scent, bright colours are used to reserve a patch of territory under the sea. With many large families of reef fishes, such as the wrasses and parrot fishes, dozens of species live close together on the same stretch of reef. Distinctive, high-contrast colour patterns ensure instant recognition and appropriate behaviour. With these fishes, dominant males establish territories from which they exclude all other males of their species, but share with a harem of females. For such fishes, conspicuous male and female colour patterns are important.

Even juveniles may have their own distinct patterns, to allow them space in which to grow up. Many young wrasses and parrotfishes start life with female coloration and sexual characteristics; only when they are big enough to defend a territory do they reverse sex and take on male colours. Some opt for an alternative strategy: for most of the year the males assume a less dramatic colour pattern, only to display special patterns during courtship. In such cases, fins and tails are especially useful for gaudy display. For these drab fishes colour is a means of expression, only appearing as a signal when needed.

At night another colour transition occurs: nocturnal feeders emerge, many of them flushed crimson; in dim undersea light this colour appears black. And the daytime feeders settle on the reef, their bodies often blotched, mottled or barred with vertical bands, to make them less conspicuous in the dark.

Some small wrasses perform a valuable grooming service on the reef: their needle-sharp teeth can nip parasitic lice from the gills and fin-bases of larger fishes. Accordingly, these 'surgeons' are never eaten and display a bold stripe along their sides to proclaim their Red Cross role. Colour combinations vary from species to species, but the cleanerfish insignia, on all the world's reefs, is a horizontal band of distinct contrast: yellow on white, black on white; white on crimson or some such.

Whereas some fishes seek to camouflage themselves, others use colour as a warning. The pufferfishes have very toxic flesh and their distinctive coloration ensures no predator would ever mistake them for dinner.

The more we study the colour patterns of reef fishes, the closer we come to understanding the complex communities in which they live. It was recently discovered that the patterns of spots and bold markings that many reef fishes display on prominent areas of their bodies vary with each individual, like a signature or the optical code on a bank cheque. As a result, all the fishes living in one area learn to recognise each other. Even though to us they may well all look the same, these fishes have adequate memory capacity to know who all their neighbours are individually, and would repel any intruder, regardless of species.

Reef fishes have excellent eyesight. For millions of years, colour patterns have evolved to serve every function for which we ourselves use colour. Indeed, some fishes are so exquisite, they could well be registered as works of art!

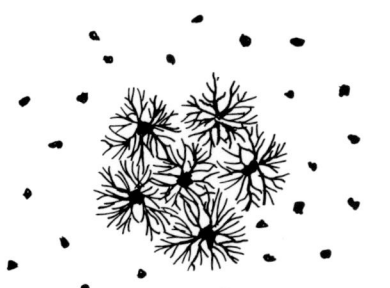

Some fishes have the chameleon ability to change colour rapidly. At the centre, colour cells with black pigment are expanded. Surrounding cells are contracted to a dot.
(N.B. Marshall, *The Life of Fishes.* Weidenfeld and Nicholson, London, 1965)

Functions of Colour in Reef Fishes
A mirror reflecting all backgrounds: flying fish.

Horizontal disruptive stripes: mado.

Advertising colours; courting male: splendid perch.

Vertical disruptive bands: striped boarfish.

Concealing eye-stripe: halfbanded perch.

Dots and Spots Acting as Schooling Signals
Single spot demoiselle and snapper.

Warning colours
Poisonous: sharpnosed pufferfish. ▶

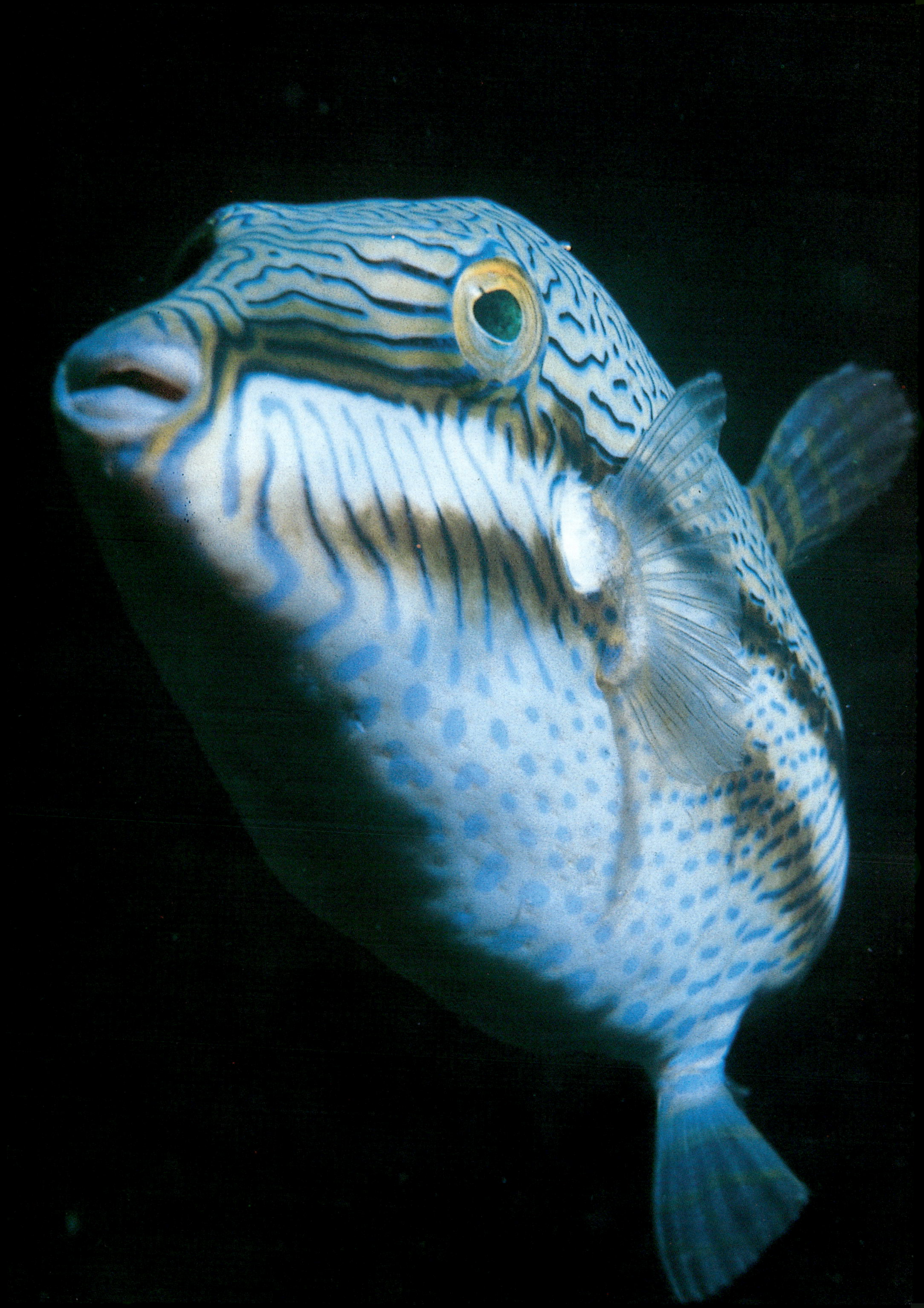

Masters of Camouflage
Scorpion fish.
Natural light: lizardfish.

Mandala wheel: reef fishes as artworks. ▶

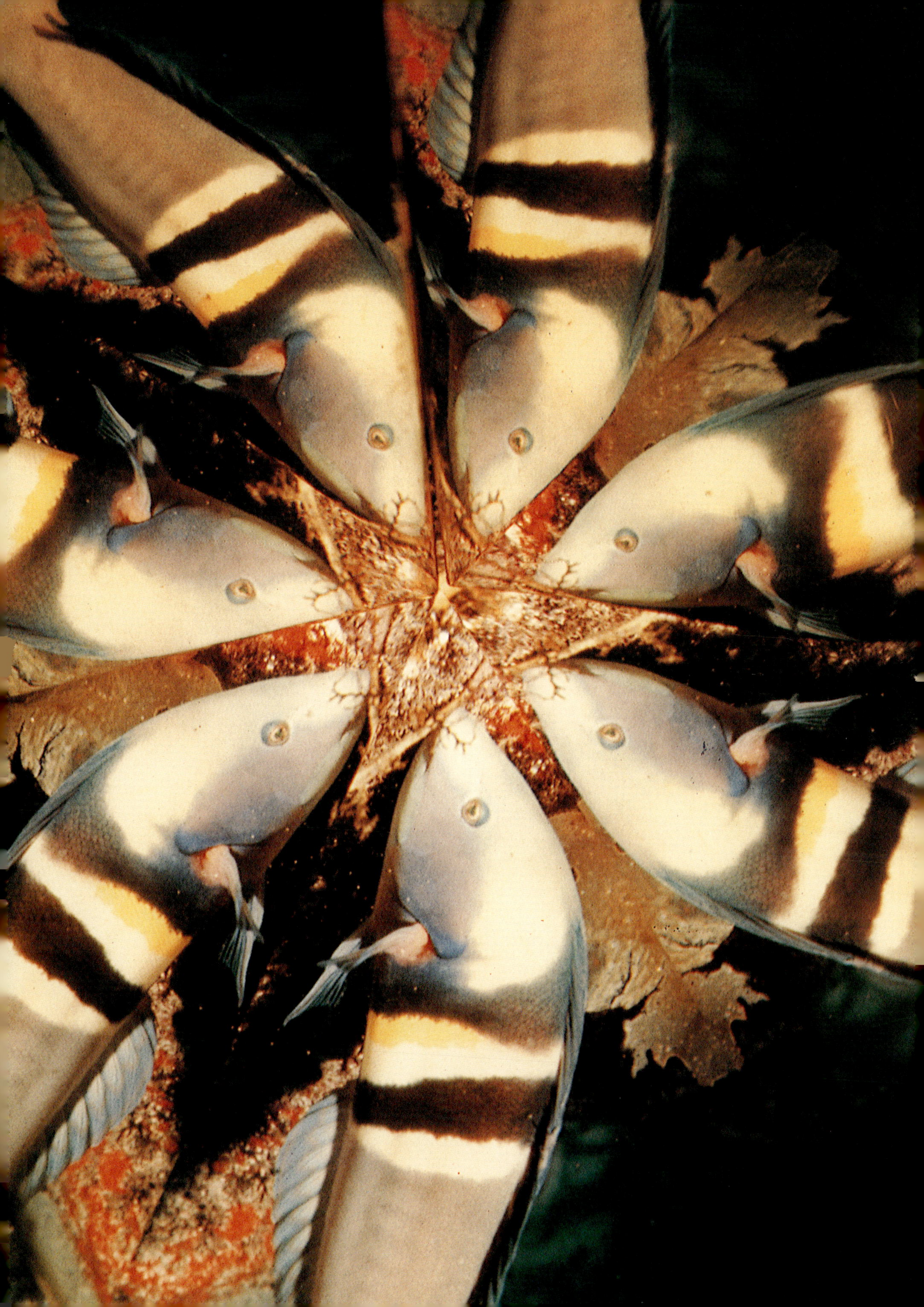

Exploring an archway, Poor Knights Islands, surrounded by plankton-feeders.

Part Two

City under the sea: portrait of a reef fish community at the Poor Knights Islands

The Poor Knights community

The reef is one of the richest zones of life on earth. Opportunities to gain a living abound in successive layers — every cubic metre is productive. The most mobile members of the reef community are the fishes. All animals find advantage in exploiting new sources of energy not available to others in a crowded community and, most flexible and adaptable, the fishes have spread into every available ecological niche — just as in a city people are always seeking new occupations and modes of employment. Each fish, whatever its speciality, needs only a few square metres of space for its support. Instead of competing with one another for a limited food resource, the reef fishes have radiated into a vast array of different species, each with its own mode of diet, its own adaptation of body form and its own habitat, so that every available energy source is exploited.

On any reef in the world the same three broad categories of habitat can be distinguished. Firstly, there are the open-water fishes, which live independent of the bottom. Secondly, there are the bottom-swimming fishes, which live close to the reef and are partly dependent on it for food and shelter. Then, within cracks and crevices, beneath seaweed fronds, in caves and under ledges are the bottom-dwellers, which are greatly dependent on the bottom for food and shelter. Ecologists studying fish habitats in any one area have found it useful to sort out the exploiters of these habitats according to their feeding patterns, grouping together all species that exploit the same resources in a similar way. As they resemble medieval craft unions, such groups have been called 'guilds'.

While I have dived on reefs of rock and coral in many parts of the Pacific, and in the Atlantic, I have spent a quarter century observing the reef fishes around the Poor Knights Islands, a group of volcanic rockpiles 24 km off the northern coast of New Zealand at 35° latitude. I now plan to examine this community of fishes in detail, as it is ideal for this purpose.

The greatest diversity of life occurs in tropical seas. A coral reef may have 2000 different species — a bewildering metropolis — but the average size of fish is only 15 cm. In cooler waters, with their marked seasonal changes in temperature and food supply, there are fewer kinds of fishes, but they are usually found in greater numbers and are much larger individually. In concentrating on the fishes of the Poor Knights Islands, I can straddle both worlds. Most of the temperate-water species, found on the mainland coast, flourish here under optimal conditions, although a few appear to suffer from competition and are more abundant further south. In addition, many warm-water species from tropical and subtropical families have found the islands favourable. This is probably due to the warm East Auckland current, which flows offshore down this coast, bringing with it larval fishes from coral reefs out in the Tasman, such as Lord Howe Island. The Poor Knights Islands, with their wide variety of deep-water habitats, caverns, archways and tunnels, offer unusual ecological niches not much used by local species. By contrast, a handful of species common on the adjacent coast are not found there at all.

Situated near the edge of the continental shelf, the Poor Knights are remnants of a string of volcanoes that once erupted along a fault line on

View from Aorangi, down into South Harbour and Southern Archway. ▶

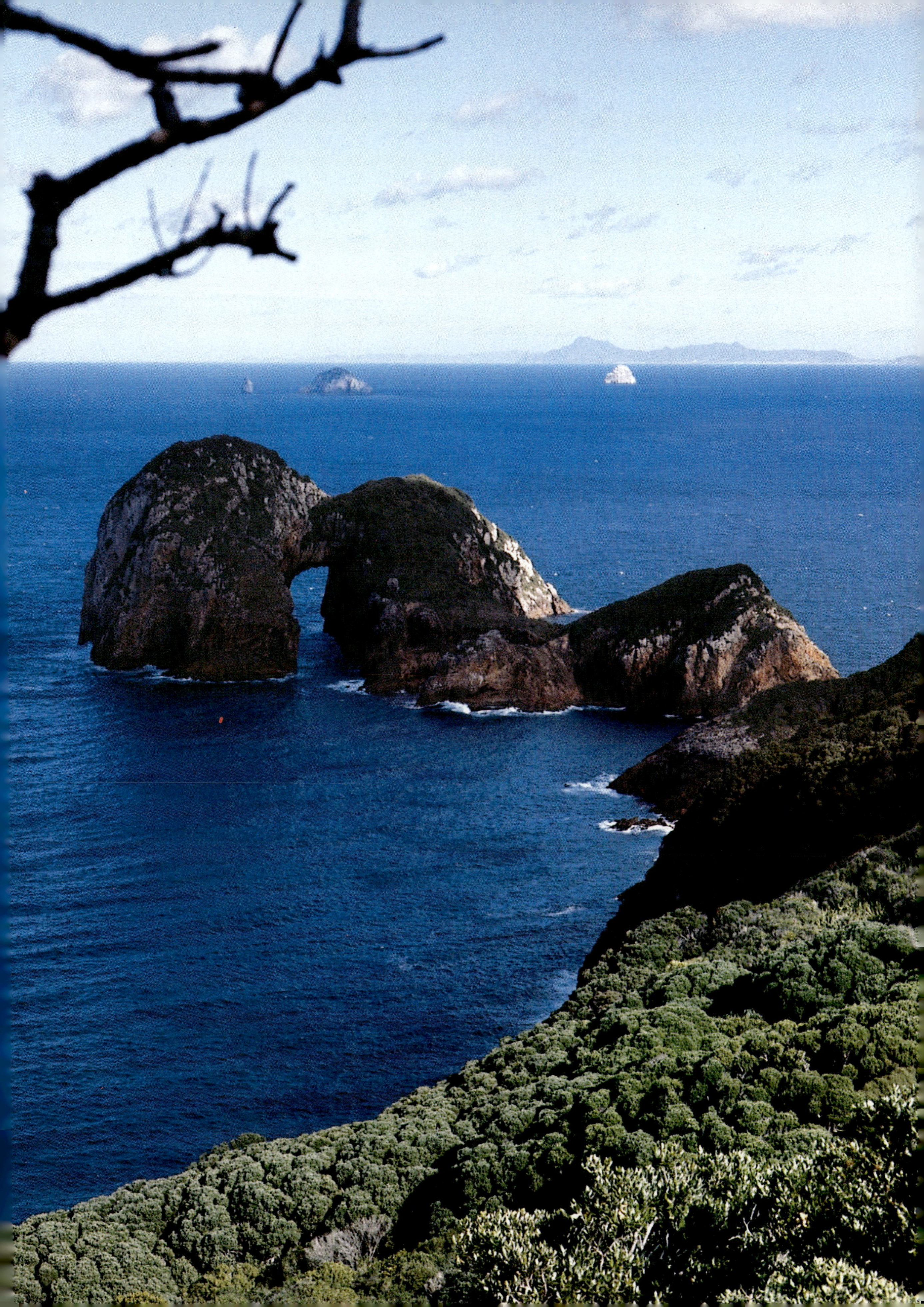

the Pacific rim. When ice ages froze so much of the world's water that sea levels fell, the surf eroded the softer portions of the volcanic rock, creating vast sea caves and archways, tubes and tunnels, chimneys and air-bubble domes. Divers find the Poor Knights ideal. The steep cliffs plunge almost vertically to around 30 m, broken by ledges, fissures, overhangs and grottos. At 50 m there is often a sandy plain shelving away gently, before a second slope carries on to depths beyond scuba range (depths which recently I was privileged to explore with a robotic submarine). Such undersea topography provides the diver with a wide range of depths within a short horizontal distance, encompassing the conditions of broad expanses of the continental shelf within a single dive.

The rich nutrient flow brimming past the islands day and night supports a wall of mouths of stunning diversity, which I have described in *The Cliff Dwellers*. In gaps between the islands, shallow, sand-floored avenues and reef outcrops provide optimal conditions for reef fishes: a constant, gentle current; shelter from wave violence, and sunlit, seaweed jungles. In such areas, diver observation of reef fish communities has been intensive and long-term.

For me, after 26 years exploring out there, the most distinctive quality of the Poor Knights, in comparison with so many coral reefs I have visited, is that I dive *in* them, not at them, and their many internal spaces give architectural dimensions to the undersea world. Sometimes it seems like a waking dream as I fly through the galleries, halls and corridors of a drowned city. The exquisite, encrusting life suggests a Louvre or a Taj Mahal, perhaps even Xanadu. For all the reef fish guilds, the diversity of habitat and food supply around the Poor Knights provides endless opportunities; it is a vertical city, a world tipped on edge, facing the infinity of inner space and all its drifting galaxies.

Moonrise, Poor Knights Islands: city of the sea.

POOR KNIGHTS ISLANDS

DIVING LOCATIONS AT THE POOR KNIGHTS ISLANDS

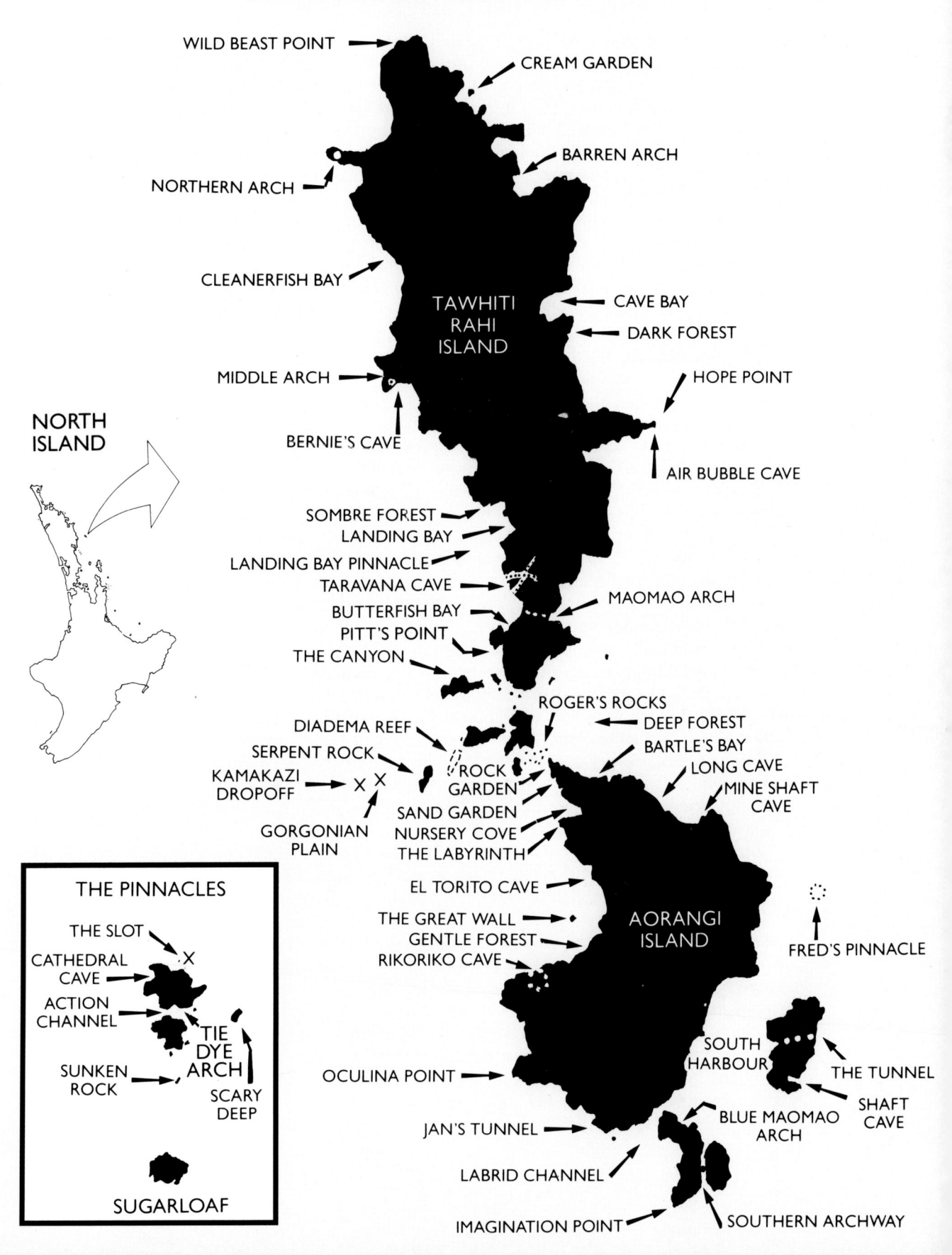

- WILD BEAST POINT
- CREAM GARDEN
- BARREN ARCH
- NORTHERN ARCH
- CLEANERFISH BAY
- TAWHITI RAHI ISLAND
- CAVE BAY
- DARK FOREST
- MIDDLE ARCH
- HOPE POINT
- BERNIE'S CAVE
- AIR BUBBLE CAVE
- SOMBRE FOREST
- LANDING BAY
- LANDING BAY PINNACLE
- TARAVANA CAVE
- BUTTERFISH BAY
- MAOMAO ARCH
- PITT'S POINT
- THE CANYON
- ROGER'S ROCKS
- DIADEMA REEF
- DEEP FOREST
- SERPENT ROCK
- BARTLE'S BAY
- KAMAKAZI DROPOFF
- ROCK GARDEN
- LONG CAVE
- MINE SHAFT CAVE
- GORGONIAN PLAIN
- SAND GARDEN
- NURSERY COVE
- THE LABYRINTH
- EL TORITO CAVE
- THE GREAT WALL
- AORANGI ISLAND
- GENTLE FOREST
- RIKORIKO CAVE
- FRED'S PINNACLE
- SOUTH HARBOUR
- OCULINA POINT
- THE TUNNEL
- SHAFT CAVE
- JAN'S TUNNEL
- BLUE MAOMAO ARCH
- LABRID CHANNEL
- IMAGINATION POINT
- SOUTHERN ARCHWAY

NORTH ISLAND

THE PINNACLES
- THE SLOT
- CATHEDRAL CAVE
- ACTION CHANNEL
- TIE DYE ARCH
- SUNKEN ROCK
- SCARY DEEP
- SUGARLOAF

The guilds

At the Poor Knights Islands, as on any reef, there are three guilds of open-water fishes: the *plankton pickers*, the *open-water hunters* and the *general predators and scavengers*. Adjacent to the cliff faces they range from just beneath the surface to within a few metres of the bottom. (Predators like mako and bronze whaler sharks are rare at the Poor Knights these days.)

Feeding on the larger plankton animals near the surface are dense schools of trevally and blue maomao, their backs often humping out, mouth parts slurping greedily as they pursue frantic, lolly-pink krill. Just beneath them long ropes of demoiselles nip copepods and other plankton creatures with deft manoeuvres. Through them all dash silvery schools of pelagic fishes, koheru and horse mackerel, in quest of similar prey. Deeper down, other kinds of plankton creatures sustain masses of perch groupers: pink maomao, butterfly perch and splendid perch. Close to the cliff hover swarms of tiny plankton-feeding triplefins. Further out, huge sunfish gulp down gelatinous forms of plankton. At dusk all these daytime plankton feeders retire and the 'night shift' members of the guild emerge: roughies or squirrel fishes, big eye and golden snapper.

Sweeping along the cliff face by day are the open-water hunters: kingfishes, barracouta and kahawai. Near the bottom, but still in mid-water, the cardboard-thin john dory stalks its prey with stealth and cunning. Close to the rock faces, weaving through thickets of seaweed or fossicking over sand plains and reef flats, are the members of seven bottom-feeding guilds.

In shallow, weedy coves, *plant grazers* with specially adapted teeth closely trim the algal turf like lawnmowers, and *plant browsers* weave among the taller sea plants, nipping off chunks of fronds and grinding them up in their pharyngeal mills. These plant eaters are black angelfishes, marblefishes, parore and silver drummer.

With their thick, rubbery lips and brush-like tooth pads the *invertebrate gleaners* rummage over rocky areas, sucking and kissing off patches of encrusted life swarming with tiny invertebrates. At first sight it seems these gleaners are weed-eating fishes as they mouth the algal turf carpeting the rocks. Members of this guild are red moki, painted moki and porae.

Invertebrate grazers scrape off encrusting organisms such as tube worms or anemones with specially adapted teeth. Some nibble like mice at tough, bristly sponges. Guild members are triggerfishes, pufferfishes, mado, bluefish and crested blennies.

Invertebrate browsers range very widely, snipping invertebrates such as crabs and shellfish from rock, sand or mud; snapper, tarakihi, butterfly fishes, boarfishes, kelpfishes and rays belong to this guild.

The *bottom grubbers* swim over mud and sand, probing with sensitive barbels and pectoral fins, and engulfing mouthfuls along with tube worms and other invertebrates. This guild consists of goatfishes, occasionally joined by trevally, blue moki, tarakihi and porae.

A very large guild, the *bottom fossickers*, swim over areas of broken rock, raking off encrusting life with sharp, rat-like teeth. All the wrasses belong to this guild, each with its own speciality and its own niche on the reef.

With their bold insignia the *parasite pickers* form a highly specialised guild, removing lice from the gills, fin bases and skin of other reef fishes. The crimson cleaner, the combfish and the juvenile Sandager's wrasse are the principal members of this guild, joined by young trevally, mado and triplefins. As they fossick for crustaceans on the bottom, these small fishes do not mind if a lice-infested patch of fish skin gets in the way; and the lice-carrier enjoys their grooming service.

To the guild of *bottom stalkers* belong the morays, congers, rock cod, groupers, scorpion fishes, lizardfishes, triplefins and blennies. Many are night predators. By day the scorpion fish lies motionless beneath ledges, under the fronds of seaweed or perched in a large cup sponge; out of crevices stare rock cod, morays and congers; within rocky recesses groupers rest. All await nightfall before venturing out to snap up crustaceans and small fishes.

Whenever I explore the cliff face at night, my flashlight reveals a startling change in the fish guilds. The bottom stalkers are out hunting, and the day feeders are at rest.

Poor Knights diorama.

KEY TO DIAGRAM OF FISHES ON FOLLOWING PAGES

1	Kahawai	28	Scorpion-fish
2	Sunfish	29	Painted moki
3	Koheru	30	John dory
4	Barracouta	31	Scarlet wrasse
5	Kingfishes	32	Halfbanded perch
6	Bluefish	33	Bigeye
7	Demoiselles	34	Red moki
8	Trevally	35	Sandager's wrasses
9	Blue maomao	36	Silver drummers
10	Green wrasse	37	Redbanded weaver
11	Banded wrasses	38	Toadstool grouper
12	Marblefish	39	Hapuku
13	Spotted black grouper	40	Splendid perches
14	Parore	41	Longfinned boarfishes
15	Butterfish	42	Yellow-banded perch
16	Kelpfish	43	Foxfish
17	Black angelfishes	44	Combfishes
18	Leatherjacket	45	Goatfishes
19	Spotty	46	Lizardfishes
20	Orange wrasse	47	Snapper
21	Yellow moray	48	Butterfly perches
22	Pink maomao	49	Porae
23	Pufferfishes	50	Bar-tailed goatfishes
24	Crimson cleanerfishes	51	Red pigfishes
25	Mado	52	Golden snapper
26	Lord Howe coralfishes	53	Rock cod
27	Gold-ribbon grouper	54	Mottled moray

The Fishes in Their Vertical Distribution — to a depth of 60 metres

(For key, see previous page)
Diagram by Grant Couchman

8
9
13
14
12
15
10
16
18
6
11
17
19
7
20
21
25
31
33
36
32
34
29
30
35
27
28
38
48
53
51
52
54
47
45
46
49
50

Guild of the plankton pickers

Pink maomao
Beneath the sea cliffs deep blue water suddenly glows neon pink with living shapes weaving to and fro in a frenzy. An oval patch of water seethes with radiance for a moment; but soon, before the sea birds can join in, all is quiet again. A school of pink maomao has chased its prey, tiny red euphausiid shrimps, or krill, up from the depths to the mirror of the surface, where escape is limited. Flexing their deeply forked tails and pivoting on long pectoral fins, the fishes wheel and turn, their upward, tilted mouths snapping each frantic crustacean with small, sharp teeth. Some of the fishes have black patches on tail or flank, where fungal growths mar their glowing colour. A few have mutilations from attack by kingfishes and other large carnivores.

Pink maomao pivoting on long pectorals.

In deep water pink maomao hover in black coral trees. ▶

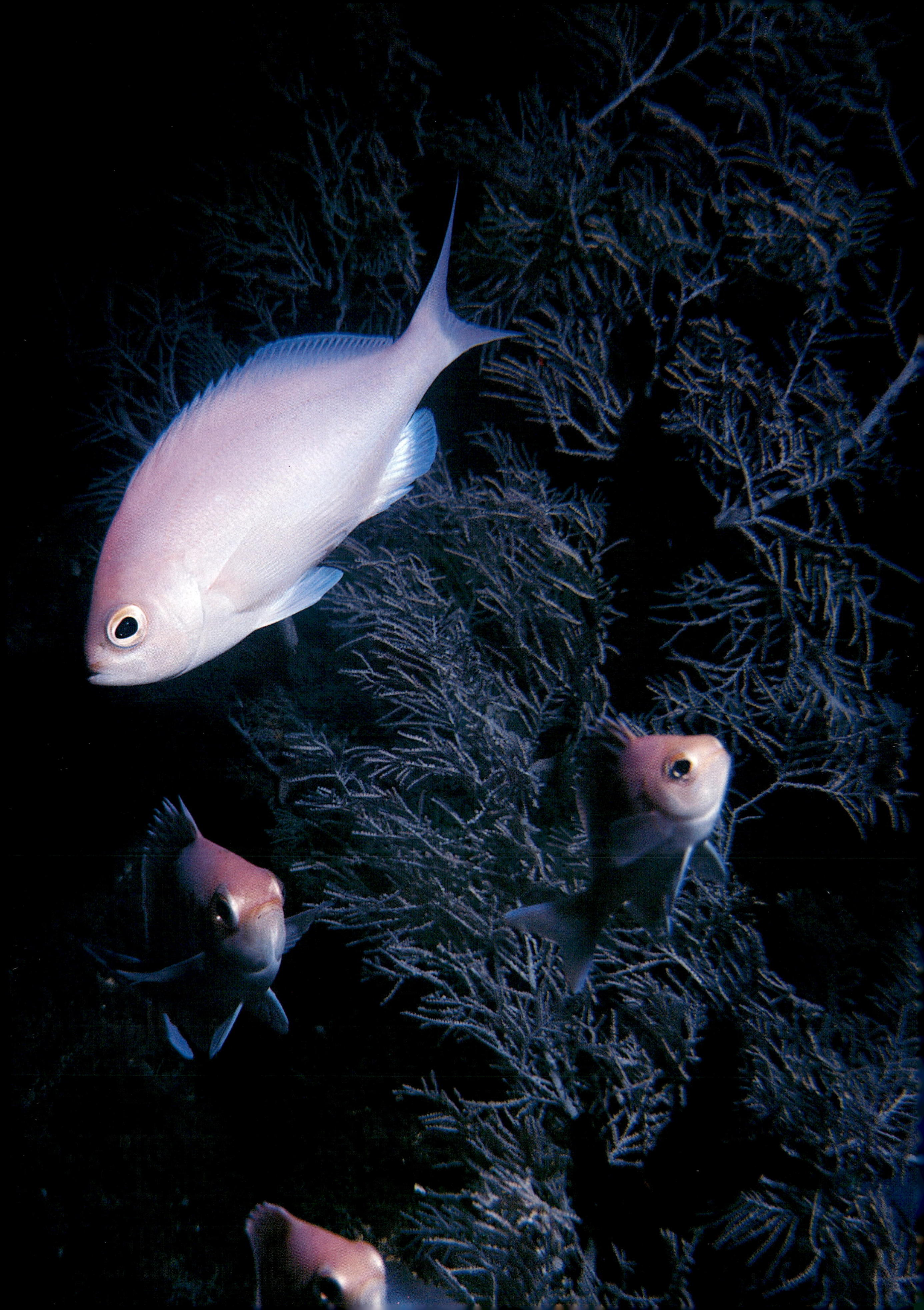

There is less co-ordination in these plankton-picking, reef fish schools than among the silvery fishes of the open sea, which swim in schools for protection. Pink maomao swim in a more casual type of school, turning and twisting as individuals and perhaps mainly aggregating because their prey is en masse.

At the Poor Knights Islands pink maomao mostly live where there is a moderate current; archways and tunnels seethe with them. At times, however, a favourite haunt, such as the Northern Arch, will be deserted; and the pink maomao will have shifted to the nearby Te Ara Ara Point, where they will be feeding intensively. Thus, while they appear to have a home ground, they move within the vicinity according to planktonic activity as it is occasioned by wind direction, tide or current.

I have seen them from depths of 100 m to within a tailslap of the surface. They mostly swim below the 10 m level, underneath schools of other plankton-feeding species. From July to December they tend to swim in a deeper zone, below 20 m. As the water warms, they are often found in the surface layers.

During the warmest months, from January to March, large pink maomao frequently take refuge in the backs of caves and beneath ledges in the upper zone. Until my bubbles disturb them they appear to be asleep; their bodies show the same white blotches as at night and they are tilted on their sides, head down, tail up, even vertical in crevices. Their senses seem momentarily dulled, perhaps by the unaccustomed warmth, but they quickly bolt out into the open as I approach with the cyclopean eye of my camera.

At sunset, pink maomao schools immediately stop feeding. They may be several hundred metres from a suitable refuge, but each night they return to their favourite roosting areas, moving in a long stream, and settle individually amongst the rocks before darkness closes in. A shallow, rocky area such as Labrid Channel becomes a very important dormitory for them, a night shelter for thousands of fishes. They seem to reach a period of deepest sleep between 11 p.m. and midnight. Despite their lidless, staring eyes, nothing seems to register. At last I can approach this flighty acrobat as closely as I wish, admiring the handsome form, now suffused with orange-red. The skin feels sandpapery — unlike that of weed-dwelling fishes, it is quite devoid of mucus.

Pink maomao actively seek cleanerfish to remove parasites, because while they have been feeding in dense plankton swarms, copepods or sea lice have fixed themselves to their fin bases and near their gill openings. At the Northern Arch, that giant keyhole in the ocean, 40 m down, 10 pink maomao are clustered around a crimson cleanerfish in peculiar poses: upside down or on their sides, seemingly entranced. The nimble cleaner dodges about, picking at a gill plate, fins and scales. As it moves away the fishes follow, repeatedly presenting themselves in its path, enticing the little wrasse to groom them; this member of the reef community is part of their pattern of health and comfort.

The pink maomao grows to 50 cm in length.

Pink maomao, active by day, and resting at night; white-blotched, night coloration.

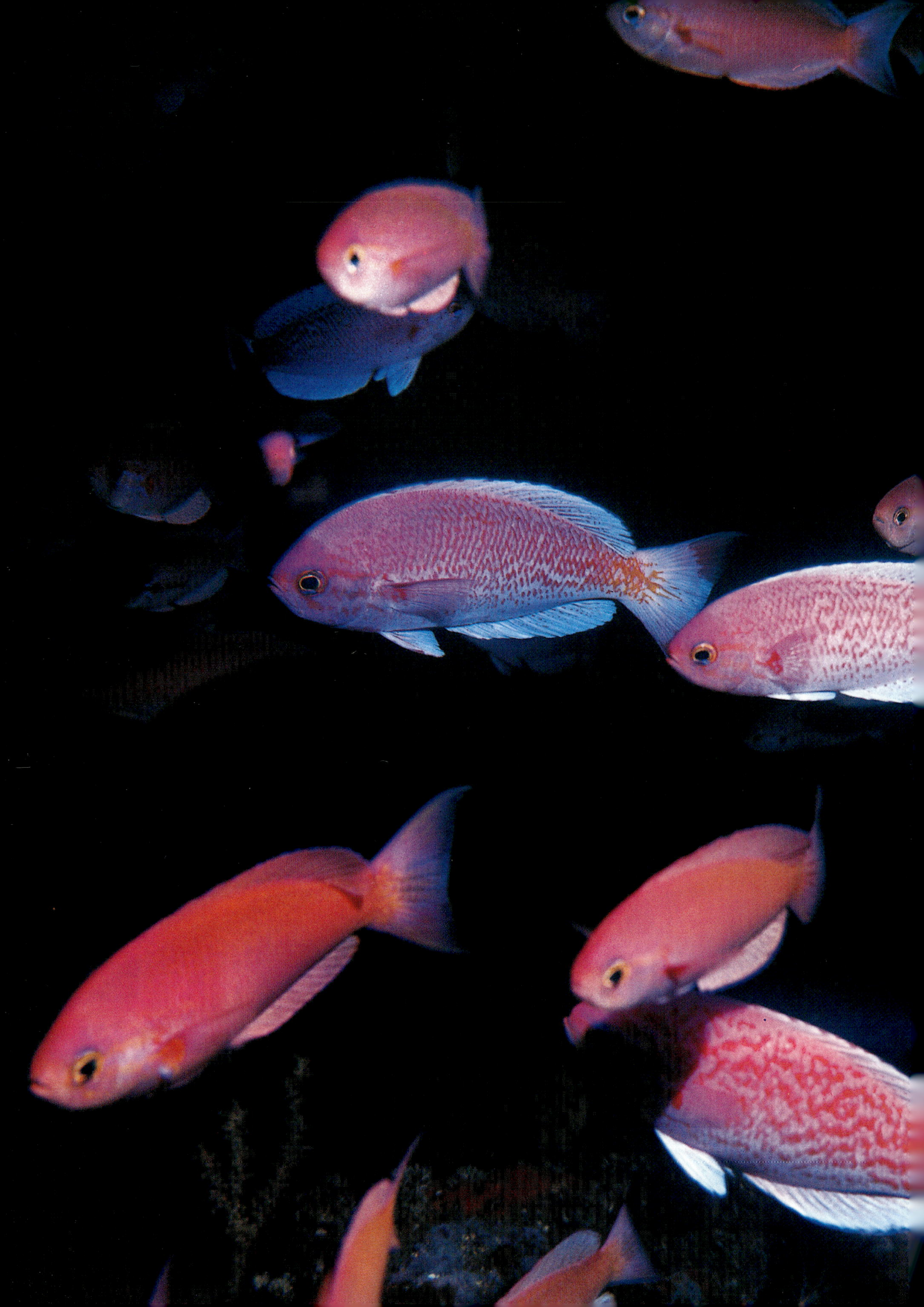

Male splendid perch, normal coloration. Only males have tail filaments.

◄ *Deep-water courtship dance of splendid perch: males in brilliant livery.*

Splendid perch

Much rarer and most exquisite of the plankton pickers, splendid perch often swim in loose association with pink maomao, but only at levels beyond 30 m. At such depths, where colours are muted, it takes an experienced eye to distinguish their beauty; only when the electronic flash is fired does a living jewel glow in my eyes for a split second. But colour is of importance to this species, and its eye must have some perception beyond our own.

Lacking the gradation of colours that make the male so exquisite, the smaller female is a uniform orange-red, with purple-tinged fins and head. In late winter the males undergo a startling colour change: their bodies become latticed with a glowing mosaic pattern. The saffron-yellow patch near the tail disappears, the tail lobes become scarlet, and dorsal and anal fins are incredibly marked with brilliant spots. Such a transition had me deeply puzzled until, in mid-October, the answer came.

A strange ritual was taking place at a depth of 60 m, adjacent to the richly encrusted pinnacles and crags of the sea cliff. A school of some 30 splendid perch was rising and falling just above the rocks. Some were liveried in the bold lattice pattern, their gaudy fins widespread. Here and there these fishes were pairing with smaller ones in less attractive colouring. I realised the gaudy fishes were the males, and the plainer ones, females.

Often a female appeared just above or below a male, as he pirouetted around her displaying his dorsal and anal fins to make his body appear a third greater in depth. At times two or three males met in an aggressive display, turning around one another as each fish demonstrated virility and majesty with imperious gestures, his body taut and curving. Then these males spiralled up with one or two females, spawned and returned to the school. No human ballet can surpass the expressiveness and finery of this undersea courtship dance.

The splendid perch grows to 30 cm.

Butterfly perch

Another of the plankton pickers, the butterfly perch has a similar lifestyle to the pink maomao, but it is not limited to plankton feeding: crabs and small shellfish also form part of its diet. This is probably why it has a smaller, deeper body (up to 30 cm) and, besides schooling in mid-water, it spends a lot of time swimming very close to the cliff face, oriented towards it rather than swimming horizontally. In a sea cave, butterfly perch often orient themselves to the roof, actually swimming upside down, which can make them difficult to photograph without the diver feeling dizzy.

Probably because they select a different range of plankton animals, they are seldom seen pursuing prey up to the surface as do the pink maomao. Plankton feeding offers a variety of lifestyles and members of this guild have adapted exquisitely to each variation in the food supply.

At night, butterfly perch descend to the reef. A deeper red suffuses their skin and they nestle in the folds of a castle sponge, lie in holes or even swim very quietly, like somnambulists, just off the bottom.

Butterfly perch resting at night, dorsal raised to maximise size.

Butterfly perch by day. ▶

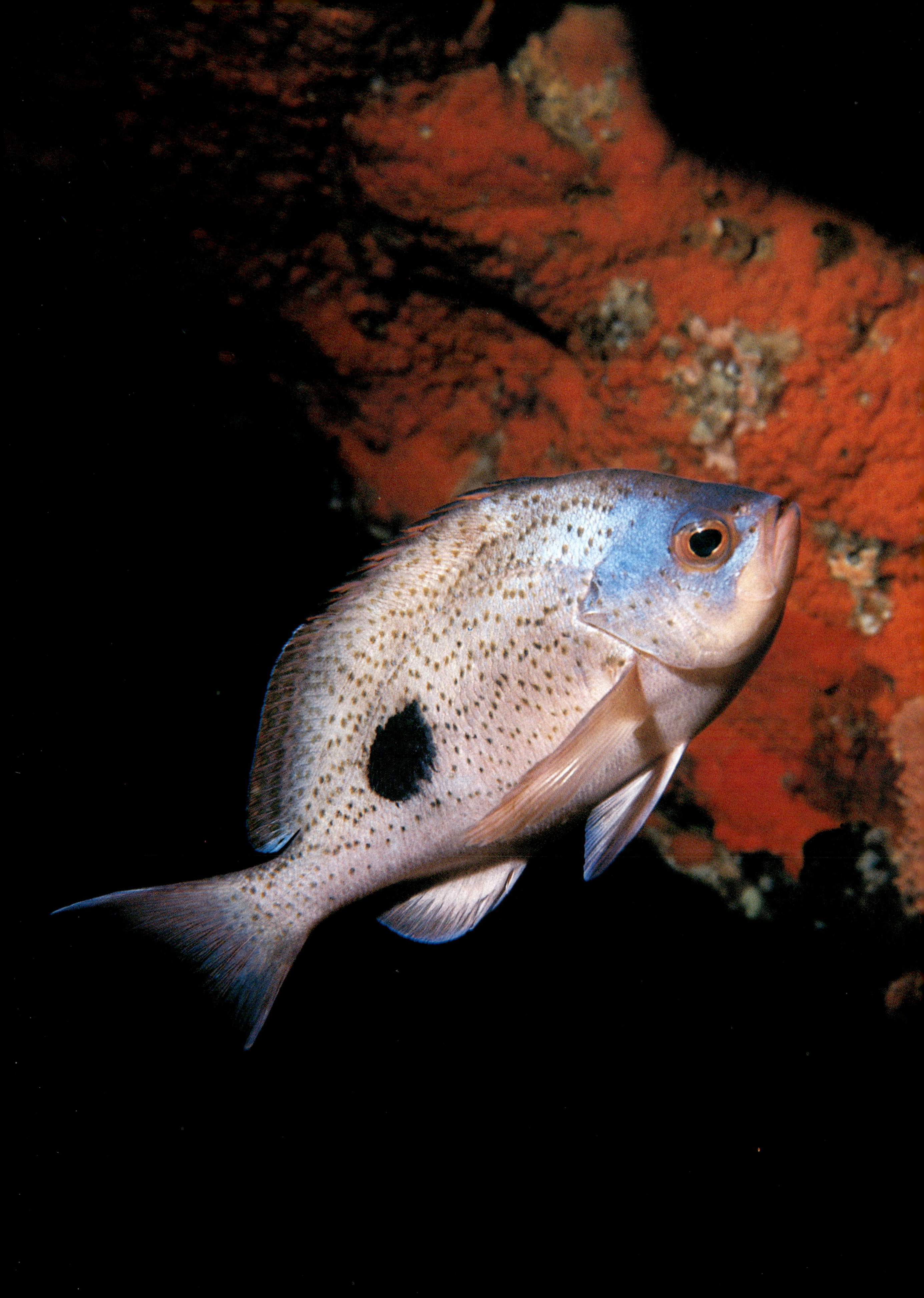

Demoiselle

Demoiselles, which grow to 20 cm, are the swallows of the sea. As plankton feeders, they are adapted to agile swooping and darting as they seize food carried on the current. Their broad, transparent, pectoral fins act like sculls, boosting them forward after prey. In manoeuvring, their deeply forked swallow-tails open and close like scissors, giving the fishes perfect poise as they pivot in mid-water, small jaws and brush-like teeth snapping rapidly. With a large eye just above the mouth and only a single set of nostrils, these are highly visual animals.

Twin dots on the flank are schooling signals and assist cohesion. In dense schools of up to 500, the demoiselles gain protection when kingfishes attack. The predator has difficulty selecting a single target from the mass of identical fish bodies and the myriad dots probably help confuse its aim.

Demoiselles have a diet consisting almost entirely of copepods, small planktonic crustaceans that feed on plant plankton from the surface down to 70 m. Demoiselles rely on a moving mass of water for a steady supply of copepods. To obtain this moving water handy to the refuge of the reef, their schools face into the currents around rocky headlands, in archways, above pinnacles and alongside steep cliffs. In such areas eddy currents and turbulence concentrate the plankton swarms.

Over the winter months, demoiselles tend to move deeper and their iridescent blue becomes a greyish blue tone. In June, at 70 m I have seen dense schools of demoiselle, along with pink maomao and butterfly perch. In early spring, for some reason, they often crowd beneath ledges or roost in the fronds of *Sargassum* weed like birds in a tree.

During November they start to show an interest in rock surfaces. Schools break up and individuality asserts itself as males begin to prepare and guard nesting sites, their tails glowing with white streaks to attract females. From a schoolfish the demoiselle has become a fierce little aggressor, boldly guarding its chosen territory against all comers and, particularly, males of its own kind. For the next four months demoiselles spawn sporadically, and frequent hatchings of larval fishes enter the open-water plankton or leave to join other juveniles sheltering beneath rock ledges and kelp fronds.

Twelve metres down, a male demoiselle hovers over a rock shelf. Close beneath him is a patch of pale green eggs from a previous spawning. His sexual colours are displayed: the inner edges of his tail lobes glow with neon-white radiance and each blue body scale, especially around the head, is flecked with black. Rapid scissoring of his tail, with its white inner margin, signals his readiness to spawn again.

Nearby move some young trevally, two female pigfishes, spotties, leatherjackets and triplefins. Above his nest clings a halfbanded perch. All around, on every available patch of rock, other demoiselles are nest guarding. Every half metre there is a nest. Periodically the male I am watching makes a fluttering dash at any fish that moves too close. In his absence tiny triplefins dash in and steal a few eggs.

Then I notice a lighter-coloured demoiselle amidst the school feeding on plankton overhead. It swoops down purposefully towards the nest, only to be repelled. About every sixth time the male tolerates the visitor, recognisable as a female by the black ovipositor tube in front of her vent. Four times the fishes meet side by side, either head-on or both facing the same way.

Demoiselle school plankton feeding.

Over his nest site male demoiselle, dorsal erect, awaits females.
Male removes objects from nest site.

As they skim the nest site, their bodies pressed together shiver and vibrate and his twin dots fade momentarily. From the female's ovipositor-tube eggs are being extruded, which the male fertilizes after chasing her off.

Now the male resumes his nest-guarding pattern, vigorously quivering over the eggs, on his side or upright. His tail oscillates and his pectorals perform graceful undulations like a dancer manipulating a delicate fan. Suddenly he charges a pigfish four times his size, the scissor tail streaming out, the points close together. In the space of six minutes he spawns six times with the same female. But demoiselles are promiscuous and the nest collects the eggs of many females, which are cruising over the male territories and spawning repeatedly. If he finds few females visiting him he makes an excursion up into open water. There he approaches another demoiselle, using the same rocking movements as when he invites a cleanerfish to attend him. He tries to entice the female to his nest.

At night the male remains on guard over the nest, only occasionally being displaced in the darkness. His duties continue until hatching occurs at night after five and a half days. Towards the end he becomes much less aggressive, showing little nursing activity and spending much time hovering about a metre above the nest. After the eggs have hatched he remains close by for several hours. Over the summer he may spawn up to three more times, depending on population density and the pressure of space — demoiselle populations are often limited by the available nesting space.

The aggressiveness of a group of nesting demoiselles makes life difficult for other members of the community. I once watched a red moki attempting to browse on the rock-encrusting animals near a nursery. Every time he ventured to feed, a demoiselle charged out and put him to flight. After eight fierce attacks the red moki took refuge beneath a ledge, abandoning all attempts to feed. On another occasion, however, a gang of four leatherjackets attacked and consumed the eggs of three nests in turn, ignoring their frantic guards. If a stone or foreign object falls on a nest, or if a hermit crab crawls across it, the male will make vigorous attempts to remove it. Demoiselles will persist with amazingly large objects.

By early April all spawning has ceased. Emerald-green juveniles 1 cm long hover close to the rock face. Unlike the adults, they swim with dorsal fin erect, to maximise body size, and extend their fin spines for protection. Initial growth is rapid: over 10 cm in four months. During winter, growth slows markedly and the young fishes, light green in colour, come together in mid-water to feed.

At dusk, demoiselle schools descend like birds to the reef. During twilight they hover in dense swarms beneath ledges and in caves. As darkness closes they settle down in crevices with fins erect, quite alert — but motionless. As night advances their colour becomes a midnight blue, their sides often blotched deep green or barred with dark, vertical streaks. Like most plankton pickers, demoiselles spend a great amount of time each day seeking the grooming services of cleanerfishes. I see a characteristic cloud of demoiselles radiating like wheel spokes. At the hub there is a cleaner weaving about, pecking gill covers, fin bases and bodies as the fishes rock gently at oblique angles, all fins extended in seeming ecstasy. If the cleaner breaks off to hunt elsewhere, the demoiselles pursue it, posturing extravagantly in their efforts to arouse a cleaning response.

Male and female demoiselles make up to 14 courtship passes during spawning.

Female demoiselle deposits eggs on nest site prepared by male who will guard them until they hatch.

Juvenile demoiselles hover in black coral tree.

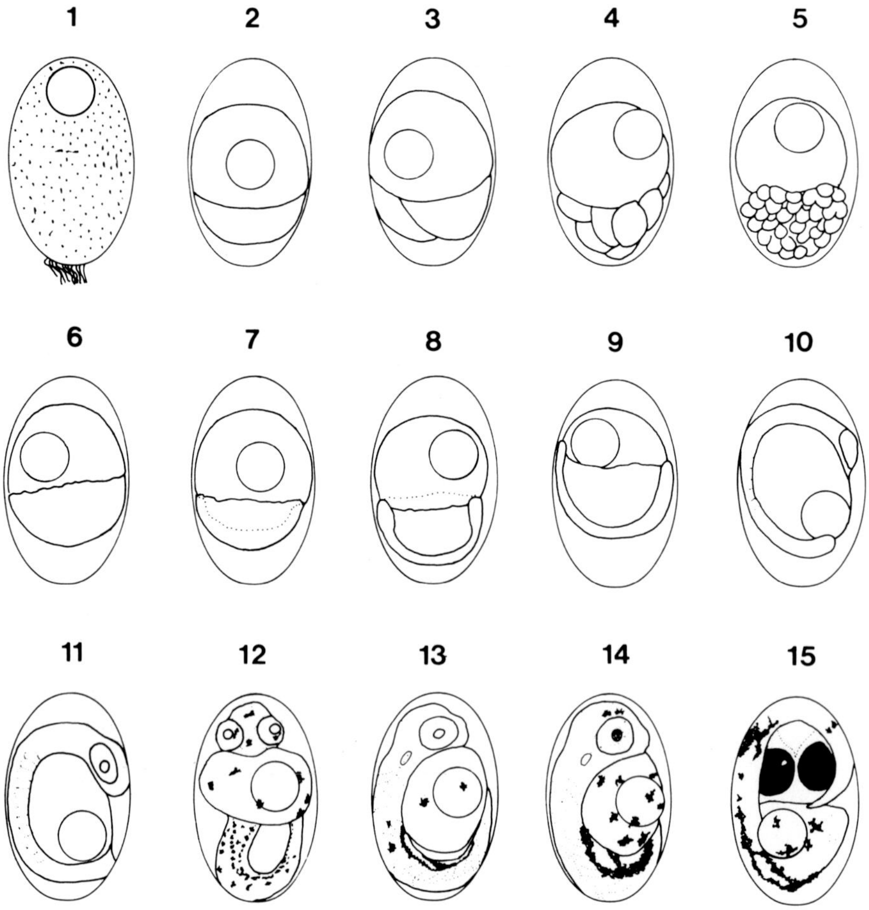
1
2
3
4
5
6
7
8
9
10
11
12
13
14
15

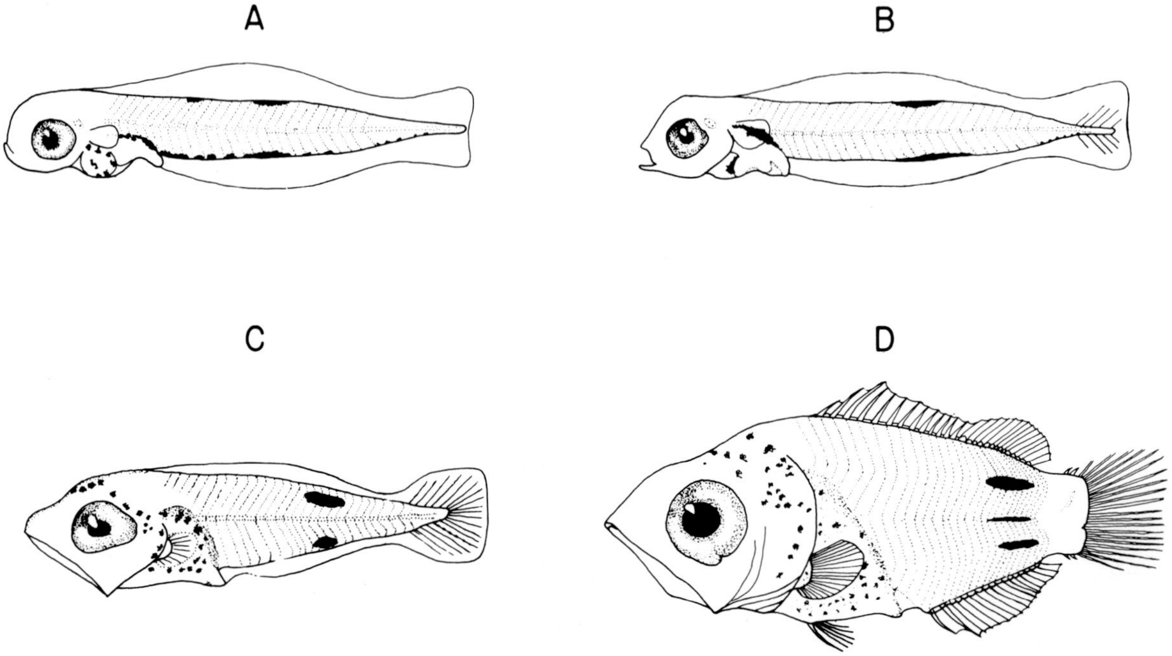
A
B
C
D

An early stage demoiselle egg, attached to weed by adhesive tendrils. Multiple oil droplets.
(Courtesy of Dr M. Kingsford. N.Z. Jour. Mar. & F.W. Research, 1985, Vol. 19: 429-438)

Opposite above: *The development of a demoiselle egg.*
1. *Unfertilised egg and oil droplet.*
2. *First hour after fertilisation.*
3. *At 1.10 hours: first division.*
4. *At 2.15 hours: 8-16 cells.*
5. *At 3.10 hours: 64 cells.*
6. *At 7 hours.*
7. *At 11 hours.*
8. *At 15 hours.*
9. *At 18 hours.*
10. *At 23 hours: head and eyes develop.*
11. *At 28 hours.*
12. *At 45 hours: movement and pigmentation.*
13. *At 50 hours: head enlarges.*
14. *At 85 hours: embryo largely fills egg capsule.*
15. *At 112 hours. At 127-137 hours, the larva hatches.*

Opposite below: *Demoiselle larvae.*
A. *Newly hatched; mostly translucent; yolk sac present. Bright blue eyes.*
B. *At 144 hours: yolk sac gone. Well-developed jaws.*
C. *Head and trunk much developed; enlarged mouth.*
D. *Adult fins have developed; no scales; 7 mm long.*
(Courtesy of Dr M. Kingsford. N.Z. Jour. Mar. & F.W. Research, 1985, Vol 19: 429-438)

Blue maomao
Bright blue ellipses explode at the surface in a feeding frenzy. Myriad tiny pink euphausiid shrimps skip about with no hope of escape from the nimble blue maomao, foreheads humping above the surface, mouths slurping audibly, bodies as tight packed as sardines in a can.

Their vee-shaped tails give them great dexterity; they can brake sharply with their pelvic fins, veer to either side with their pectorals and seize their planktonic prey individually with their small, finely toothed mouths, in much the same way as the fantail, an insect-eating bird, catches its prey.

Of all the plankton pickers, these swim uppermost in the water column, seldom venturing below 20 m. Beneath them, in serried layers, swim vast schools of demoiselles and, a little deeper, solid schools of the quite unrelated pink maomao, butterfly and splendid perch. Blue maomao live in a vulnerable habitat and they quite often suffer predation. I have seen a kingfish make an explosive rush into a mass of blue maomao, its whole body lashing with waves of energy, and snap one up that strayed from the school.

At night blue maomao move into the foot of the cliffs. Unlike pink maomao, they do not fall into a deep sleep, but hover just clear of the bottom in rocky hollows, or cruise very slowly among the rocks. Compared with most reef fishes, they are surprisingly active at night. When our powerful movie lights attract dense swarms of night plankton, blue maomao and sometimes koheru arouse themselves and join in a midnight feast. At night all their pelagic predators have withdrawn to spend the hours of darkness in loose formations in mid-water. Even then the blue maomao are not safe. They have been found in the stomachs of scorpion fishes and other stalkers of the night.

In summer, juveniles appear in small groups close to the rocks near the surface. Until they are about 10 cm long they have yellow anal fins and belly.

A closely related species, but slightly smaller, is the sweep. It schools along with the blue maomao and is almost identical, but for its uniform grey colour and slightly deeper body. It grows up to 25 cm long.

Blue maomao are assiduous in seeking the attention of cleanerfishes, especially over the warmer months. It is common to see a cleaner wrasse flitting over the rocks, with a retinue of blue maomao seeking any opportunity to cluster round and posture in the typical tilting attitude which seems to release a cleaning drive in the wrasse.

A more unusual behavioural trait is one I call 'skimming'. A group of blue maomao will often dive-bomb a patch of sand among the rocks, skimming off it on their sides and ascending to await another turn. A group will persist in this activity for some time, taking turns to skim the same patch and always presenting the same side of their bodies. On cliff faces I have seen them skimming on a patch of weed or sponge. I do not believe this is parasite removal or spawning activity, but it may be a form of ritualised grooming, such as we see with birds and monkeys.

On one occasion, within a rocky canyon I saw a mass of some 300 blue maomao so closely packed they were virtually touching. The sphere extended to within 2 m of the surface and 1 m of the bottom, in water 8 m deep. Beneath the fish cloud about a dozen fishes at a time were skimming on the rocks and rejoining the sphere. They let me observe them from within a metre range without disturbance. They were barely moving, a dreamy, close-packed mass of electric blue. Further on I encountered a second, similar mass. As I passed them, a larger number accompanied me, swimming ahead, alongside and behind me, almost all the way back to my boat — a mystifying ritual in which I had felt accepted!

The blue maomao grows to 40 cm.

A flurry of blue maomao.

Trevally

As a part-time member of the plankton-feeding guild, the trevally has a deeper, more compressed body than its close relative, the predatory kingfish. Such lateral compression of the perfect cylindrical shape of pelagic fishes increases the surface area and hence adds to drag. Therefore the trevally sacrifices some speed for its compressed shape; but it is much better adapted for its other roles — the vertical tilting action of vigorous plankton feeding and for bottom feeding. It grows up to 60 cm long.

In summer trevally are most conspicuous in close-packed schools, backs humping above the water as krill and other plankton creatures are gulped down. Around the Poor Knights, resident schools used to be immense — as large as a football field. The noise of their feeding and the roar as large predators torpedoed through their midst added to the excitement of witnessing such frenzied activity. Then, one year, I had to watch helplessly as a commercial vessel spent two weeks harvesting them with a giant purse seine net. Since then, only crumbs of the original armada remain.

Trevally are versatile and, when suitable plankton food is not abundant, they forage on the bottom, sucking up sediment to sift out worms and other small organisms, before blowing the detritus out through their gills.

As the trevally grows beyond 40 cm, its back becomes dark blue-green. Sharp, bony scutes on either side of the tail become more prominent and the head develops a hump. Such large adults abandon school feeding and forage in small groups around rocky headlands. Slow-growing and long-lived, such fish may exceed 45 years in age.

Juvenile trevally, up to 15 cm long, form part of the rocky reef population moving about in small groups, along with blue maomao and koheru. Like these fishes, they frequently skim on sand, rock or the bodies of other fishes, for prolonged periods. Very small individuals, 2 cm long, sometimes remove parasites from blue maomao and black angelfish. They boldly pursue kingfish, much like their relatives, the pilotfishes, do.

I once saw a group of young trevally pursuing a large scarlet wrasse, persistently enclosing it in a huddle of silvery bodies, until it just gave up and hovered passively at the centre. The behaviour of fishes often mystifies me and I am left with a strong desire to spend more time in their society.

Groups of reef trevally gradually merge to form open-water schools of the same year-class.

Koheru hover, hopeful of cleanerfish attention.

Koheru

The koheru is a small, plankton-feeding schoolfish up to 50 cm in length. Its near cylindrical, finely streamlined body is too short for it to have the speed of the longer kingfish. However, by dodging about in closely co-ordinated schools, koheru can usually elude predators. The yellow-green colouring of their flanks tends to merge the fishes together, making target selection difficult. In younger koheru more of the body surface has this yellow coloration, but it can be intensified or suppressed in a flash. When marauding kingfish move into sight, koheru will dodge down to the shelter of the reef — an unusual move for silvery, pelagic fishes.

Koheru feed on smaller plankton animals than trevally do — mostly copepods — and they seldom school on the surface, preferring mid-water. As they mill around at high speed, their bodies rustle with sound energy and their flexible jaws extend intermittently to form a sucking tube.

Juvenile koheru swim in much denser schools. While the adults dodge about at random within the aggregation, the juveniles move with more co-ordination, often streaming up towards the surface and down to the reef in shimmering, silvery ropes. A lone baby kahawai can often be seen swimming with them.

Both juveniles and adults frequently rub themselves on the bodies of other fishes, even sharks, and they often form an escort around a diver, perhaps enjoying the protection of his or her bulk. Small groups of adults seek the attention of cleanerfishes. They hover in mid-water, bodies twitching, tails arched down as they receive close inspection.

The koheru can easily be confused with the jack mackerel, which has very similar colour, form and lifestyle. The jack mackerel does not have the yellowish streak along its back; its lateral line dips sharply midway long its length and its pectoral fins are so long they reach to the dip in the lateral line. The jack mackerel grows to 45 cm.

Sunfish

Amongst the plankton world that nourishes so many of the Poor Knights communities, is a bizarre pelagic creature that occasionally joins the reef fishes during its ocean wanderings. A relative of the triggerfish, puffer and porcupinefish, the sunfish is the most outlandish of all — just a head with huge anal and dorsal fins and a tail flap. The fins may extend 4.75 m from tip to tip. Its spinal cord is no more than 25 mm long — this for a creature that can reach nearly two and a half tonnes, the largest bony fish in the sea. It grows to 1.5 m in length.

The sunfish form is an oval disc with two opposing fins towards one end, bridged by a hinged, crescent-shaped flap which serves as a rudder. The scientific name *Mola* is, appropriately, Greek for millstone. Such an enormous fish has only a tiny mouth with powerful, bony-ridged jaws. I have seen it feeding on soft-bodied plankton, salps and jellyfishes. Why it has such formidable jaws, ideal for crushing shellfish and crustaceans, is a mystery, but it may also feed on the ocean floor.

At least it *is* known that sunfishes begin their lives in the deep ocean, rising as they grow. When it hatches from its buoyant, planktonic egg, the larval sunfish has a tail just like any ordinary fish. But as it develops, the upper and lower tail lobes fuse around the end. During its helpless, juvenile period the sunfish is protected by an armour of strong spines, five of which grow into long horns protecting the middle of the back, the snout, the chest, and either side of the body.

At the next stage the fish begins to deepen, the spines reduce and a new tail develops, connecting the abbreviated back and anal fins. As the spines are discarded, the tail shrinks like that of a tadpole. By the time it is about 12 mm long, the body has assumed the basic adult form.

The sunfish's propulsive system is equally unusual. The two long fins flex in unison from side to side, each describing a figure of eight, counteracted by the broad tail surface. With the inertia of such bulk it takes time for this finning system to build up speed, and for this reason divers have found it possible to catch and examine sunfishes. Once the dorsal fin is seized the vast creature relaxes completely and grinds its jaws with a strange creaking noise. The tough, gristly skin is several centimetres thick; a diver described it as feeling like 'fossilised towelling'. Inside its mouth are goose barnacles, alongside huge isopods, which it allows us to remove — if the vice-like jaws were to close they might sever a wrist! Other parasites swarm around the tiny gill slits and eyes. No wonder sunfishes are seen on the Californian coast receiving the attentions of cleanerfish. Perhaps these parasites account for the explosive leaps the sunfish can make, launching its enormous mass completely out of the water, several times in succession. I have seen one scratching its side on the bottom at 30 m.

Sunfishes join the Poor Knights plankton pickers over the summer months, but one year I watched a dozen feeding on a huge agglomeration of chain salps in late June. In recent years their numbers have reduced with the advent of wasteful fishing methods, such as drift-nets. Until humans encroached on their world, sunfishes were extremely well adapted to escape any potential predators and probably had a very low mortality rate.

Largest bony fish in the sea: why does the sunfish have such powerful jaws when its diet is plankton?

Golden snapper

By day, dusky brown shadows hover in the twilight of an undersea cavern. Swimming slowly in mid-water, seldom near the surface and never resting on the bottom, the golden snapper hide their burnished, shot-silk bodies in the gloom of caves. In deep water they hover, barely moving, above the peak of a rocky pinnacle. These are nocturnal feeders, awaiting the nightly invasion of the upper sea layers by swarms of animal plankton: copepods, crustacean larvae, krill and arrow worms, and the small fishes which feed on them.

Planktonic crustaceans, essential diet for many night-feeding fishes, perform a nightly vertical migration. Triggered by the fall in light intensity, the animal plankton rise each evening from the deeps to feed all night long on the rich plant plankton in the surface layers, dropping down again with the first rays of sunrise.

Animal plankton use this light/dark change as a mechanism to enable them regularly to change their environment. Unable to move more than a hundred or so metres per day under their own power, these tiny animals may, by sinking and rising through layers of ocean water moving at varying speeds and even in different directions, travel a couple of kilometres or more by morning to reach a new patch of plant plankton. Otherwise they would swiftly exhaust their local food supply.

The golden snapper is part of this food chain and regulates its living pattern according to the movements of the large plankton. Thus it is normally found in deep water, right down to 200 m offshore, where plankton-carrying currents are richest. Golden snapper schools move very slowly and do not follow any closely co-ordinated pattern. Unlike many other schools, they may include individuals varying widely in size, the average being from 30 to 40 cm.

Their reflective coloration serves as a daytime protection from predators, rather than as camouflage from their night-time prey. Beneath each translucent scale there is a layer of vivid orange-red pigment. Depending on the angle of vision, the fish either appears as a dark brown shadow in the dim light or shines like a copper mirror. Sea water filters out all red light in the first few metres, and this is why so many night-feeding fishes are bright red.

The schooling behaviour of the golden snapper seems more useful for the safety of numbers than an advantage for feeding; hence the presence of schools in dimly lit regions, where they would be least conspicuous. Further defence is provided by sharp spines on the head, fins and gill plates, and the heavily armoured scales with serrated, razor-sharp edges.

The mouth has bands of minute teeth in both jaws. The jaws are protrusile, with an upward, gulping action for seizing prey silhouetted against the starlight or lit by the pale blue fire of luminous plankton.

The golden snapper reaches 55 cm in length.

Golden snapper, night feeder of the plankton.

Slender roughy
Close relative to the golden snapper, the slender roughy is a smaller fish which inhabits the deeper waters of the continental shelf and the abyssal waters below. At the Poor Knights it comes well within the range of skin-divers. By day it lurks beneath low rock ledges in the darkness.

Its two-toned body, light above and dark below, is an example of reverse countershading, adapted to daytime concealment. Occasionally, on overcast days or when light is poor because of turbidity, the roughy is seen in schools in the open like the golden snapper, but normally it seeks shelter all day, only emerging to feed at night, like its larger relative. Its mouth opens almost vertically, well served by the large, forward-positioned eye. In size it would not reach more than about 12 cm.

Slender roughy hover in caves by day, hence their light-coloured backs and dark bellies.

Big eye

Beneath any ledge, in the gloom of a cave or under a large rock, these gregarious little reef fishes swarm during the daylight hours, hovering in groups of a dozen and up to 150, heads to the light, darting to and fro as if afraid to venture out.

Within half an hour after sunset the water becomes alive with them; they flit about like beetles, or lie motionless in mid-water, frozen in the torch beam. By day they appear to be a dark, chocolate brown; but when they are illuminated at night, iridescent pink and purples appear.

Big eye live at all depths, from 70 m to within 2 m of the surface — wherever a suitable daytime refuge is available. Each group appears to use the same shelter, day after day. In very large caves, such as the enormous Rikoriko Cave at the Poor Knights, big eye and slender roughy mill around together in the permanent twilight, even by day. On summer nights they enter rivers on the adjacent coast, swimming well upstream into mangrove forests to feed on crab larvae, shrimps, amphipods and other animal plankton.

Easily confused with the slender roughy, which shares its habitat and mode of life to a certain degree, the big eye is distinguished by its deeper, more compressed body, shorter-based dorsal and longer anal fin. Its eye is much larger, more than half the head length, and it is positioned directly above the mouth, which opens vertically like a trap door. If I switch off my diving torch at night, once my eyes adjust I can see a miracle: the big eye are feeding selectively on tiny motes of plankton that can be detected by undersea moonlight — and even by starlight!

Like many fishes that live in caves, big eye often swim upside down. Orientating themselves by a back-to-the-light reflex called 'dorsal light reaction', they place their backs towards the light source and where light bounces off the sandy floor of a cave they will readily swim upside down. That this is not simply an orientation to the nearest surface has been proven in aquarium experiments, where the direction of light can be altered to cause the fish to roll on its side or upside down.

From early January, juvenile big eye begin appearing, in groups of up to 150. By late March they may double in size, reaching up to 3.5 cm in length. At this stage they are *not* nocturnal fishes. In broad daylight they school amidst the kelp glades, swimming with a jerky motion, beating their tiny, invisible, pectoral fins. Black marks on the tips of dorsal, anal and tail fins probably function as schooling signals, while their body colour merges well with the background. Why the juveniles feed on plankton in the open by day, instead of sheltering in caves, can only be surmised. Perhaps they are safer in the open than risking predation under the noses of adult fishes.

Large big eye reach up to 15 cm in length and tend to live in deeper water.

Nothing is wasted in nature: the flow of plankton past the Poor Knights Islands is undiminished, by day or night. The nocturnal members of the plankton-pickers guild are as well adapted to exploiting this food source as the day shift.

Another of the night feeders. Hordes of big eye hover under ledges by day. At night they feed selectively by starlight.

Guild of the open-water hunters

Kingfish

The kingfish is a roving carnivore that preys on trevally, koheru, blue maomao and other plankton feeders. This lifestyle gives rise to its elliptical, streamlined form. Driven by rapid flexures of its rigid, vee-shaped tail, the finely scaled, flexible body responds fluidly to a very powerful set of muscles. A kingfish on the attack is a rare statement of beauty and strength. The fish's whole structure is involved. Such a high energy burst requires extra oxygen use; mouth and gill flaps remain open for prolonged periods to increase water flow over the gills. An extra set of muscles act as power boosters. For normal cruising, red muscles receive oxygen from the blood stream; but for short bursts of speed, white muscles draw on oxygen stored chemically in fatty tissue and they oxidise this fat so rapidly the kingfish can treble its speed. Otherwise its energy output would be limited to the amount of oxygen available from the water — about a twentieth of the oxygen present in the air.

To soar or dive through 70 m of ocean in less than a minute the kingfish needs an especially small swim bladder. As the fish descends, the gas-filled buoyancy organ is compressed and its body becomes a little heavier, but its pectoral fins act like the wings of a jetplane and give adequate lift to compensate. As a further aid to buoyancy the kingfish skull, like the body tissues, is full of oil, providing incompressible lift. If its swim bladder were adjusted to deep swimming, like the hapuku and the groupers, a sudden ascent would cause the gasbag to expand faster than the blood system could absorb excess gas. The kingfish would then rise distended to the surface, unable to submerge.

Occasionally, when I am scuba diving, a squadron of kingfishes come wheeling around me, making several tight circuits before vanishing again into the blue. The rumble of my exhaust air may be the attractant. A clue is given by the kingfish's brain: as with many open-water fishes, the centre for smell is quite small, while that for hearing is very much enlarged. Kingfishes, trevally and koheru can 'hear' disturbances in water from a great distance. Sound travels four and a half times faster and much further underwater than it does in air. All vibrations in this dense medium are picked up by sensitive nerve endings along the fish's lateral line, where silvery and dark coloration meet, and transmitted to the brain. A school of plankton feeders would create a static-like buzz on the kingfish's lateral line. Small wonder my exhaust bubbles arouse the kingfish's curiosity through its highly tuned receiving system.

An unusual trait of kingfishes is the habit of 'standing by' an injured companion, thus exposing themselves to risk, as do dolphins and whales.

These days, kingfish schools have dwindled sadly. Before heavy commercial fishing invaded the Poor Knights region, somewhere within hearing there was always the slap of trevally tails — their backs and snouts awash, the plunging of gannets and the dark and silver torpedo shapes of the kingfishes, up to 2 m long, dashing through the school to grasp their prey with their finely toothed jaws and swallow them whole.

Open-water hunter: kingfish.

Kahawai

Kingfish, trevally and koheru have flexible bodies, with fine, silvery scales, but the kahawai is covered with large, coarse scales that inhibit body flexing. Its main source of power is the broad tail and its movements are more directed and unswerving. In its juvenile stages it is a plankton feeder; the adult is adapted to chasing small school fishes, yellow-eye mullet, pilchards, piper and whitebait, as well as shrimps, krill and swimming crabs. Because such prey are more abundant in coastal waters, the kahawai is only marginal at the Poor Knights, but forms large schools inshore in summer. It grows up to 60 cm.

Kahawai.

John dory
Cardboard thin, its sides patterned with rapid-change camouflage, the john dory is barely visible head on. It is a master of illusion: a sea-going mouth with an eye spot on its side that distracts from this amazing organ. The high dorsal, with its extended rays, and the outspread tail are motionless in the water, stabilising the fish so perfectly that no movement or changing light patterns draws attention to its neutrally buoyant, circular body. It is constantly oriented directly at the prey. All propulsion is provided by hardly perceptible undulations of the opposed anal and soft dorsal fins. Like a spectre it glides over the reef, often tilted obliquely to mimic a scrap of weed drifting on the current or, with the aid of the false eye spot, some other harmless fish.

Its forward-mounted, protruding eyes provide true bifocal vision, rare in fishes but essential for accurate estimation of distance. Other fishes overcome this visual problem by approaching a target with slightly alternating turns of the body, but such movements would spoil the john dory's hunting technique. It stalks to within about 30 cm of the quarry, which is usually a small pelagic or juvenile reef fish up to half its own size. The jack-in-the-box jaws expand in a flash. The broad gill plates dilate, creating a fierce suction. Into a long tube the animal is gulped and the mouth snaps shut. The small, prickly teeth are used for gripping only when prey is so big as to require a second gulp.

Time and again, as the dory is about to attack, the prey fish gets alarmed and flees for cover; but this does not deter the solitary hunter. However, despite the deceptive strategies it does not manage to obtain a meal frequently. Compared with the kingfish, which seeks similar prey, the john dory consumes very little energy and so needs less food.

John dory are usually lone swimmers; there would be no advantage for them to hunt in a school. Although slow-moving, they can readily outpace a diver when they are alarmed. But I have found that if I herd one quietly, aided by another diver, it abandons all efforts to escape. There is no apparent fear, the sharp fin spines probably rendering it immune to predation. As it hovers inches from my camera lens, it can be stroked gently with a finger.

The john dory grows up to 40 cm.

Mid-winter stalker: john dory.

To suit hunting strategy, john dory's eye spot can be intense or muted. ▶

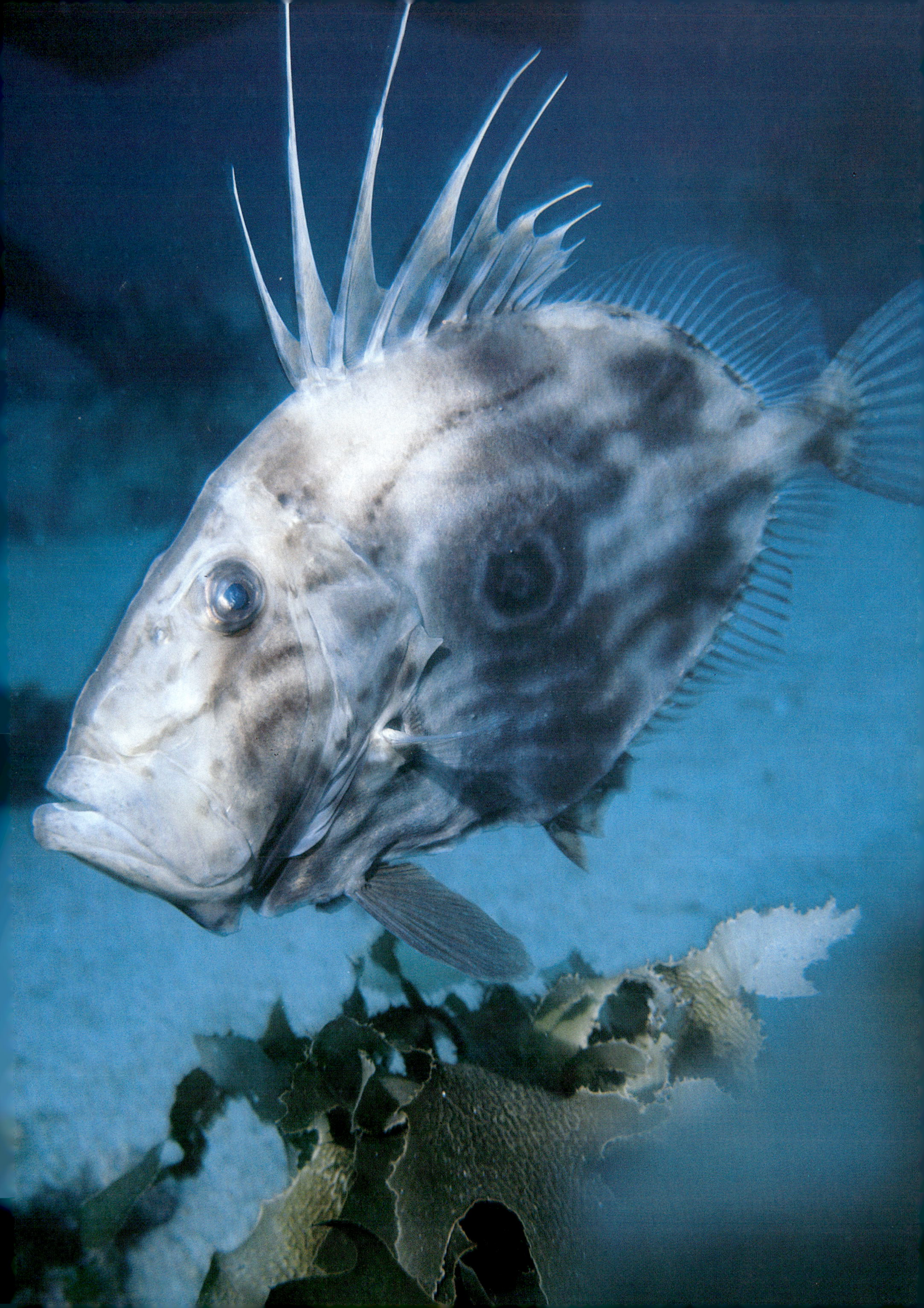

Guild of the plant grazers and browsers

Black angelfish

The black angelfish does not range far for sustenance. Each fish hovers above its territory on the reef, centred on a ledge or crevice where it seeks refuge at night. It is a plant grazer, a herbivore, especially adapted to taking its needs from the broad base of the food pyramid, where the supply is abundant, the energy yield is low and digestion is slow and difficult. Plant consumers are advanced, specialised fishes, relatively new in their evolution.

I have watched the black angelfish grazing the turf of red weed that carpets large boulders, selectively nibbling the delicate filaments of red weed that sprout on kelp fronds, and browsing on the lacy green ruffles of sea lettuce. It is a tiny ecological farmer working within its boundaries so that no patch is ever stripped bare or overgrazed. Short bouts of feeding are interspersed with turning and hovering, proclaiming its territorial rights. Its stance reminds me of a boxer dancing about on his toes, jabbing, jabbing, then dancing some more. With such a diversified feeding pattern the sea plants can grow at least as fast as they are consumed; in this way the black angelfish is able to spend its entire life in one small area of reef.

With the male there will be, somewhere within this territory, a jealously guarded nest site: a smooth, near-vertical patch of rock. Such sites are an asset that completely determines his reproductive success. Year after year he keeps it free from invading kelp plants and encrusting animals, just allowing a close-cropped mat of red and green weeds to remain, and fending off any urchins or shellfish that seek to graze it.

With the longer days of spring the male black angelfish becomes more aggressive and territorial. There are threatening gestures, head-buttings, side-swiping skirmishes and rushes to repel rivals during the winter months; and the frequency of such behaviour increases until, by November, spawning and nest-guarding begins.

Two black angelfishes swim in vertical circles alongside a steep rock face, their chunky bodies occasionally touching and always very close together. Movements are short and quick. Sometimes they quiver. Often they change direction to rotate the other way. At times they are nose to tail, but mostly they are side by side, facing the same way. Then, from the belly of the female a black ovipositor tube extends, attaching sticky eggs to the stubble of weed the male has prepared. He moves over the eggs, ejecting milt to fertilise them.

After spawning, both fishes hover above the nest, but eventually only the male remains, the white patch on his shoulder aglow, signalling his strong territorial claim to all members of the reef community. One male may spawn with several females and there are often three or more overlapping circles of eggs of different colours, showing developmental stages.

Looking closely, I see that the eggs are well fixed to the algal carpet in a circular patch around 60 cm square. They are golden spheres embedded in a jelly-like meshwork. Above them the male hovers, finning gently and constantly turning to maintain a close vigil. Nearby, egg-stealing blennies are poised on their pelvic fins, waiting for any chance to dash over the rock

Black angelfish browsing his weed patch. ▶

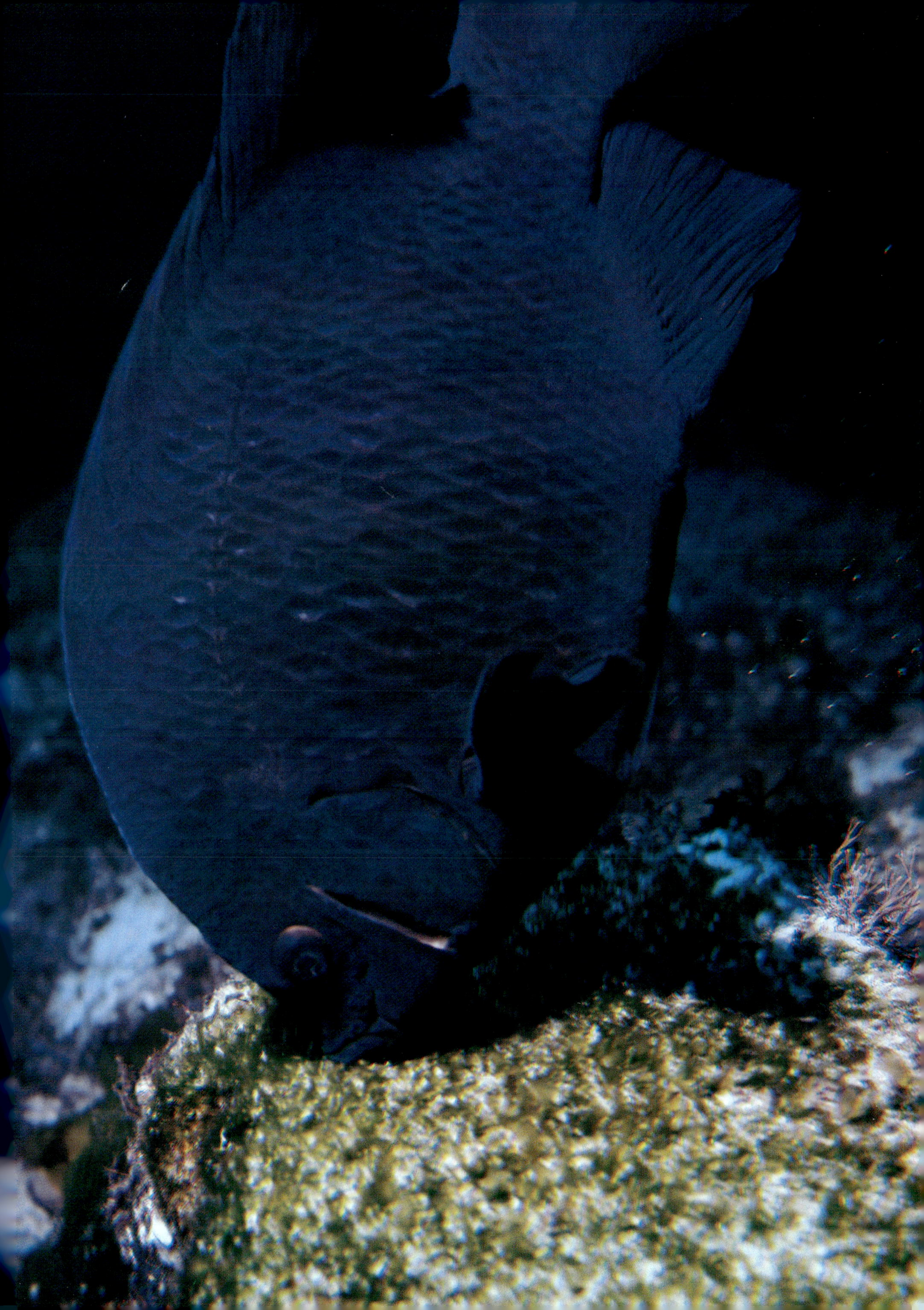

Male black angelfish guarding nest site.

face and gulp a few eggs. Other reef fishes in the vicinity are also aware of the nest and would rob it at first chance.

For the guardian, the critical distance seems to be a metre; within this range even fishes with no hostile intentions will be driven off, the male pursuing red moki, marblefishes and demoiselles several metres from the nest and then rushing back. Quite often a thief will have robbed him during his brief absence. If the pressure of other fishes is heavy, his aggressiveness becomes frenetic. I have seen one so distraught he charged repeatedly head-on at nearby rocks. At such times a grunting sound is emitted, an additional threat signal. Occasionally, like a bolt from the blue, a horde of leather-jackets may swoop down and engulf every one of his precious eggs, ignoring his utmost efforts to repel them.

Nevertheless, for such a small fish with limited egg capacity, this spawning pattern ensures a higher survival rate in the turbulent conditions of a rocky shore. The more usual group-spawnings of reef fishes can suffer very high mortality from predation or dispersal of spawn by sudden storms. Because nest-guarded eggs can be relatively large, newly hatched fry are quite big and less vulnerable to predators. Within 10 days the eggs are all hatched. Spawning continues over mid-summer until late January, when it tapers off.

*Challenged by a model, the male black angelfish's white 'ear' patch flashes white.
White 'ear' muted, black angelfish groomed by juvenile Sandager's wrasse.*

Initially the juvenile is chrome yellow with iridescent blue markings and a black spot ringed with blue on its dorsal fin. It has a false eye or *ocellus* to distract predators. Such bold coloration may also protect the young from the aggressiveness of parent fishes, which repel others of the species yet allow juveniles to live within their territory.

Over the ensuing 18 months the juvenile grows rapidly. The yellow fades to grey, the *ocellus* disappears, the blue lines lose intensity, the first dorsal fin increases in height and the body deepens. At 10 cm it is greyish black with vestigial blue squiggles on the upper part of its body. At about 12 cm there is just a little blue near the eye and flecks on the anal fin. At 15 cm all blue markings have gone. Below the lateral lines there is a copper colour. From 16 to 30 cm the body deepens considerably and the rear dorsal fin rises twice as high as the rest, so that the adult is almost rectangular in form. Such a short, deep body with sharp dorsal spines is almost impossible for a predator to swallow. It is also highly manoeuvrable in narrow rocky places, although for prolonged fast swimming the drag would be excessive. A great many reef fishes have this form.

Throughout its juvenile period the fish inhabits the same small crevice in the shallows, seldom venturing out more than a few metres to feed. Amazingly, once it reaches adult size, there is no further growth for the rest of its life!

Such is the premium on good nest sites that a young male may have to wait for another to die before he can spawn. Suitable nest sites seem to determine population densities. The greatest number I have ever seen was in a bay full of large, irregular boulders, almost every one of which was an ideal home for a black angelfish. Their constant aggressiveness was frenetic.

At night the black angelfishes retreat into crevices, fins erect, hovering quietly, alert and never resting on the rocks. The white 'ear' fades — except where three fishes share the same hole. The significance of this white patch intrigued me for some time, and at first I thought it was a sexual display signal. Then I found it persists all year around in dense populations. One day I discovered I could make the white patch disappear; if I advanced towards the fish, the patch faded and it slowly swam away. Just as a dog will offer its throat to a superior, presenting a vulnerable area to an aggressor is a classic appeasement gesture. Minutes later the patch had returned. It seems it is a territorial signal, more apparent during the spawning season when aggression is at its peak, but persisting among dense populations, where territories are close together. Such signals are truly forms of communication — the language of the sea.

The black angelfish reaches around 28 cm in length.

Black angelfish eggs; ten days to hatch.
Juvenile black angelfishes undergo a sequence of colour changes.

Parore

Parore are wary, furtive herbivores, rather like wild sheep. In weedy, shallow bays, uncommon at the Poor Knights, they dart about in loose schools of up to 30. Rarely will they allow a diver within close range. As soon as one parore senses a movement, the whole group streams along the reef, keeping to the shallows. As they glide through a dappled kelp glade, the vertical bars on their silver-grey flanks disrupt the body outline.

From a hiding-place I watch them feed. Close-set, incisor-like teeth with three cusps shear off sections of brown frond with a side-swipe of the head. They crop the thin lawn of red algae up in the shallows and nip off blades of tender greens. I once saw them gorging on pelagic salps in mid-water, their stomachs bulging with the gelatinous creatures. Parore mainly feed at dawn and dusk. At night, schools break up and they rest in crevices alone, their bodies a dark brown, splotched with yellow.

Juveniles, perfect replicas of the adults, often shelter close to the body of a larger fish, only feeding when the protector pauses to graze; the adult often jerks its head as if in annoyance at its persistent mascot.

The parore can reach 40 cm in length, and it has a broad, muscular tail.

A parore school, like wary sheep.

Marblefish

The marblefish has the small, down-turned mouth of a weed eater. Its cryptic camouflage is well suited to the shallow kelp forest, where it lurks alone or in small groups. Seldom seen feeding, it prefers to graze during the early morning and late evening. The body is well adapted to bottom grazing: triangular in cross section, with thick, fleshy pectoral fins for thrusting the fish along as it feeds like a lawn mower, clipping off the algal turf with tricuspid teeth. Concentrating on one type of weed at a time, it fills its capacious gut with small particles, which it spends most of its time digesting.

During the day, it often rests at the entrance to a small cave. On seeing a diver, it rushes at him or her in a clumsy, lumbering tail drive, body weaving sinuously, before veering aside and dashing back out of sight. Shortly after, it may make a second inspection before hiding altogether.

Juveniles are olive green, while the adults are a darker brown, varying in tone according to surroundings. They grow up to 60 cm.

Marblefish camouflaged for its weedy habitat.

Silver drummer

The silver drummer is a weed eater that prefers exposed, turbulent areas. For this reason it is a marginal species at the Poor Knights where vertical cliff walls reflect waves with minimal disturbance. The drummer's rudder-like tail can cope with the violent wave action, white water and fierce backlash which many fishes avoid. This adapts it to browsing on the fine brown and green algae and tender reds that flourish on wave-swept rocks, where tall, brown seaweeds find it difficult to anchor. A severe storm will strip off the finer seaweeds, but they grow fast and the rich supply of nutrients in exposed areas soon restores the sward once the seas moderate.

At the Poor Knights, silver drummers are usually seen in small groups dashing about in great haste, dodging under rocks to hide for a while, then speeding to and fro for no apparent reason. They are seldom seen feeding, as they gorge themselves in rapid bouts at dawn and dusk. The juveniles live in the most turbulent, bubble-filled white water and are appropriately coloured: dark green with horizontal lines of light spots.

They grow to 75 cm.

Silver drummer schools browse fast-growing weeds in turbulent shallows.

Butterfish

Among writhing blades of kelp, dark shadows weave and glide. Fins like streamers undulate in the thresh and ply of surges with a silent beauty only a seaweed forest can offer. In this fluctuating world the butterfish blends so perfectly as to vanish before the eyes, melting into a loose scrap of weed.

Butterfishes browse on the erect, canopy-forming seaweeds. Teeth fused into bony ridges, they mouth tender fronds, nip out a disc and macerate it with the grinding teeth in their throats. For this diet of larger seaweeds they have little competition: other herbivores mostly seek finer algae.

Butterfishes have a long spawning season, commencing in early July and ending in late February. Over this eight-month period, spawning takes place several times. On exposed rocky shores, subject to heavy storms, this pattern of extended partial spawning is an excellent adaptation to ensure the survival of eggs. Many reef fishes in temperate zones share this strategy, so that larval development and early growth take place in summer.

Outside the spawning season, males mostly live in depths beyond 10 m, while females and juveniles inhabit the shallows. Called 'disjunctive sex distribution', this pattern spreads the range of feeding in a population and leaves the most tender food sources to younger fishes.

During the spawning period, both sexes exhibit a violet-blue chinstrap on the lower jaws, and blue dots and whorls on the gill flaps. Those of the male are more splendid and he bears similar markings on his elongate anal and dorsal fins. Males establish territories, repel other males and court females by using bold fin displays. Over the months prior to spawning, females build up a store of fat in the intestine. When spawning begins, these fat reserves are converted into eggs; the older the butterfish, the more eggs she can produce. Younger fishes need a large proportion of their food for growth, while older ones feed primarily to maintain their functions.

Juveniles go through three colour phases. When they are very small, the slender butterfishes are a uniform red-brown, with a pale median stripe. They are extremely shy and seldom leave the shelter of the kelp forest. Wafting to and fro by means of invisible fins, a juvenile beneath a clump of weed suddenly fades from view and reappears; such is the value of its camouflage. As they grow, butterfishes become a rich golden brown with a degree of countershading — darker above and lighter below. By this stage they are more active and often group together above the weed canopy.

With sexual maturity, in their fourth to sixth year, butterfishes undergo three more distinct colour changes. By the time they reach 45 cm, most have taken on the final colour pattern; the back is very dark, almost black, and the median stripe is a series of lighter patches. This camouflage enables the adults to evade predation, while swimming low over the kelp canopy rather than hiding among the fronds. They move sinuously, sculling their pectorals and undulating their dorsal and anal fins, only using the tail for sudden bursts of speed when they are alarmed or are in rough water.

All butterfishes begin life as females; during earlier stages of development there are no males at all. At around 40 cm in length, in the fifth or sixth year, sex reversal occurs and some females transform into males, in a ratio of two to one. In this way, fishes with good survival capacities get to contribute most to the breeding stock; immature males would compete for food yet contribute very little to the population.

Butterfishes reach about 75 cm in length.

Juvenile butterfish undergo complex colour changes.
Male butterfish has graceful elongate fins for bold courtship displays.

Guild of the invertebrate gleaners

Red moki

In the half light beneath a rocky ledge, fleshy pectorals fan the water and broad tails undulate. Gradually the fishes turn to reveal pale, 'chumbling', fleshy lips, and red and white flanks like football jerseys in a scrum.

Red moki are slow, home-ranging fishes growing up to 60 cm long. They live in small groups or alone wherever suitable shelter is offering. Females forage over shallow reefs down to 15 m. Beyond this depth, large deep-bodied males inhabit caves and tunnels, which they defend against rivals. At dusk, disputes may occur which result in the resident rolling on an interloper, pushing him into the bottom or biting him. During autumn, females visit these lairs at dusk to spawn. Males herd females into their territory, chasing and biting their tails if they try to leave. One April, I saw a pair beneath a ledge showing intense interest in each other. One 'kissed' the other's tail and they rubbed along each other's bodies. During spawning the female is prostrate while the male vibrates over her, belly to belly.

Red moki refuges seem to be permanent and they spend most of the daytime within them. Stray individuals may be seen foraging at any time, but most adults feed intensively for up to an hour at dawn and dusk, resting between meals. At night they remain alert in their shelters, dorsals erect to discourage predators, their body colours muted to a uniform brick red.

Young red moki spend most of the day feeding in the open and divide the shallows up into small territories. As specialised bottom gleaners, red moki have an extremely varied diet, taking in a whole range of small,

Red moki refuge.

Living in deeper water large adults may have muted coloration. ▶

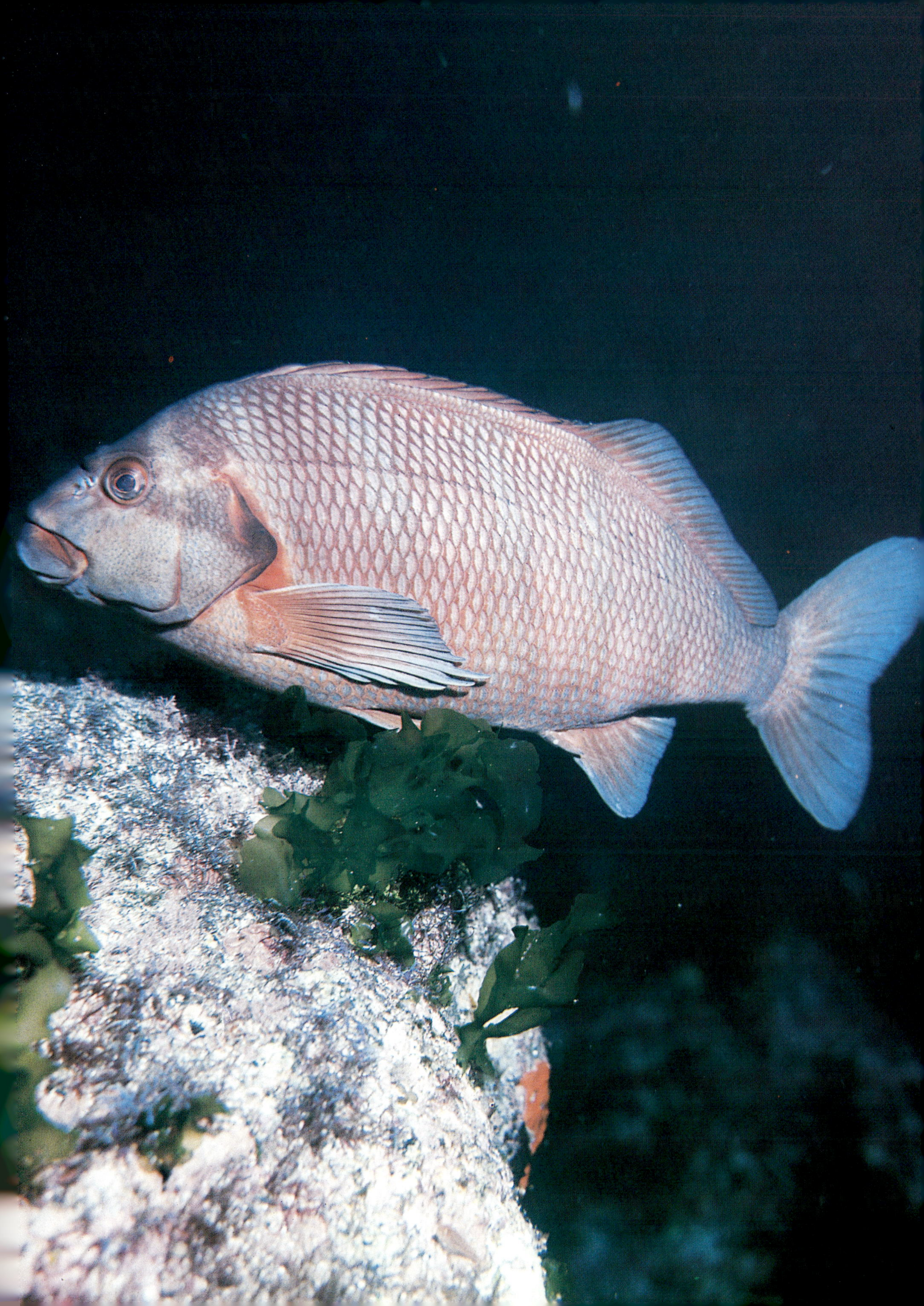

invertebrate animals. Crustraceans are the most important, including amphipods, isopods and crabs. Echinoderms eaten include sea-urchins and brittle stars. The urchins taken are usually very small and live well hidden within the thick carpet of coraline red seaweed. At times the red moki eats enormous quantities of juvenile sea-urchins; up to 60 have been counted in the gut of one small fish, like beads on a string.

Although it is seen munching away at the weed carpet, the red moki should not be mistaken for a herbivore, for the food it seeks is exclusively animal: molluscs, chitons, tube worms and polychaete worms.

When it is feeding on encrusting animals such as limpets, small paua and chitons, the red moki reveals its special bottom-gleaner attributes. Head down-tilted, using its large pectorals to manoeuvre close to a vertical or sloping rock face, it bounces down on to the rock with an audible chunk. The fleshy lips 'kiss' the food item off. Its jaws have bony plates of rasp-like teeth, which assist the suction of the mouth. This enables it to remove limpets, which teeth alone would not be able to prise loose. Few reef fishes have access to such a range of diet.

The red moki colour pattern is a good example of disruptive camouflage. The irregular, vertical patches of brick red contrasting with white break up the body contour and concentrate attention on the pattern rather than on the fish, as it moves among the stalks and fronds of a kelp forest or over the variegated, encrusting fauna of the rocky reef. In juveniles the pattern is extremely well defined. Large fishes, up to 60 cm, often become uniformly brick red, as most moki do at night. Such individuals may be 60 years old.

The red moki used to be a very common inshore species, with densities of about 2000 per kilometre of rocky coast. Until the gillnet and speargun it had few predators and therefore it produces relatively few young. Reduction of such reef fishes has serious effects on coastal ecology.

Bottom gleaner: red moki feeding.

Painted moki
Close relative to the red moki, but more strikingly patterned and with twin sets of protruding horns on its head, the painted moki lives close to areas of rock and kelp, but does not spend so much time resting beneath ledges as does its cousin. It is a straggler from Australia, where it moves in large schools. It reaches around 50 cm.

Painted moki, a straggler from Australia.

Blue moki
Occasionally, in deep, sandy canyons beyond 30 m, very large solitary blue moki are seen at the Poor Knights; these are stragglers from southern waters, where they live in schools. Similarly, the bastard trumpeter, a common reef fish in Tasmania, has been sighted on very rare occasions at the Poor Knights. Blue moki grow to 90 cm.

Porae
From the edge of the tide to depths of 60 m and beyond, porae glean the bottom for crabs, brittle stars, urchins, worms and shellfish. With their full, fleshy lips and inturned teeth they nip off limpets and clumps of calcareous seaweed swarming with tiny animals. Their feeding style is similar to the red moki, but they range out over open sand, often kissing at a patch, filtering out any small creatures and ejecting the rest from their gills. While bottom feeding they use especially adapted, long pectoral fins as props.

   Although they are usually seen as a solitary fish or in small groups, they sometimes congregate in large numbers. In The Canyon at the Poor Knights a resident tribe of 20 porae has lived for many years in a deep, sandy arena. In midsummer I have seen them resting on the sand. Just above them the thermocline made a distinct interface, with warm water above and icy cold water below. The porae appeared to prefer drowsing in the cold zone.

   At night, all fins erect, body blotched with a sleeping pattern, they wander through the kelp glades like sleep-walkers. They grow to 60 cm.

Porae find food by gulping at the bottom.

At night porae rest in the open; protective dorsal spine erect. ▶

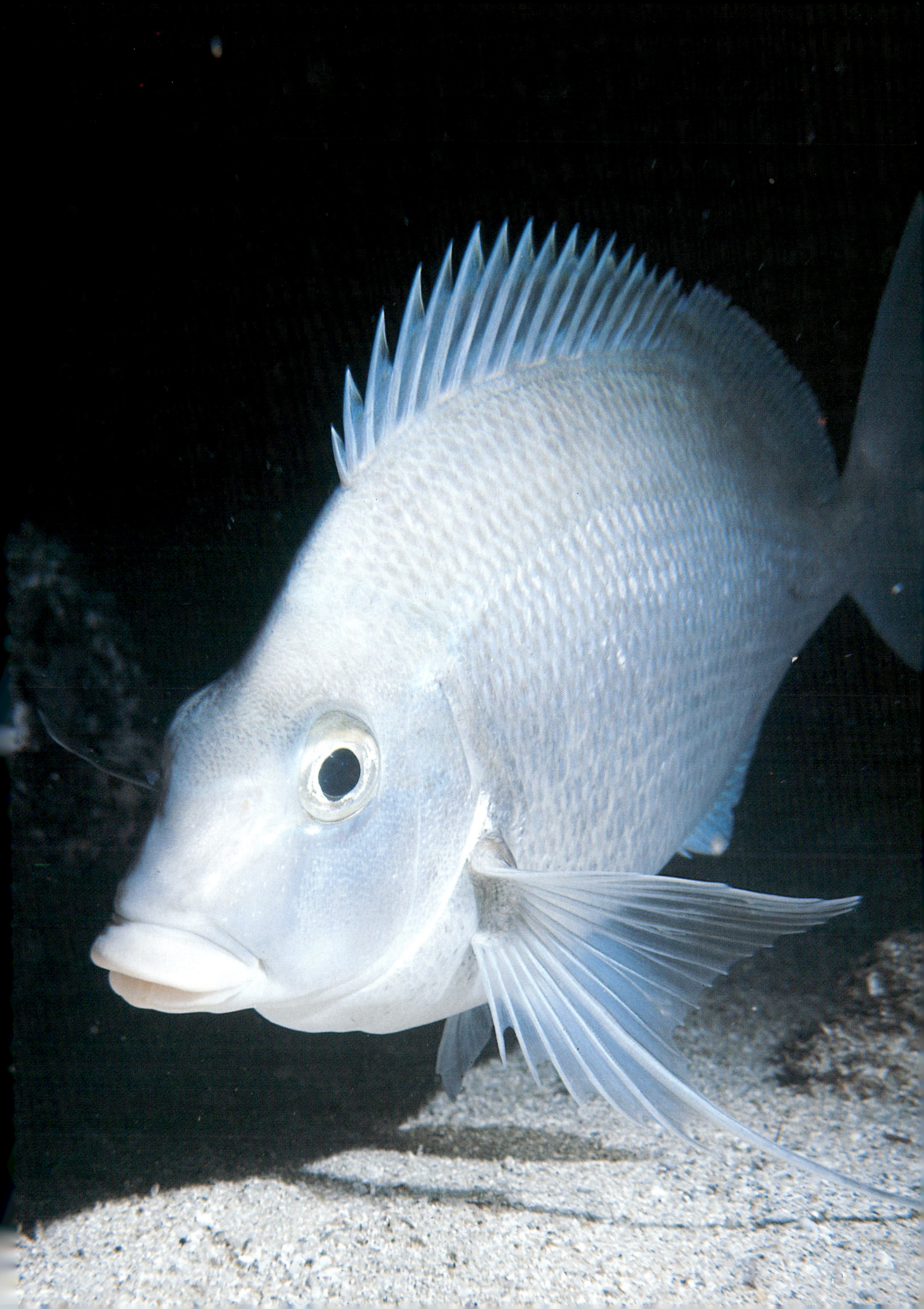

Guild of the invertebrate grazers

Leatherjacket

The leatherjacket, or triggerfish, is one of the few fishes with the audacity to bite a diver. As I operate my camera, one of these diamond-shaped clowns will nip my fingers experimentally. I have seen them grazing sponge tissue with great gusto, a diet few fishes would accept because it is full of needle-sharp spicules and toxic slime. With their chisel-like teeth and powerful jaws leatherjackets will even attack a sea-urchin, gradually nipping the spines away so they can smash the shell and gorge its contents.

In spring, colonies of giant salps sometimes arrive at the Poor Knights. These are weird, 15-m long, lolly-pink colonies almost a metre in diameter, drifting with the current like alien spaceships. Within their transparent walls several leatherjackets are busily munching their way to the exterior, gnawing great holes in the sides. Once, when we were laying concrete under water, leatherjackets sneaked up and gulped down our cement. While we were firing explosive bolts into the rocks, they would persistently take mouthfuls of cartridge grease, only to spit it out solemnly. Their catholic taste may be the secret of their success — they are found everywhere, from the shallows to 100 m. It has been calculated that, where abundant, these bottom-biting fishes modify 20 per cent of the rock face every year, helping to maintain the patchwork-quilt diversity of life forms we enjoy.

The leatherjacket has virtually no predators. As well as its rigid body and tough skin, it has a large serrated dorsal spine for defence. Along the hind margin there is a deep, vee-shaped groove into which fits another wedge-shaped spine. When the first spine is erected, the second spine, the so-called 'trigger', locks it firmly into position. Unless muscles retract the trigger, the main spine cannot be depressed. Any predator that swallowed such a meal would damage its intestines horribly. When the fish is alarmed, or even when on the defensive, as when feeding or putting on a sexual or aggressive display, the dorsal spine is raised like a flag. This is the only remnant of the spiny dorsal fin common to most fishes.

The leatherjacket has no pelvic fins. Backward-angled, soft dorsal and anal fins ripple with waves, driving it forward or, when required, in reverse. The tail forms a stabilising vane, as on a helicopter. Gill openings, vulnerable areas in most fishes, are reduced to tiny slits. The body is encased in a thick, inflexible hide, the normal scales having been modified into bony spinules, like coarse sandpaper. Such rough skin, without any of the usual protective mucus, demands its price: adult leatherjackets sometimes develop black, cancerous growths, which erode parts of the body and may lead to early death. At night leatherjackets shelter in narrow crevices, their skin mottled with white and their dorsal spines erect.

During winter and spring, males establish territories around themselves, repelling other males and attracting a female by putting on an elaborate display of sexual colours. The head develops light blue markings with dark, oblique bands radiating from the eye. The dorsal spine is waggled up and down suggestively and the wide-spread, lemon-yellow tail is waved vertically. The female's body is a mosaic of dark mottlings.

Courtship is intensive, with daily bouts week after week, frantic pursuits,

Male leatherjacket in display colours. ▶

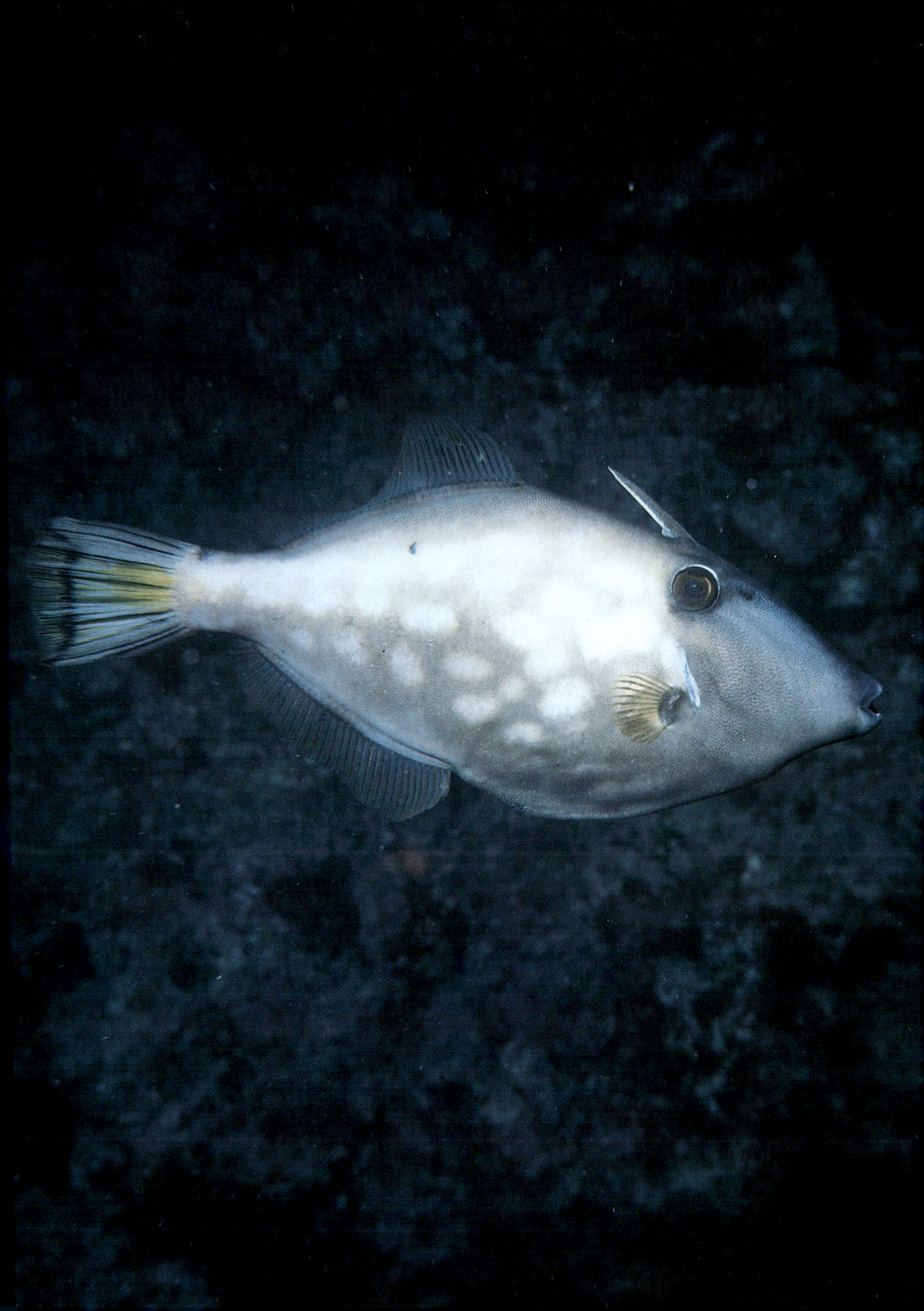

nibblings and even clicking sounds. An actual spawning has yet to be observed but nests of untended eggs have been found. Once the female's eggs are ripe and ready, spawning could occur at first light, to avoid egg predation by plankton feeders.

Juveniles appear in summer, minute replicas about 50 mm long, bright green, which are almost impossible to see as they shelter amidst the kelp. Growth is rapid and they attain adult size (25–35 cm) in two years.

A resting leatherjacket at night, dorsal spine erect, dark mottled for protection.

Well camouflaged, juvenile leatherjackets hover close to weed.

When grazing the spine is often erect, a warning signal — 'It's mine'. ▶

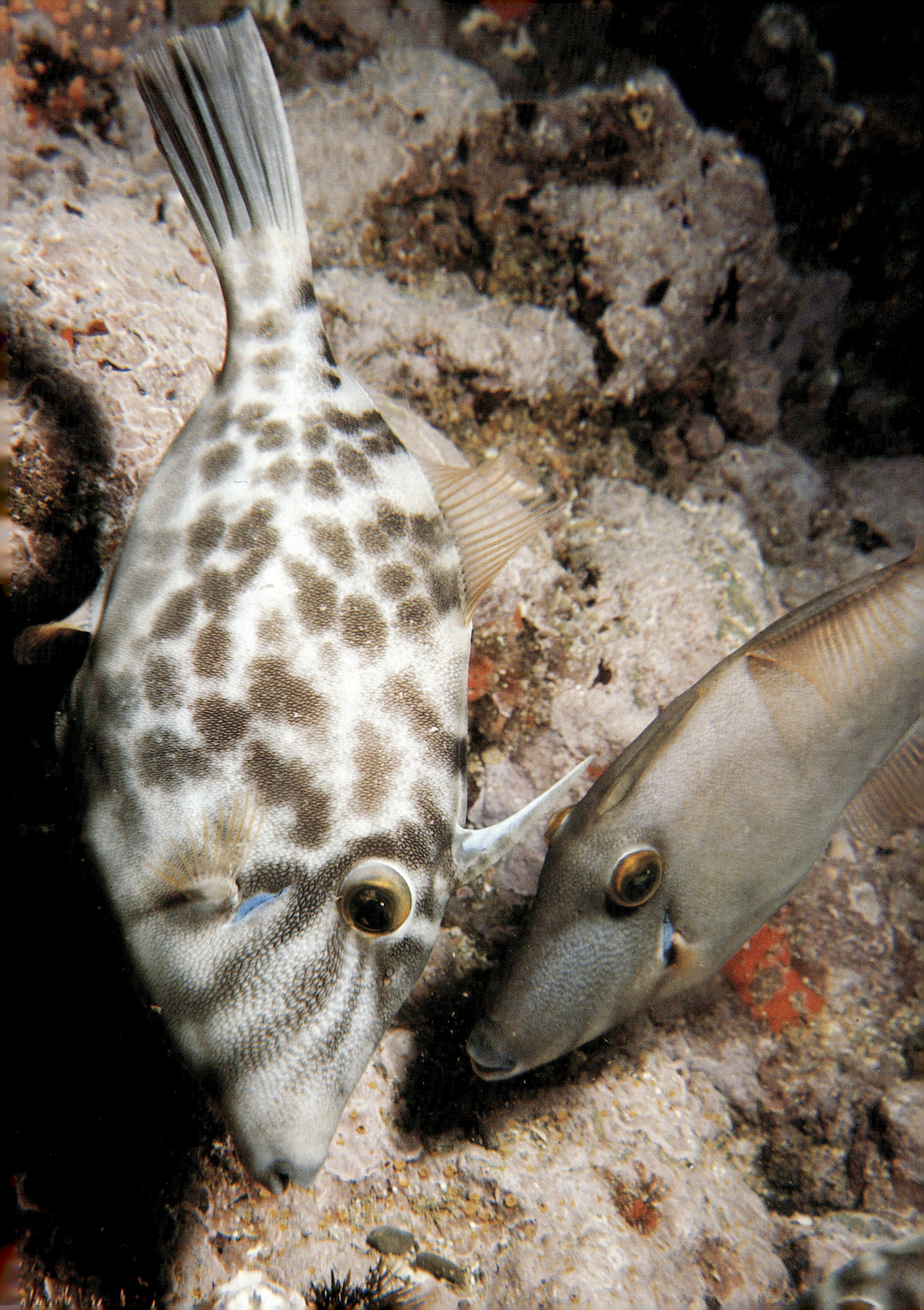

Sharpnosed pufferfish can hover, turn and reverse like a helicopter.

At night, protected by toxic flesh and warning coloration, the sharpnosed pufferfish roosts boldly in the open. ▶

Sharpnosed pufferfish
Another versatile bottom grazer, the tiny sharpnosed pufferfish is most prevalent where there are many caves and rocky galleries. At Nursery Cove, Poor Knights, up to 50 pufferfishes inhabit one rocky area called The Labyrinth, at 25 m. In other areas they are often seen 5 m above the sand, plankton feeding. I have seen individuals hovering around bushes of *Sargassum* weed, studiously keeping to the shady side, where small mysid shrimps often lurk. When I approach with my camera, the little fish hides behind the nearest stem, motionless, facing towards me. Each time I move it shifts a little so that the stem of weed always remains between us. It seems unaware that the only part of its body concealed is its eyes: all the rest is plainly visible.

Perhaps it is not all that concerned. When disturbed, the puffer can inflate its swimbladder with water, moderately increasing its body size. The white band on its side is a warning. Parts of the puffer's body, especially the liver, are deadly poisonous.

Like its relatives the porcupine-fish and sunfish, the pufferfish has teeth fused into a solid parrotbeak, divided in front. This suits it to a very broad diet, with sponge a specialty. Its gills are just tiny slits, as the rigid skeleton would restrict the respiratory action of bony gill covers. To compensate, the fish has a rapid cycle of up to 150 movements per minute — so fast, I cannot see it breathe. It has no spiny dorsal fin at all, and only the skimpiest of tails, which it uses for displays of courtship and aggression, much like the leatherjacket. Propulsion is by means of the opposed dorsal and anal fins. The rear part of its body is so shaped that these fins give adequate forward thrust. It grows to only 15 cm.

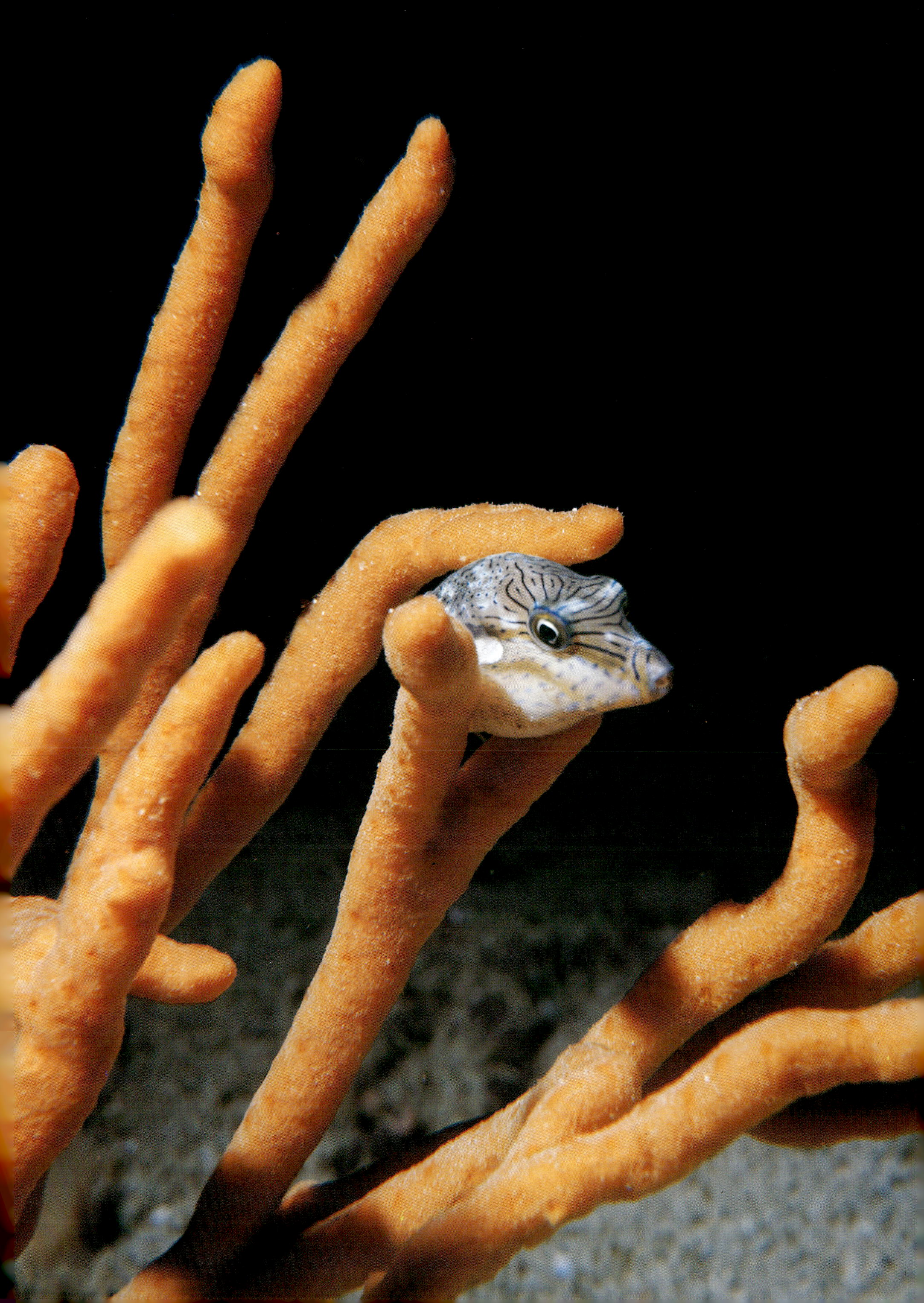

Mado

Dazzle-striped yellow and brown, the mado darts amidst plankton-feeding fishes near the cliff face. For some time it was thought to be a plankton feeder like its relative, the blue maomao, which it resembles, but this has been disproven. The clue came from its teeth. Both blue maomao and mado have small teeth in bands in both jaws, but in the mado the outer band is enlarged and pointed. The head itself is more protruberant and suited to grazing rather than plankton feeding. Closer observation showed that the mado is a grazer of encrusting invertebrates.

In all the places that I have seen mado in the greatest numbers, there has been a cave complex in the vicinity — masses of tumbled rocks or labyrinthine galleries. At such places, mado swim in random schools down to depths of 40 m. In these shaded areas, expanses of rock surface are left bare of the larger seaweeds that depend on higher illumination.

With the reduced competition for settling space and with protection from violent water movement, the rock surfaces near cave entrances become encrusted with a patchwork quilt of filter-feeding animals: gorgonians, hydroids, anemones, solitary corals, sponges, tube worms and ascidians. These in turn provide shelter for tiny crustaceans, and echinoderms such as brittle stars. This richness of marine animals, all feeding on plankton, or upon one another, explains why invertebrate-grazing fishes such as mado reach peak populations in shaded, rocky areas. The mado's diet consists of polychaete worms, anemones, and small amounts of hydroids, amphipods, shrimps and delicate red seaweed.

Juvenile mado may act as cleanerfish. For a small mado, a crustacean parasitic on the skin of a fish would be just as acceptable as one crawling over a sponge. Juveniles up to 8 cm long have been seen cleaning demoiselles, blue maomao and the male red pigfish. In each case, the customer had to initiate the response with repeated posturings. Then the mado would give a dainty, desultory peck here and there, swimming off a little way until confronted again by the host fish, eager for attention.

Mado grow to 25 cm.

Mado and bluefish are invertebrate grazers.

Bluefish.

Bluefish

The bluefish spends a great deal of its time lurking under cover, especially amongst those heaps of tumbled rocks which form a maze of galleries and passages in shallow areas. Such apartments may shelter a dozen bluefishes of varying sizes, along with red moki and cave-dwelling fishes. The bluefishes come and go constantly, rarely staying still for more than a few minutes and seldom actually resting on the bottom. They seem to prefer areas where large expanses of shaded rock provide ideal feeding conditions. Their powerful bodies and rudder-like tails adapt them well to the violent water motion that can afflict such a habitat.

Closely related to the mado, the bluefish grazes encrusting animal life: shellfish, brittlestars, tube worms and crustaceans. As I have never seen it feeding, it is likely this takes place at dawn and dusk. Like its other relative, the seaweed-grazing parore, it has tricuspid teeth, but in the bluefish these are set in several rows in each jaw. At times its brilliant blue body spotted with gold can darken rapidly to appear almost black. As a reef dweller the bluefish grows very large: up to 75 cm in length and 9 kg in weight. It probably spawns in midsummer. Juvenile bluefish are similar to the adults, but are an even brighter blue with light spots.

Guild of the invertebrate browsers

Snapper

As a wide-ranging carnivore that lives at all depths down to 200 m, the snapper is an extremely adaptable fish with a very broad feeding niche. Browsing on invertebrates, and even small fishes, its diet includes about 100 different species of marine animal. When a certain food becomes scarce it can turn to many alternatives; in this way the effect of any temporary scarcity is reduced and a large population can thrive.

Crustaceans are generally the main snapper food, especially crabs, and over rocky areas they find great numbers of tiny sea-urchins and tube worms. Large snapper generally feed on bigger, hard-shelled creatures such as limpets, but I have seen them following bottlenose dolphins and consuming their faeces! They are opportunists, ready for anything.

For the diver the snapper is an elusive fish. Its silvery pink coloration has a mirror effect that enables it to blend with all backgrounds. In open water, where I most frequently see the snapper at the Poor Knights, it has an evanescent, illusory quality. By the time my mind registers its presence, it has gone. Before the days of marine reserves, snapper were extremely wary of divers and it took me many months to get a good picture of one.

Ultra sensitive, it can detect a scuba diver's bubbles from beyond visual range, from vibrations reaching its lateral line. Often the only sign of a snapper is the random pattern of iridescent blue dots on its body and the blue flecks over its eye. These seem to be close-range schooling signals enabling fishes to keep together while schooling, yet having minimal visual appeal for an attacker. As the snapper gets older, these schooling signals vanish and it lives alone or in small groups.

The snapper is an excellent example of a group-spawning fish. When surface water temperature reaches 18°C in summer, large schools aggregate in open water. Males become swarthy, almost black, and they rush around among the females, both sexes rising in groups to release eggs and sperm together. Over a period of about four months repeated spawnings may occur, enhancing the possibility of success.

Juvenile snapper resting at night.

As invertebrate grazers snapper have the widest range of diet in the reef community.

The eggs look like very fine boiled sago, each a transparent sphere enclosing a buoyant globule of oil and a yolk. Within 45 hours the drifting embryo develops. The tail thrashes and eventually ruptures the egg membrane. Larval fishes drift on the current for about a month before settling to the bottom and developing pigmentation.

Initial growth is rapid. In reef areas juveniles establish small, exclusive, feeding territories. From 15 cm upwards young snapper gather in silvery schools of uniform size and age called 'year classes'; when a successful spawning occurs the resultant young fishes form a dominant year class that can be followed year by year as they develop.

Like most fishes, snapper do not have a maximum size but grow at a gradually reducing rate. Growth varies from place to place depending on temperature and food supply. A series of warm summers will accelerate growth, but, generally, a snapper spawned at Christmas would average 10 cm after one year; after two years, 14 cm; after three years, 21 cm; and after four years, 26 cm. Thereafter growth slows and the length relationship varies considerably. A snapper aged around 50 measured only 59 cm; another, aged 60, was 90 cm.

Until their third or fourth year all snapper are females, then about half reverse sex to become males. Old snapper leave the school and often mooch around alone. The forehead develops a slight hump, the jaws and teeth strengthen, the skin becomes a uniform grey and they feed around the cliff faces in the shallows, prising loose large shellfish with their canine teeth and crushing them with double rows of smooth molars. Whereas school snapper, preferring warmer conditions, move offshore in winter and inshore in summer, the large adults often remain in harbours and shallow bays during winter. Their strong teeth enable them to exploit food sources for which there is little competition.

At night snapper rest on the bottom, fins erect. I once saw a small snapper in a saucer-shaped depression it had created in the sand, its body barred with vertical brown bands. A resting adult allowed me within touching distance — unthinkable by day!

The snapper grows to around 80 cm.

Tarakihi

At the Poor Knights, the tarakihi appears as a solitary, marginal fish swimming in deep, sand-floored canyons. It has a broad diet similar to that of the snapper, but it is more adapted to browsing invertebrates in areas of fine, soft mud. Like its relative the porae, it poises its body at an oblique angle propped on elongate pectoral fins, grubbing gently in mud or sand and adjusting its position with small fin movements. I have seen it browsing the leathery, grey tube worms that flourish on low, flat reefs in open sandy areas. Tarakihi also eat small urchins, shellfish, crabs and other crustaceans, and feed in mid-water on krill and other plankton animals.

The tarakihi is really a deep-water fish, most abundant between depths of 50 and 200 m. Whereas snapper prefer warmer waters, which they find inshore in summer and offshore in winter, tarakihi are the opposite: in summer their schools are most common in depths from 100 to 200 m, and in winter from 50 to 100 m.

The tarakihi may sometimes be confused with the porae, but it has several distinctive features: the black saddle on the nape of its neck, which is a schooling signal, the shorter snout and the thinner lips. Like the porae it has enlarged pectoral fins, the uppermost of the six rays being very long, almost extending to the anal fin. The teeth are smaller and slender, forming velvety bands, and the mouth is slightly down-turned.

In their fourth to sixth year, when they are around 30 cm long, tarakihi reach maturity. As water temperatures begin to fall in autumn they migrate to spawning areas, especially off East Cape between Hicks Bay and Lottin Point. The males congregate in separate schools from the females, resting near the bottom in deep water. When the females' eggs are fully ripe the two sexes come together in mid-water. Around midnight spawning commences, groups of both sexes rising together from the main aggregation to mingle and release eggs and sperm before rejoining the others. It is likely that each fish spawns several times in a night and this continues at intervals for several weeks.

By producing multiple batches of fertilised eggs, this extended partial-spawning strategy increases the chances of survival should some disturbance occur: a violent storm or an attack by egg-devouring fishes. It also means

Solo here, tarakihi form dense schools in deeper waters.

that the eggs of each female are likely to be fertilised by a number of different males, with all the genetic advantages that entails. The female can produce one million eggs. If spawning is interrupted she reabsorbs them into her body and produces another batch when conditions are favourable.

The fertilised eggs, each supported by a globule of oil, float to the surface and hatch within about three days. For up to ten months the larval fishes drift with the currents, dispersing widely.

In early summer they begin settling to the bottom in rocky areas. From a tiny fish with beetroot-red sides, dark grey back, bright silver below and lacking the characteristic black saddle on the neck, normal coloration develops.

Initial growth is not rapid. At age two, juveniles reach around 19 cm; at age five, 31 cm; at age ten, 37 cm. From this point growth is very slow, so that a large fish over 60 cm could be more than 30 years old. Females grow faster and bigger than males.

At the Three Kings Islands in New Zealand's far north, I once encountered a great armada of tarakihi 30 m down. At that time this was an unexploited area. They wheeled around me with seeming curiosity, as trevally and kingfish do. These were very large, old fishes, all 60 cm long, with a purple tinge to the upper parts of their bodies. When I rubbed my fingers together they crowded around and tried to nibble them.

Lord Howe coralfish

Almost always in a male/female pair, Lord Howe coralfishes live in or near sea caves and archways from 3 m down to 60 m. They seem to prefer places of low illumination, supporting a rich growth of filter-feeding invertebrates.

With its short, laterally compressed body, about 20 cm in length, the coralfish is extremely well adapted to manoeuvring around rocks and corals. The sharp dorsal spines, which it erects when alarmed, would make it virtually impossible for a predator to swallow. The mouth, at the end of a long snout, is full of tiny brush-like teeth with which it can reach into crevices for crustaceans, or nip off the individual polyps from gorgonians, soft corals and other coelenterates. This specialised diet explains the limited habitat preference.

The resemblances of mouth, snout and body form between this fish and the long-finned boarfish are an example of convergent evolution; each species has quite independently developed similarities of structure and form to enable it to manoeuvre and forage in similar food niches.

It is not known whether the Lord Howe coralfish actually breeds in New Zealand waters. There are seldom more than two pairs in any one location and no juveniles have yet been sighted. If these fishes were as common as related species of coralfish in the tropics, we would be likely to see their typical aggressive behaviour, when the male defends its territory. Aggressiveness and territoriality explain the brilliant coloration of tropical fishes in comparison with the camouflaged or muted colouring of most temperate-water fishes. The coralfishes have brilliant colours and bold patterns to signal their presence to others of the same species from the greatest possible distance.

On a coral reef, where the intensity of life is so great, body coloration serves as a species-spacing mechanism to keep the animals within territories or feeding ranges. Hence the aggressiveness of the coralfishes, and the necessity for a male to form a permanent bond with a female and drive off all others of its own sex. At the Poor Knights, such behaviour is less obvious because the coral fish is at the extreme of its range and the food supply is abundant.

At night I have seen the coralfish at the back of a cave, fins erect, alert, with no change in coloration. It grows to 25 cm.

Lord Howe coralfish live in a permanent pair bond. ▶

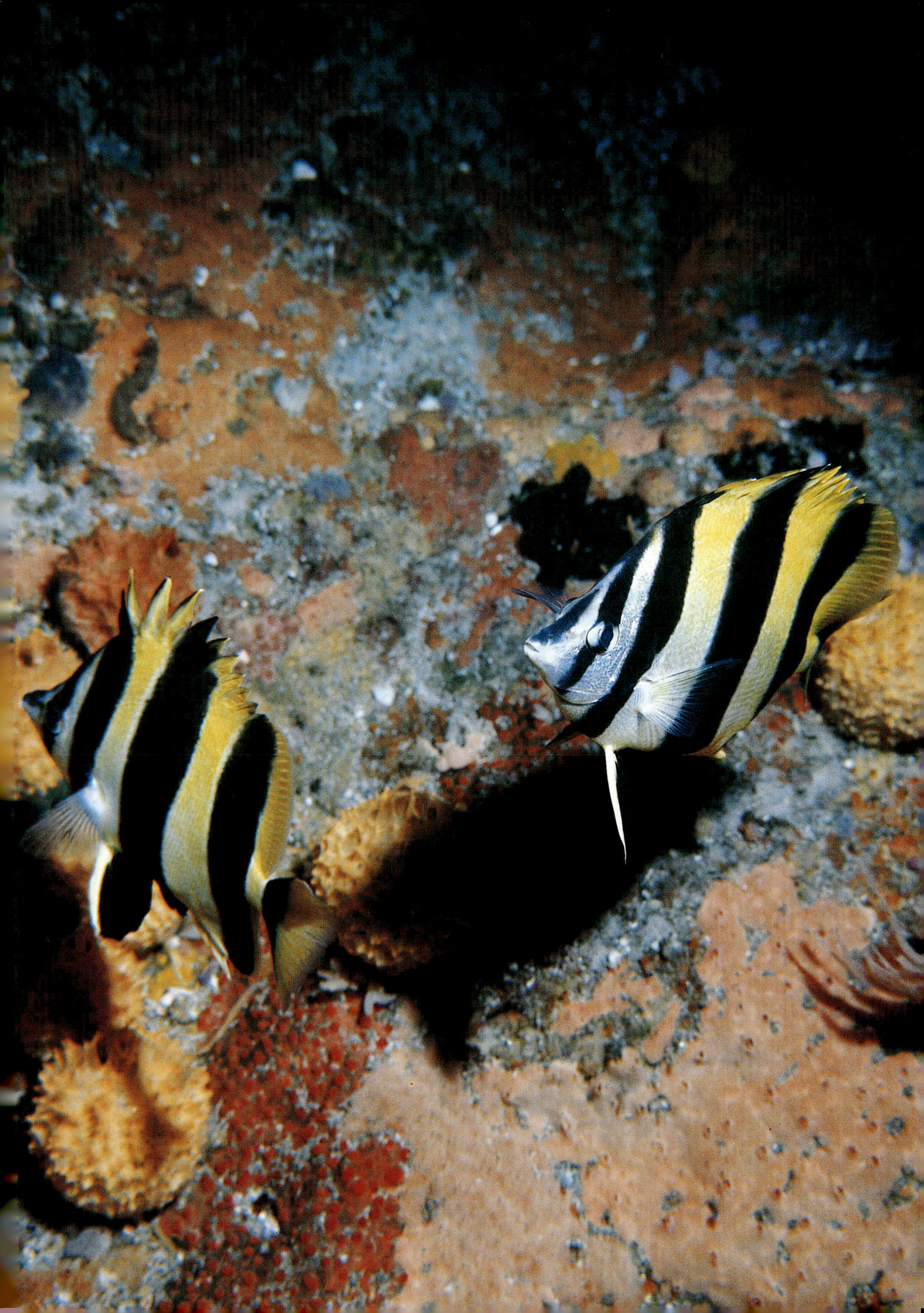

Long-finned boarfish: probably a male/female pair.

Tall stabilising fin assists the long-finned boarfish as it probes crevices. ▶

Long-finned boarfish
With its curving, translucent dorsal fin and slender snout, the long-finned boarfish has something of a dreamlike quality as it hovers near the tubes of candelabra sponges. Because it lives at depths where the diver's senses are a little narcotised, this fish seems entranced and other-worldly as it glides slowly along the cliff wall in the sponge-dominated zone beyond 30 m.

Besides its defensive value, the lofty dorsal fin gives the neutrally buoyant body great stability, enabling the protruding snout to be finely inserted among the branching and bulbous sponge shapes to snap up brittle stars, worms and tiny crustaceans. The small, conical teeth are arranged in bands on both jaws, the outer row being enlarged and slightly curved.

I have never sighted this fish above 30 m and it occurs right down to 140 m. It is extremely home-ranging; the same individual has been observed around a deep pinnacle at the Poor Knights for over three years. Long-finned boarfish are frequently solitary, yet are also often seen in pairs, probably male and female. Occasionally aggregations of up to six fishes have been sighted. These boarfish grow to 30 cm.

On rare occasions a relative, the striped boarfish, has been seen at the Poor Knights near archways and caves. This tropical species has six vertical brown bands and bright yellow fins, and reaches 55 cm.

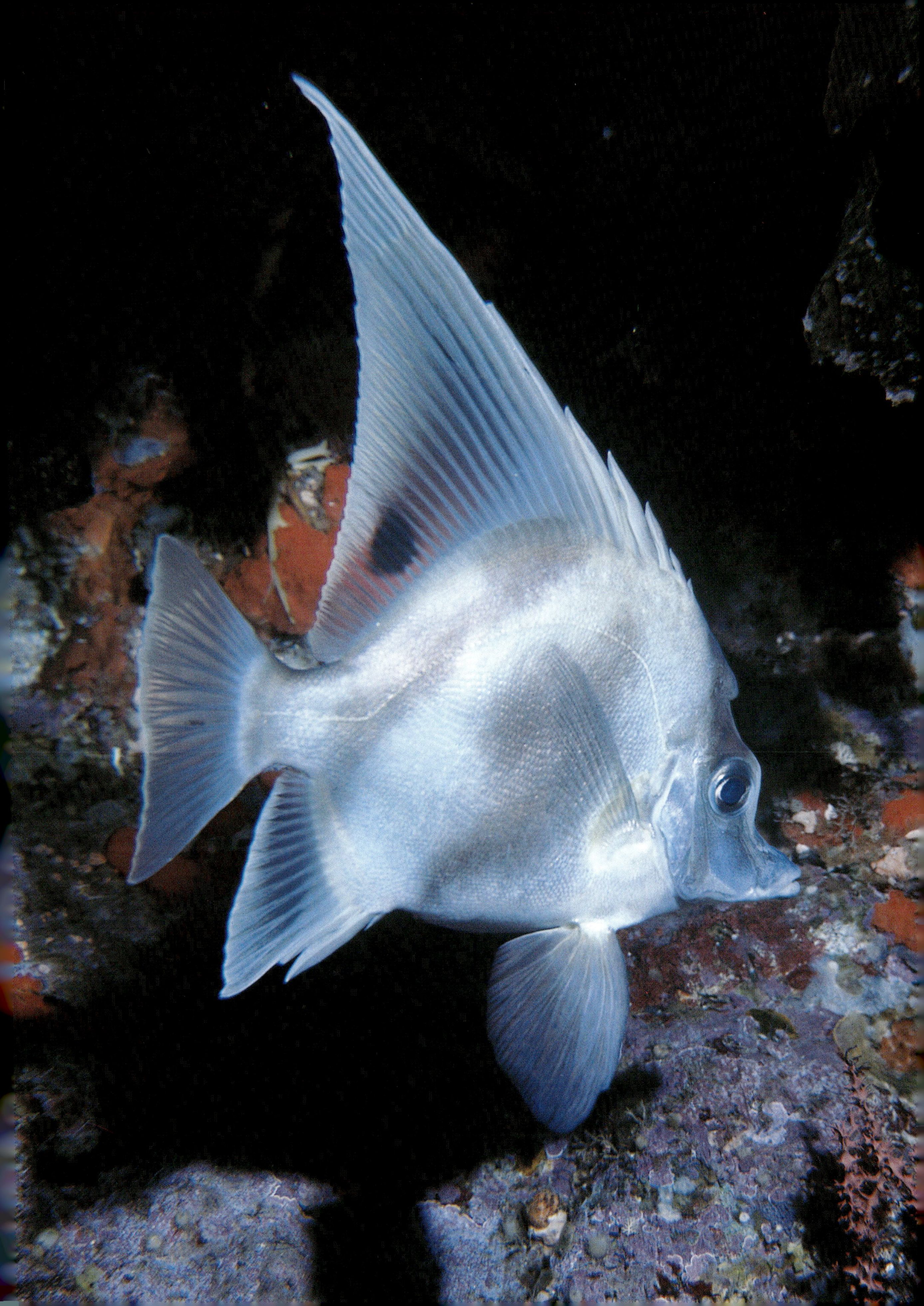

Kelpfish

This small fish looks rather like a little grouper. It is quite gregarious and commonly lives in tribes of four to eight members, of varying sizes. At the Poor Knights it is not seen in large numbers, but on the adjacent coast it is very abundant. With so many species at the Poor Knights, many coastal fishes may find severe competition for their particular food niche, or their habitat may be limited.

The kelpfish lives in very shallow water, right up to the low tide mark and rarely beyond 25 m. Because this zone is subject to heavy wave action, the kelpfish must withstand severe buffeting and there are few fishes so well adapted to life in turbulent water. Its pectoral fins are so greatly developed they function like hands. Protruding rays can hook on to the bottom and the fins seem to clasp the rock. The kelpfish rests in narrow fissures or tunnels where water surges back and forth. The fish hugs the rock on every sort of incline, bracing itself with all its fins and facing into the current.

The diet of the kelpfish includes all sorts of small marine animals: crabs, brittle stars, shellfish, worms and small blennies. As it lives in shallow water, where light levels are quite high, the olive-brown, pepper-and-salt, obliterative camouflage is perfectly adapted to merge its outline with surroundings; this probably assists also when it is stalking prey. The younger fishes have a reddish tinge.

It required a special effort for divers to discover when the kelpfish feeds. Since by day it normally rests in caves or beneath ledges, we assumed it was a nocturnal feeder. On night dives, however, we were confounded; there it was, still resting in its cave. It was necessary to make observations just on dusk before we were able to solve the problem. In the undersea twilight the kelpfishes were actively foraging over the rocky bottom, searching for the first crustaceans and brittle stars to respond to the diminishing light levels and leave their daytime refuges. Increasingly, we were to realise that the first and final hours of daylight are the feeding times of many species.

In winter the kelpfish moves into deeper water, beyond 15 m. As this is a fish that also lives where coral reefs flourish, it may be seeking warmer conditions. It grows to 35 cm.

Flounder

It is hard to believe that the flounder begins life as a normal, upright fish. As it develops from the larval stage, one eye migrates to the upper side of the body, leaving the underside blind. So, in actual fact the adult flounder swims on its side, with the continuous dorsal fin fringing one edge of its body and the extended anal fin on the other. It skims the bottom with undulating ripples running along its body and fins, scanning ahead for prey with its protruding eyes. The flounder is excellently adapted for feeding on invertebrates in sand or mud, such as crabs, shrimps, worms, shellfish and even tiny fishes. For defence, its skin has special pigment cells that enable it rapidly to match the colour of its surroundings. It needs no swim bladder and only leaves the bottom during courtship and spawning activities.

Because of this superb camouflage and because most sandy areas at the Poor Knights are at considerable depth, flounder are not frequently sighted there, although they certainly are part of the reef fish community. They grow to around 50 cm.

Kelpfish hunt mainly at dawn and dusk.
Cryptic camouflage par excellence: the flounder.

The eagle ray swims with flapping wings.

Eagle ray

At first sight the eagle ray may look rather evil, like some advanced military aircraft, especially when it rises on its wing-tips using the downthrust of its gills to gain height, before it accelerates off across the bottom. Rays are members of the shark family that have adapted to bottom feeding. They have no solid bones, the body being supported by soft cartilage.

Out on the sand I often see large craters of freshly disturbed material. This is where eagle rays have been feeding on giant heart urchins and hat urchins. Their teeth are fused into powerful, crushing plates, rather like the jaws of a vice, and they can smash up quite solid shellfish and crabs. Often a small band of wrasses and young snapper will follow them to glean any fragments of flesh left over from the feast.

The finely barbed spine at the base of the tail is coated with toxic slime; a diver who tried to grab an eagle ray by the sides for a ride was severely stung on the arm. Despite their malevolent appearance, rays offer no threat to divers, provided we respect such an excellent defensive system. They reach sizes of up to 1.5 m across.

Sting ray

Like giant butterflies silhouetted against the blue twilight, huge sting rays wheel and dive in the Northern Archway. These summer aggregations are probably for breeding. At times I have seen up to 50 of these black diamonds in one archway. They are not aggressive towards divers, despite the terrible wounds their tail sting can inflict on a wader unfortunate enough to stand on one. However, they can be very curious. My diving partner almost drowned with sudden laughter when one settled on my head like an enormous sombrero, while I was taking a photo of the cliff face.

Their tropical relatives, the manta rays, which sometimes visit the Poor Knights in summer, are especially adapted to scooping up plankton with the lobes on either side of their capacious mouths. Mantas have no sting.

In summer, large numbers of sting rays aggregate in shallow coastal bays, possibly for mating purposes or to give birth to their live young. At such times they may suffer fierce attacks by orca, which descend on them with cleverly co-ordinated hunting techniques, making it hard for the rays to escape slaughter. Sting rays can grow up to 2 m across.

The eagle ray has a rounded head.
The sting ray has a pointed snout and swims with undulating fins.

Guild of the bottom grubbers

Goatfish

Like a blind man dabbing his cane, the goatfish moves slowly over the bottom, its barbels flitting rapidly in front of its mouth, probing for tasty, soft-bodied invertebrates. In all the world's oceans the goatfish is a bottom grubber that frequents sandy areas near reefs. The twin barbels hanging beneath its chin like the beard of a goat are well provided with sensitive taste buds. The mouth is protractile, angled downward, and the fish gulps its prey along with a fair amount of sand, which is expelled through the gills. The tiny teeth are unsuited to crushing shellfish or larger food, but can seize small fishes that hide on the sand.

The goatfish has the chameleon ability to make lightning-quick changes of both colour and pattern. Beneath its skin, nerve fibres run to tiny colour cells. When the eye perceives that the background is light coloured, a message to the colour cell causes the pigment to contract so that the fish becomes white in a few seconds, with a thin pattern of red or blue lines to disrupt its outline. As the goatfish moves up from the bottom over weed and rock, the pigment cells expand and it flushes ruby red. It also assumes this colour when at rest at night.

The goatfish is a particularly keen patron of the cleanerfish. First, it often assumes a white coloration. As soon as it gets near the cleaner wrasse, it rests, as if by reflex, on the sand or hovers at an angle half a metre above and opens its mouth fully, enabling the cleaner to enter and extract parasitic lice. Quite often the cleaner ignores the goatfish and continues on its way, nipping at rock encrustations with its tiny, sharp teeth. The goatfish then has to set out again to entice the cleanerfish. Making its presence known, it settles down hopefully in exactly the same posture. While being cleaned it may flush brilliant red, perhaps to render the skin parasites more visible by contrast.

On one occasion, a goatfish followed a cleaner, the juvenile Sandager's wrasse, for some time. Eventually the cleaner entered the mouth of the goatfish and emerged with a very large isopod, which it began to dash on the rocks and devour. I have seen a group of five goatfish solicit the attention of the specialist cleaner wrasse, the combfish, arranging themselves in a circle on the sand, heads pointing inwards like the spokes of a wheel. The three goatfish nearest the cleaner were bright red, while the others remained pale like the sand.

At night goatfishes rest in the open on sand, or under rock ledges. Their bodies are pinkish, with darker red splotches forming cryptic camouflage, through which runs a red band along the lateral line. To maximise size, both dorsal fins are erect.

Goatfishes mostly move about in loose schools varying from about five to 15 individuals of different sizes, from about 7 cm to 30 cm. I have never seen them more than about 2 m above the bottom. Within kelp glades, they are more often seen swimming above the rocks and sand. They range in depth from the shallows down to 60 m.

About twice as big as mature females, male goatfishes (17 cm) are seen in courtship colours during December and January, with a blue tinge to their bodies and fins. At this time, males establish breeding territories, repelling other males and courting females with elaborate displays of their

Master of colour change: goatfish ('red mullet') by day, and resting at night.

Black-spot goatfishes swim in protective schools and feed en masse.

handsome fins. If a female's eggs are ready for spawning she is receptive. Weaving sinuously the pair rise together, the male straddling her back with his pelvic fins. A few metres above the bottom they spawn and return to the sand. Pale-coloured juveniles first appear in February, probably from the previous year's spawning, and spend most of their time feeding on the sand, all fins erect.

Occasionally two other species of tropical goatfish arrive at the Poor Knights in larval form, transported by ocean currents from islands to the north. Some survive to maturity, but they do not seem to breed here.

In the tropics, the black-spot goatfishes normally swim in schools. The herd instinct is so strong in the individuals I have seen at the Poor Knights that their juveniles join up with any fish that will accept their company, mostly local goatfishes. Sometimes one swims alongside a juvenile Sandager's wrasse that bears a similar black spot near its tail. Whatever species they team up with, the black-spot goatfishes look most conspicuous with their bold yellow and red median stripes and the black schooling signal near the tail. As they develop, they aggregate in small groups of their own kind. However, survival in this new world must be difficult: the largest black-spot goatfish I have seen was solitary and one gill flap had been torn off by a predator, exposing the gill filaments — but otherwise, the fish appeared quite healthy. They grow to 40 cm.

Another tropical visitor is the bar-tailed goatfish, growing up to 15 cm. This is a fast-moving species, darting about in small, tight schools, its coloration especially adapted to rapid swimming over a bright, sandy bottom. Its pale skin and the dazzle markings on the abdomen combine to render it nearly invisible, and the asymmetrical red bars on the tail provide just sufficient signal for the school to maintain cohesion.

An unbelievable colour transition: the black-spot goatfish by day, and by night.

Guild of the bottom fossickers

Wrasses

The wrasses are a brilliantly coloured family of reef fishes comprising some 450 species. They are found in all the world's seas, chiefly in the tropics, but some more sombre-coloured species have adapted to the temperate zone, where they live in great abundance. Closely related are the equally successful parrotfishes, which have fused beaks for crushing corals and live almost exclusively in tropical waters; and the butterfish, which uses its fused teeth for browsing the tall seaweeds in cool seas.

At the Poor Knights Islands, the wrasse family is represented by at least 10 species. But since each has a variety of growth phases, this means we have about 33 exquisitely patterned, different-looking animals forming the most complex and fascinating society in the area.

Wrasses are mostly solitary fishes, which fossick over the reef using their sharp teeth to detach small invertebrate animals found on rock surfaces. They are characterised by their rat-like front teeth, thick lips and very flexible bodies. In the gullet there is a 'pharyngeal mill': upper and lower sets of grinding and cutting teeth in the throat, with which food is crushed before it enters the stomach.

Wrasses are the most important group of fish cleaners. Some remove parasites only during early life, but for other, smaller wrasses this is the main source of food for adults as well. It is their minute, canine teeth which enable them to play their important fish-cleaning role. With larger wrasses the teeth would be too damaging; the surgery too drastic!

Wrasses have complex social patterns.

Wrasses are home-ranging, aggressive towards invaders. ▶

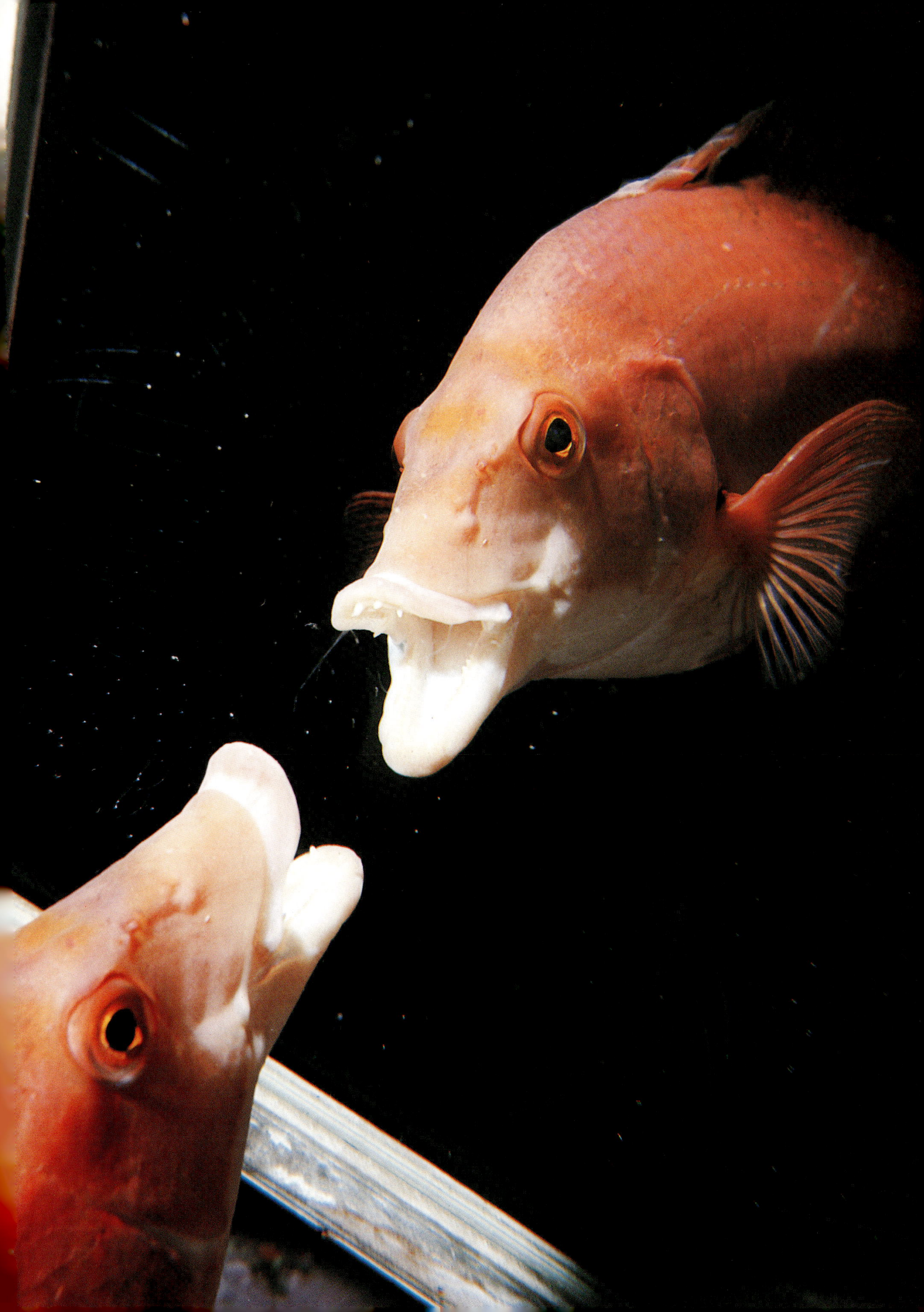

The usual brilliant coloration of the wrasses plays several important roles in their biology. Most of them are sexually dimorphic, the males having a different form and colour pattern from the females. Many are home-ranging and aggressive towards any of their species that infringe their territories. For this purpose, colour serves as a warning — a 'species-spacing mechanism', as ethologists call it. Many juvenile wrasses, and especially full-time parasite pickers or cleaners, have a special pattern, basically a contrasting median stripe, which serves as a guild sign to fish needing attention. Within each species small variations in colour pattern enable individuals to recognise each other, for the purposes of the 'pecking order' and other social relationships.

While some species range to depths of 130 m, most of the Poor Knights wrasses live in the upper levels. As home-ranging fishes, they usually stay in a single small area for long periods. They all have similar fin arrangements and a distinctive swimming style: 'wrasse stroke', sculling along by pectoral fins alone. There is very little tail movement, except for bursts of speed or changes in direction, and the dorsal fin is mainly used for aggressive or sexual display.

All wrasses are carnivores. Although it is popularly supposed that some eat seaweeds, since they live amongst them, there is no evidence to support this, other than incidental swallowing with animal food. Each species appears to have certain preferences, yet draws sustenance from a wide range of invertebrates. Crustaceans, especially crabs, hermit crabs and amphipods are important, along with shellfish, chitons, echinoderms, polychaete worms and barnacles.

The spotty has a preference for bivalve shellfish, while the scarlet wrasse eats mainly crabs and hermit crabs, and Sandager's wrasse, from a very broad range, shows a bias towards brittle stars and chitons. In this way each species has its own place in the food web, so that pressure on available food is spread widely over the more nutritious kinds of invertebrates. Linked with this is the tremendous speciation of the wrasse family, evidence of their capacity to adapt to many available ecological niches in the reef environment. In a special way, such speciation is helped by their marked sexual dimorphism and colour transitions. By changing colour, a species can very readily acquire visible differences while retaining similar bodily characteristics such as fin ray numbers and scale counts. It is as simple as donning different football jerseys! Being closely linked with reproduction, such changes would be swiftly favoured in natural selection. Any small change in appearance and food selection would give a quick advantage in reduced competition with others of the species.

There are a great many species of wrasse in the Indo-Pacific region and this intensive speciation may have occurred when a population, having spread to an island remote from the rest of its kind, soon became geographically isolated. Then, if any mutation in colour pattern occurred, the new form would swiftly have become reproductively isolated from its kin if it re-invaded the original area. Since wrasses mostly spawn in pairs, a sex-pair would have recognised each other, but shunned and repelled any different-looking species. A kind of reproductive apartheid would have ensued, and a new species would have evolved quite readily.

Whereas mass spawnings usually occur at one time and place, paired spawnings continue for several months. Thus one male can service a great many females. In a wrasse population, patterns of courtship and sexual display begin early in the spawning season. Repeated invitations ensure that spawnings occur when the eggs are quite ready. It is likely that one female spawns with several males, ensuring advantageous genetic mixing.

But why are some wrasses at the Poor Knights such brilliant colours while others are camouflaged? There is a balance between the advantages of camouflage and the need to be distinctive. Wrasses most common in temperate waters have more subdued coloration and, although very abundant, live in communities where there are fewer wrasse species. The banded wrasse and the spotty are cryptically coloured and rely on contrasting spots and markings to distinguish sexes. The scarlet wrasse is the deepest ranging. Because of the progressive filtration of colour with sea depth, red darkens to black, so red is an ideal concealing colour, common to many deep-water species. The male and female scarlet wrasses are among our least sexually differentiated wrasses, relying on changes in form and small colour distinctions. The wrasses of warmer waters, where competition is more intensive, show a marked trend towards vivid hues and bold colour patterns, with very little attempt at concealment.

If we were to take a further step northwards to the tropical reefs of New Caledonia, the progression towards brilliant poster coloration is clear. For reef fishes in areas where species diversity and population pressure is great, the advantages of brilliant coloration outweigh concealment. As with coral-fishes, poster-colour fishes are intensely aggressive: members of each species keep a measured distance from food rivals of the same species. This serves to space the species out along the reef, making the best use of each available ecological niche.

By day, wrasses fossick continuously over the reef in search of prey, seldom resting as do many other species. Their movements are only checked where territories overlap. Then hostile fin displays and aggressive pursuits break out until boundaries are observed. At dusk all the wrasses go to rest, in rock crevices, beneath ledges and even beneath the sand. Some exude a mucous envelope as a protective shield. During the hours of darkness all the wrasses seek is survival, and feeding ceases till first light.

Spotty
Like the humble house sparrow, the spotty is one of the most widespread and nondescript of wrasses, yet it has a complex society. At the Poor Knights, spotty populations do not reach such densities as they do over shallow inshore reef flats, around harbour wharves and in tidal rivers.

Its broad distribution is matched by its range of diet. One of the least discriminating wrasses, it fossicks with its sharp little teeth for small shellfish, crabs, hermit crabs and, to a lesser extent, amphipods, shrimps, barnacles, chitons and polychaete worms. Juveniles often feed on plankton.

The female varies in colour from yellowish green to pale greyish white to brown, but her body bears a regular series of four dark bars and a bold black blotch. On the yellow anal fin are two black dots.

Juveniles settle out of the plankton between December and February. Sheltering close to the kelp forest, they swim in loose, foraging schools, but space out as they grow and eventually fossick in a solitary fashion, each within its own small territory. Females mature in the August of their first or second year, depending on their growth rate. For competitive reasons, females seem to inhibit the growth and maturation of younger ones, by aggressively restricting their attempts to feed. Variable triplefins (coastal only) also compete with young spotties for food, driving them from territories and probably affecting their growth rate and reproductive output.

When females reach around 16 cm, in their third or fourth year, most change sex as soon as the spawning season is complete. With the male, vertical bars and fin dots vanish. The black spot stretches into a pattern of black spots. The gill plates are patterned with blue lines and each fawn scale on his body bears a tiny spot of blue. Males tend to live in deeper water than females, and some older ones are able to control a territory from which they repel other males: these are the most successful breeders. A perfect territory would include an area of broken rock, which offers shelter to the local females and juveniles, and a bare patch of rock, which is the courtship ground. Ideally this should be situated on the down-current side of a reef, so that when the male spawns, the fertilised eggs are taken away by the current without having to run the gauntlet of a million plankton-feeding mouths — all the encrusting invertebrates and the fishes that live over the reef flats. Larval spotties spend two months wandering in the plankton before settling to the bottom and developing pigmentation to suit their weedy environment. Those amongst sea lettuce are lime green.

Spawning takes place from late July to early December, when females move to deeper areas and the males chase them on to their courtship grounds. There the male circles the female, signalling with his dorsal. If she is ready they come together on the bottom and dash upward, almost touching. Increasing pressure in their swim bladders forces out twin clouds of eggs and sperm which mingle as the fishes veer aside and descend. The most successful males may spawn up to eight times an hour!

Long-term studies of spotties at Leigh Marine Reserve by Dr Geoff Jones have revealed some surprising aspects of their sex life. When the sex change occurs, not all spotties don the male regalia. Certain individuals mature early, to become small (8.6 cm) fully functional males, while still masquerading in female colours. Furthermore, these transsexuals have large-size testes compared to the normal male, which gives them considerable reproductive advantage. When a couple are courting, the innocent young 'female' is able to hang about in the vicinity, without being chased off by the male. No rival male spotty would be tolerated anywhere near a courtship ground. Then, when the pair make their upward spawning dash, the pseudo-female quickly joins in, adding his store of sperm to the egg cloud.

The blotches or black spots that embellish the flanks of either sex have a very special function: each individual has its own pattern, like the code on a bank cheque. Wrasses have good memories and the spotty learns to recognise the signature patterns of all the locals. Before long, the normal male distinguishes the transsexuals in his community as rivals and pursues them aggressively at every encounter. Eventually the deceiver abandons his false pose and assumes normal male coloration. Fishes are the first animals with backbones. In their society we find basic elements of much vertebrate behaviour, including our own; even the male hormone that determines sex change is the same testosterone that regulates our bodies.

At night the ever-busy little spotty rests on the bottom, sheathed in a protective mucous envelope, all its markings faded. It grows to 26 cm.

Female spotty.

Male spotty.

At night the spotty is cocooned in a protective mucous shroud.

Banded wrasse

Another wide-ranging species, the banded wrasse, lives much closer to the kelp forest than the spotty, and its colours provide good camouflage. This is a maddening fish to photograph, because it constantly dodges in and out of the weed close to the diver, but it is never still and seldom fully exposed.

It appears to be a more selective fossicker, with a distinct preference for small, hard-shelled animals: crabs, hermits, limpets, chitons, small paua, mussels, topshells and baby sea-urchins. Such creatures are found in the cracks and crevices of the rocky reef, in seaweed holdfasts and amidst encrusting growths, where the banded wrasse forages with its especially prominent, rake-like teeth.

Amidst the weedy shallows the shy juvenile varies in colour from light purple to red-brown and mottled brownish green Along its back and extending on to the dorsal fin, it has a series of six bright dots. As it matures into the olive-green female, these dots become yellowish-green wedges of colour. With transition to the male, the wedges extend more and more on to the body, along with a matching series along the base of the anal fin. Eventually the ground colour of the body breaks up into six dark purple equally-spaced vertical bands. The male has a blunter head and deeper body. Largest of the New Zealand wrasses, it can reach 60 cm in length. It tends to live in deeper water than the female, down to 30 m.

While most wrasses begin life as females, many reversing sex upon reaching a certain size, banded wrasses are not consistent with this pattern. Some actually start life as males. Once development from the larval stage is complete, others may change from female to male at any time. Those that make the transition while young will never function as spawning females. On the other hand, a few continue as females all their lives — more than 25 years. These 'super females' grow as large as mature males. Although they still retain their green female coloration, the matrons develop the deep body and blunt head of a male — and its extremely prominent teeth.

Until divers began to observe wrasses underwater, classifying them taxonomically was very difficult. In several cases different phases of development had been identified as separate species — until we actually saw them mating!

Since almost half a population of banded wrasses become males, competition amongst such a relatively large number of males is intense. During the winter spawning season, from August to September, I have often seen males hotly pursuing females, all fins raised, their yellow markings gleaming brightly during the chase, while the female's drab colour is unchanged. I would like to see what happens when a small male tries to court a super female — if indeed he dared to try.

By day the banded wrasses are continuously on the move, but about an hour before sunset they vanish. When I explore the reef by night with a diving torch, I find them resting in crevices. The body has a peculiar, furry appearance, and it is enclosed in a sheath of mucus exuded from special skin glands to provide a protective envelope for the fish.

Male and female banded wrasse.
Super female and juvenile banded wrasse.

Scarlet wrasse

The depth range of the scarlet wrasse seems to begin where that of the spotty and banded wrasse tapers off. Seen mostly below the 10 m level, these sumptuously coloured fishes are among the few wrasses I have observed beyond 60 m. As I watched the television monitor receiving images from a robotic submarine, I was delighted to see a scarlet wrasse and a foxfish swimming over the wreck of the *Niagara* (a treasure ship which lies at 130 m, a few hours, steaming from the Poor Knights). Both the red coloration and the diet of these fishes are adapted to a deeper range and to bottom-fossicking habits. They have a strong preference for hermit crabs, along with brittle stars, small urchins and shellfish. Densities of these wrasses are much greater in cooler waters than at the Poor Knights, where I have never seen them in aggregations of several fishes in every square metre, as in the South Island. At the Poor Knights there is just a fairly even distribution of individuals and pairs.

As I swim over a reef, a scarlet wrasse will occasionally follow me. Entering the territories of others of its species, it suffers furious attacks, but still continues in my wake. I sometimes lie on the reef and watch individuals for lengthy periods, and I find that when they patrol territory borders they swim along regular and predictable pathways. Their course is rather like a clockwork train: over a ridge, around a rock, between two kelp thickets and along a sandfloored canyon. Since this fish is nearly always moving, it is a difficult subject to photograph. But with one individual, its path was so certain I was able to set my camera and flashgun at a fixed range along its course and take a dozen exposures as it finned past each time. Sometimes, in deep water, I have seen large males resting within deep recesses during the day — most unusual for a wrasse.

There are three growth phases. The slender juvenile is like the female, in that both have rows of red and yellow scales on the lower part of the body. The female is a brighter red and loses the three pale spots that the juvenile bears on its back. In about the third year, a sex change occurs.

Male scarlet wrasses have the typical deep body and blunt head, while the tail becomes markedly lunate. The multiple red and yellow stripes on the belly of the female are replaced by a uniform red, often with a salmon-pink cast. Basically, scarlet wrasses have the least distinctive sexual coloration of all those described here.

When spawning occurs in springtime (August–November) I often see bold fin displays and vigorous pursuits, but never an actual spawning. This is one of the most aggressive wrasses and will nip a rival viciously with its sharp teeth. Elsewhere, the male is seen courting and spawning with a group of females, but such a gathering would be unlikely at the Poor Knights, which seems to be at the limit of their range. They grow to 40 cm.

Male scarlet wrasse, with filaments on tail lobes.
Female scarlet wrasse.

Orange wrasse
In May, off the end of a long reef extending westward like a tongue from the Sand Garden, a group of 30 male orange wrasses can be seen hovering above the kelp forest, circling and sparring intermittently with each other. Beneath, among the kelp stalks, are similar numbers of females. From time to time four or five females soar up into the male throng; if the males are not receptive they chase the females down again. Occasionally a male courts a female, both fishes arching around each other tensely, all fins erect. Then rapidly, with eel-like sinuous swimming movements, the pair ascend side by side about 3 m, before turning and releasing twin clouds of eggs and sperm. Both fishes then rejoin their groups. This pattern is often varied by group spawning movements, when one or two others accompany the spawning couple in their upward rush and all the fishes spawn together. As with the spotty, some of these are pseudo-females, males masquerading in female coloration, sneaking in on the spawning to gain advantage with their outsize testes.

In the vicinity, male wrasses of other species circle; spotties, banded and scarlet wrasses, all act in a disturbed manner as if there were some hormone release in the water which caused them to respond to the sexual activity of the orange wrasses. Such group spawnings by orange wrasses have been observed in this same location throughout their unusually long spawning season (March–October) and for year after year. Later in the season, paired spawnings similar to those of other wrasses also occur. The double spawning pattern ensures a wider distribution of spawn, which increases their chances of survival.

The orange wrasse is a subtropical species that has adapted well to the kelp forests of the Poor Knights. Juvenile and female fishes are a brilliant apricot orange, with silvery cheek straps or gill covers that continue along the body as five rows of white flecked scales. Six vertical white bands may also be apparent, but they vary in intensity.

At around 15 cm in length, sex reversal occurs. The male has a much deeper body, brick red to mauve with a checkerboard pattern of four black and five white squares on his back extending partly on to his dorsal fin, and a splatter of red dots on his green-tinged cheeks. During courtship and aggression, this checkerboard pattern gleams with signal intensity. All phases have a dot at the pectoral base, black in the female, teal blue in the male. There is another colour form, in which the male has a handsome green head, but no checker pattern; this is either a transitional stage going towards the male, or else a super female.

Orange wrasses feed on small crustaceans. Small females supplement their diet as fish cleaners, attending to porae, blue maomao and black angelfishes. They grow to 25 cm.

Male orange wrasse.

Female orange wrasse.
Super female orange wrasse.

Male green wrasse.

Green wrasse

Another subtropical visitor, the green wrasse does not seem to breed successfully at the Poor Knights, but arrives as a larval fish from the reefs to the north. It is a very large and handsome wrasse reaching about 60 cm. Its diet is mainly shellfish and small crustaceans.

There are three distinct phases of growth. The juvenile is brown-green with a green-tinged head and ten horizontal bands of silvery yellow dots along its sides. The female is dark brown and develops a pretty 'scribbled' scale pattern of horizontal lines and vertical squiggles. The male is a most impressive fish, with a powerful, blunt head and elongate, wedge-shaped body. He is dark olive green with boldly contrasting light yellow dorsal and anal fins, which are used for aggressive and sexual displays. At the base of the leading dorsal spine there is a prominent black dot, only visible when the fin is erect, in a signal mode.

Females and juveniles lurk among the seaweed fronds and are well camouflaged, while the males swim boldly in the open near the weed.

These are home-ranging fishes and in July, during their spawning season, I have seen a male chase a rival from near the surface down to 50 m and beyond. All fins were erect like gleaming banners, maximising the size of the attacker and signalling his aggressiveness.

Not all females reverse sex and some continue to grow, with female form and colour, into huge maiden aunts, or super females. One of these, whom we called 'Lola', became very friendly and curious. For many years Lola was regularly encountered in the same small area of the Sand Garden, lolling in clownish ecstasy amongst the kelp fronds. With her body at an oblique angle she fell slowly, then wriggled, rose, and repeated the stance: 'Lola the circus fat-lady'. In this state she showed no fear and I could bring my camera as close as I wished. But when my wife Jan was looking at her at close range, a sudden disturbance sent Lola hurtling into her arm in blind panic, gouging the wetsuit rubber with her large canines. Poor Lola!

Female green wrasse.
'Lola', the super female green wrasse.

Red pigfish
With its ruby-red body, an iridescent, blue-black ocellus on its imposing dorsal fin and a white patch towards the tail that intensifies as a signal when it is aroused, the male red pigfish is one of the most majestic of wrasses. Despite its beauty, the narrow, concave forehead and extended snout have led to this unflattering name. Undaunted by our label, the male red pigfish is a proud and boastful fish, up to 50 cm long, patrolling its home range and displaying its fine livery to the females within its harem.

The female red pigfish is a paler version of the male, but still very pretty. The ground colour of her body is pinkish white, with yellow on the abdomen overlaid with three rows of red dashes and ten red lines. If the dashes are closely examined it will be noticed that each bears a 'signature' squiggle at the centre, varying with each fish like a bar code, and providing for individual recognition within the female dominance hierarchy. Juveniles are similar, but with a pure white ground and yellow fins. The male has a striking lunate tail, while the female's is truncate and the juvenile's gently rounded. Sex reversal occurs at around 30 cm in length.

Red pigfishes range in depth from the shallows to 60 m, foraging for a wide variety of small invertebrates, their long narrow jaws and sharp teeth being especially suited to extracting hard-shelled prey from narrow crevices: small shellfish, chitons, crabs, amphipods, brittle stars and ascidians. They even eat quite large sea-urchins, a difficult prey, as it demands the breaking of many sharp spines to gain entry. At night the red pigfish rests in narrow crevices and tunnels, its fins erect and its colour unchanged.

From July to September is their spawning time. Initially there is much sexual display and aggressive posturing. Males repel others that venture into their territory and make passes at females in the area. When approached by a male that has its dorsal and anal fins erect, the female will also erect her fins and will arch her body in a taut bow, and will curve towards the male just before dashing off, with him in hot pursuit. The male will approach females day after day, testing their readiness and the ripeness of their eggs.

In July I once saw a male chase a female until she veered upwards. The two fishes ascended, belly to belly, gyrating and swerving. The male had his median fins erect and was twisting in a peculiar way until almost upside down. After rising some 6 m the pair spawned, parted and returned to the bottom to repeat the ritual. I was never more amazed than when, one warm January day, I saw a female approach and court a male. Standing on her tail she sank vertically before curving seductively around him, all fins elegantly displayed.

When it is receiving the attentions of a cleanerfish, the red pigfish extends all fins and drifts trance-like in mid-water. Being tail-heavy, it sinks to the bottom. Quite often it may entreat a cleaner by posing in this way, only to be ignored because the cleaner is 'on strike'. The poor red pigfish remains, looking absurd standing on its tail, fins erect, eyes staring, and alone.

Female red pigfish.
Male red pigfish.

Fox fish
When I first sighted a fox fish in deep water I thought I was suffering from double vision, affected by the depth. A red pigfish that had *two* white patches on its back! For several years my notebooks recorded sightings of a 'strange, two-dotted pigfish', swimming in deep, sand-floored canyons. Eventually I managed to photograph one 50 m down in the Canyon at the Poor Knights. At that depth, with its muted colour, it looked just like a red pigfish. Viewing my transparency produced a shock; its true colour, brought to life by the electronic flash, was a glowing orange-red, quite different from that of the red pigfish. Besides, it had sulphur-yellow pectoral fins, a pure white abdomen, twin white patches on its back, and its head was convex and blunt. Had we first sighted this fish in the shallows, where our minds are not fuddled by nitrogen, there would have been no doubt as to its uniqueness. Since then the fox fish has always been observed beyond 30 m, usually in pairs, so it is likely the male and female forms are similar. I once saw one swimming over the hull of the *Niagara*, which lies on its side at 130 m, not far from the Poor Knights. The fox fish grows to 40 cm.

Fox fish.

Male elegant wrasse.

Elegant wrasse
During the seventies, when the fishes of the Poor Knights were being intensively explored by diving biologists, new species were sometimes discovered by a process of gradual realisation that these were different from their companions. In this way it was eventually grasped that the extremely abundant crimson cleanerfish was not the juvenile of some other wrasse, but a distinct species.

At intervals of several years, gyres of warm water break away from tropical currents to the north and bear down on New Zealand, bringing with them an influx of exotic species in larval form. Such was the case in the early seventies, when five new wrasses were discovered in close succession at the Poor Knights. (As I write there are indications such an influx is recurring.) These inner-space travellers settle out of the plankton on reaching a suitable habitat, and develop into females. Some survive several winters to become males and may even spawn. But eventually they die out, perhaps because they are unable to produce sufficient spawn to win the lottery of current dispersal at southern latitudes.

Such an arrival was the elegant wrasse, first discovered at Nursery Cove in February 1972 and subsequently found in both male and female forms. Young elegant wrasses, yellow with rows of blue dots, move about in loose schools feeding rapidly in short bouts before speeding away to another site. The exquisitely coloured, gold-and-blue male is solitary, moving from group to group of females. These wrasses are common at Lord Howe Island, in the mid-Tasman Sea, where so many species, marginal at the Poor Knights, abound in normal populations. The elegant wrasse grows to 25 cm.

Rainbow fish

In the only calm, shallow bay at the Poor Knights, which divers have named Nursery Cove, the kelp bed cuts off at 15 m in front of a gently sloping sand plain, sprinkled with clumps of rock and tall seaweeds. It is here that many new arrivals at the Poor Knights have first been discovered. When I eventually travelled to Lord Howe Island, where so many of these exotic species abound, I was intrigued to find this cove most closely approximates the colonists' normal habitat. And that was where the rainbow fish was first sighted in August 1971.

Underwater, where light is muted, the female rainbow fish appears red-pink with 10 horizontal blue bands. Most noticeable are the three black dots on her fins: one near the front of her dorsal, another near its rear, and the third at the base of the tail, above the midline. With wrasses, such dots seem to have a signal function, perhaps assisting species recognition on a busy reef.

Larger than the female, at first glance the male is a bluish coloured fish, and retains only one of the fin dots, that at the front of the dorsal fin. Most distinctive is the strangely shaped and elaborately patterned tail, semi-lunate in form, the upper lobe extending almost to a thread. For sexual or aggressive signalling this tail is virtually a flag, the upper third a brilliant yellow, the lower part a burgundy red. In actual coloration, which only emerges when the fish is taken from the sea, the male has a dark green back with a burgundy-tinged abdomen, overlaid with 10 rows of bright blue dots, the upper rows coalescing to form continuous bands. Dorsal and anal fins are rich burgundy red, with blue and green patterning. This is one of the most intricately patterned and brilliantly hued fishes in New Zealand seas.

Rainbow fishes always swim in male/female pairs, which is unusual for wrasses, and live within the same small territory all their lives. It is thought that pair formation begins as soon as the fishes settle out of the plankton. Then, after about a year's growth, whichever fish is the larger reverses sex to become the male.

In winter 1971, where the sea floor meets the kelp forest in Nursery Cove, a male rainbow fish was swimming just above the glistening white sand, within a metre of the rocks and erect seaweeds. He approached the female, spread his median fins slightly, and undulated horizontally alongside. Six times he repeated this ritual, approaching each time from behind and afterwards swimming off about 2 m before returning. On the last two occasions he became very agitated and seemed to be pecking her flanks. She then spread her median fins, and very swiftly they both swam upwards, bellies almost together. Just over a metre above the bottom they parted and as they turned they shot out little white clouds of eggs and sperm which intermingled and dispersed. They then returned rapidly to the bottom and the male moved off over the sand and rocks.

Over the ensuing years all the lovely rainbow fishes gradually disappeared from the Poor Knights, but in spring 1990 a new attempt at colonisation was taking place. They grow to 18 cm.

Male and female rainbowfish.
Male and female blueheaded wrasse.

Male Sandager's wrasse.

Sandager's wrasse

I have to confess that of all the fishes at the Poor Knights Islands, the Sandager's wrasse has intrigued me the most. Of the wrasses out there it is the most markedly polymorphic; the juveniles, females and males are quite different in colour and form. Even the transitional stages between each growth phase can be clearly recognised.

The slender juveniles are boldly emblazoned with the insignia of the parasite pickers' guild — a white body with a golden-yellow median stripe and a significant black dot at the tail base. During the sixties we studied this cleanerfish, its habitat, diet and which fishes it cleaned. But we were mystified. Although it was abundant all around the Poor Knights, there just did not seem to be any males, nor any mature females, amongst these strange little fishes. Then it dawned on us: these cleanerfishes *were the juveniles* of the Sandager's wrasses!

When the juvenile reaches around 15 cm, its transition to the female form begins. The yellow band takes on a russet tinge and gradually separates in the middle. The body then deepens and eventually the two portions of the broken band become salmon-coloured patches on a white body. The black dot at the tail base spreads and loses intensity until it fades away. These changes in pattern and form are partly a function of growth; it is as if the original wrasse were a rubber balloon fish, which alters its pattern as it is inflated. As the black dot on its tail base disappears, the fish ceases to be a cleaner. Its golden insignia has gone, which means that demoiselles and other eager clients no longer press for its services. Besides, its strong teeth are now too long to remove skin parasites without damaging the patient; it has become a mature female.

The female Sandager's wrasses, of varying sizes, fossick for invertebrates over the rock faces and across the sand at the foot of the undersea cliff, in loose aggregations of from 10 to 20, accompanied by similar numbers of juveniles at all stages of growth. These females are not part of any male harem, but wander freely through all territories.

Somewhere on the fringe of the group will be a deep-bodied, blunt-headed male, about 40 cm in length. This is an extremely handsome fish in comparison with the slender, milky-white, twin-patched females. His grape-coloured body is embellished with a multi-coloured saddle: alternating pairs

Sandager's wrasse juvenile: a cleanerfish.

Sandager's wrasse — transitional sub adult.
Sandager's wrasses — female with juvenile.

of white and deep maroon bands, a wedge of saffron yellow, a red pectoral base and mauve cheeks. These proclaim his masculinity to the females in his area and to all other males. No male can enter his territory without provoking a vigorous aggressive display, although injuries are seldom inflicted. In areas where these wrasses are abundant it is rare to see males closer to each other than from 7 to 10 m and on the adjacent rocky coast, where sandy dormitory areas are scattered, there may be nearly a kilometre separating rival males.

The pattern of the saddle colours varies with individuals, and this plays an important role in the community: each male is instantly recognisable, even to other species. Since all Sandager's wrasses commence life as females, there are no young males. Amongst a group of females there seems to be a hierarchy or pecking order maintained by daily contact and individual recognition. It also seems that, with the death of the male, the dominant female in any group is released from male dominance. In response to male hormones then released in her body she undergoes a sex change and replaces the male. Experimental research involving injections of the male hormone testosterone into a tagged female has proven that such reversals can be induced biochemically, so that within two weeks a mature female becomes a fully functional male.

Sex change occurs outside the summer spawning season. In winter I once saw two females in the process of transition. Both were still slender females. One had a dark saddle on her creamy white back; the other had the salmon colour of a male, but the saddle colours had not developed.

Spawning takes place from December to March. During this period I see frequent sexual displays and aggressive pursuits. The male parades around his territory, erecting his fins to accentuate body size and masculinity. If he comes across a female ready to spawn, the typical wrasse-style spawning ascent occurs.

Close observation of these wrasses has provided a wealth of insights into the learning capacities and social organisation of reef fishes. An eagle ray was seen swimming slowly over the bottom with a female Sandager's wrasse cruising along beneath it. Whenever the broad wings swept too close to the bottom the wrasse would come out and move alongside, but would slip back beneath at the first opportunity. Eventually the big ray settled down on a patch of rock to crunch a shell in its grinding jaws. As it chomped audibly on the gastropod the wrasse swam around trying to look under its wings; if the ray lifted its head for a moment the fish sought to slip underneath. I was mystified at its behaviour. Then a number of other females and larger juveniles came along and did the same thing, weaving all around the ray. Two juveniles set to work cleaning the ray's back. Suddenly a violent fight erupted just above it. Two young females, 30 cm long, faced each other and then charged with open mouths and bared teeth. They thumped together, then swerved aside and immediately swept in again to renew the attack. During the fight they changed colour. The normal dark patches went white, while the white areas flushed salmon. This was a complete colour reversal, and I crept in to snatch a photo of the 'negative' fish.

Ten attacks were made before one fish got the upper hand and chased the other away. Then the victor returned. The eagle ray was just lifting off, having finished its meal, and several wrasses ducked underneath to start nibbling at the shell fragments. As the ray flapped away two snapper and a cloud of Sandager's wrasses moved in on the crushed shell and tatters of flesh. For these fishes there had been no reason to fear the ray, which could not hurt them, its tail being only a defensive weapon. Its crushing jaws would have been unable to glean all the crumbs — only a wrasse could pick the shell clean. Fishes are evidently aware that rays can provide them with morsels to eat, and the pugnacious female did not like sharing her prize with a rival.

Aggressive female Sandager's wrasse assumes negative coloration.

After a night dive at the Poor Knights we were puzzled. Where had they gone — all the Sandager's wrasses and combfishes that we saw there during the day? We had seen other wrasses resting in crevices and all the night feeders were foraging in the open. We knew the pelagic species had withdrawn to the open sea for the night. But we could not find a single specimen of the two species of the genus *Coris* that we had been observing during the day.

During the winter of 1971 we determined to solve the riddle. We would enter the sea before sundown and stay with the wrasses until we found out where they went, even if it took relays of divers. An hour before sunset we began our vigil, hovering on the surface above a tribe of Sandager's wrasses. As daylight faded, their foraging movements intensified within one small area of broken rocks and sandy clearings. They did not seem to be feeding at all — just milling about aimlessly. A frenetic activity ran

Sex Change in Wrasses
Dominant female Sandager's wrasse.

First stage of sex change: male saddle develops.

Sex change advanced: saffron wedge appears.
Completed sex change: male wrasse that began life as female.

through all the other reef fishes in the vicinity. Pelagics boiled around us; blue maomao jostled for the attentions of a crimson cleaner; and demoiselles, snapper, red moki and marblefishes all seemed infected with an urge to move around at random over the reefs and along the sandy valleys, through tunnels and under ledges.

The Sandager's wrasses gradually began to localise their movements, until small numbers hovered over patches of coralline sand between the rocks, occasionally dipping down to the bottom, passing under a rock outcrop and returning. All the other reef fishes were disappearing and the sea grew still and dark. With the last squibs of light we saw some Sandager's wrasses dive beneath a rock in a flurry of sand. The largest female seemed to bully the others, who all vanished before she withdrew. Last to go to rest was the male, hovering over a secluded sandy alcove. We knew there was an extensive low cave there. It was quite simple — they had probably just holed up in a very narrow fissure or confined space and we had not looked hard enough in the past.

When it was pitch dark we returned wearing scuba sets. We descended with torches to the cave. Our beams probed every recess in that cave and every other cave in the vicinity, but not one Sandager's wrasse could be found. A whole tribe had vanished! Then someone began delving with their hand in the coarse sand under a ledge, and withdrew it with a shock — an involuntary reaction at touching something moving. Further probing, and the sand seemed to smoke in a straight line. Something was wriggling beneath it. Suddenly a sand storm erupted and four female Sandager's wrasses leapt out and dashed off into the dark, crashing into rocks in their blind panic.

This discovery shed new light on the habitat requirements of these fishes. On many sections of rocky coast, they are absent. Clearly they need areas that provide plenty of rocks among which to fossick by day, and coarse sand close by where they can hide at night. We could hardly believe our eyes: that an active reef fish could spend hours beneath several inches of sand seemed incredible. But members of the genus *Coris* may be especially adapted to wriggling on their sides under sand. Unlike many other wrasses they have small, firm scales and very flexible bodies. Their gills seem to be perfectly capable of pumping a sufficient flow of water through the coarse sand particles, to support a resting fish.

The diet of Sandager's wrasses includes most of the small animals that encrust rocks or live in crevices — especially brittle stars, amphipods, chitons and gastropods, along with limpets, bivalves, polychaete worms and small crabs. For the juveniles, parasites are not the major source of food. The juveniles do not actively solicit customers with a special display dance as do some tropical cleaners, but simply clean any fishes which present themselves as the juveniles fossick after small bottom-living organisms, which they nip daintily off the rocks. They mainly clean demoiselles, but also blue maomao, parore, black angelfishes, goatfishes, spotties, banded wrasses, porae and koheru. I once watched one enter the mouth of a goatfish, rip out a large sea louse and dash it against a rock until it was dead, before swallowing it. At times a juvenile has been seen cleaning females of its own kind. These juvenile Sandager's wrasses really belong with the next guild.

The Sandager's wrasse grows to 45 cm.

Demoiselles solicit grooming from Sandager's wrasse juvenile.

Guild of the parasite pickers

Combfish

Few fishes have given me more surprises than this master of rapid change. The combfish is a parasite picker, closely related to the Sandager's wrasse. A small, specialised cleaner, it never grows beyond suitable proportions for this role. It bears very prominently the guild signal for a parasite picker: a chocolate-black median band, scalloped or comb-shaped along the lower edge. There is also a short red band along the head in front of the dorsal fin. With the juveniles, the black median band extends right to the end of the tail. At maturity (about 8 cm) the combfish develops a beautiful golden-yellow tail, which contrasts with the body to make this little fish even more conspicuous as it sculls along, lazily beating its transparent pectoral fins.

These are home-ranging fishes and have been observed in the same place for many months. Such areas become recognised by the other reef fishes as 'cleaning stations'. Typically they are in rocky areas, close to sand, under which the combfish spends the night like the related Sandager's wrasse.

Cleaning intensity varies from day to day. On one occasion, a combfish in the giant Rikoriko Cave was seen to clean 16 fishes in a 54-minute period within an area no larger than a small house. As it moved about its home range it was completely preoccupied with cleaning and sought out fish after fish, pecking at fin bases, gill covers and mouths. It spent five minutes with a goatfish, pecking at it 50 times. This goatfish was initially vermilion; it paled to white and then flushed vermilion again, perhaps to make parasites in various areas stand out in contrast. (Parasitic crustaceans such as sea

Combfish: male or female.

Male combfish in courtship or aggression colours.
Female combfish. *Juvenile combfish — no yellow on tail.*

lice come in swarms during periods of intensive plankton bloom. They are usually transparent, or coloured like the host fish, as this gives them a survival advantage.) The combfish then cleaned some demoiselles with six pecks each; and then cleaned two porae, a male orange wrasse and a male Sandager's wrasse. While being attended the demoiselles were poised in a rosette, all focused on the cleaner, fins extended, as the little fish wove to and fro amongst its customers.

Four days later, in the same area, this same fish was watched for two 40-minute periods. Although five goatfishes followed it around assiduously, it refused to clean any of them, but kept nipping at the bottom and roaming about its area. The clients would deliberately place themselves in its path, open their mouths, expand their gill covers and erect all fins, but the combfish would only give them a cursory examination and swim on its way.

Combfish pursued by eager clients: black-spot goatfishes.

Trevally seek attention.
Mouth agape, a goatfish is inspected for sea lice.

The goatfishes kept up their expectant poses for some time after the cleaner had deserted them. Perhaps they had already been deloused, and only sought the grooming service for the pleasure it provides. Next day the cleaner serviced only three fishes in a 45-minute period.

Grooming for no reason, and perhaps the extended sessions of 'skimming' practised by blue maomao, could induce a biochemical euphoria in the client fish. Studies of monkeys have shown that mutual grooming stimulates production of endorphins, the brain's own opiates, which have a narcotic effect. It would explain the blissful appearance of fishes being cleaned and their insistent drive for more attention. Trout are known to produce endorphins under stress. Further study is needed here, but it may be difficult to create pleasurable experimental conditions for fishes.

The combfish is a subtropical species, abundant at Lord Howe Island and only a sporadic coloniser at the Poor Knights. We first saw it in 1969, as a 35-mm juvenile, which had probably reached the islands in larval form. Unaware that it was just a juvenile-phase fish, for months we watched the tiny stranger dancing around a small clump of rock at 35 m; it looked very like the widespread tropical cleaner, *Labroides dimidiadus*, and this is what we mistook it for initially.

Then, in February 1972, we came upon some extremely large combfishes, up to 22 cm long. They had a much more prominent comb pattern along the middle. One day I saw one looking even more peculiar: its back was bluegrey instead of the usual white. The black band had vanished! Through its eye and curving down along the gill edge was a chocolate-black crescent; the belly was yellow-brown and the tips of the pectorals were dark blue. This strange fish was displaying its fins to a normally coloured individual slightly smaller than itself; clearly these were male and female combfishes. But where did this big male come from? I was to discover that, with these wrasses, the male looks exactly like the female until the spawning season (February to June), when he can change his colour pattern in a split second.

I see the black lateral band disappear and this strange, sickle-headed creature emerges, dancing around the female, all fins erect and body tautly curved. As soon as the female begins to respond to his advances, he positions himself above and slightly behind her, his pelvic fins straddling her dorsal. Together the two wrasses rise some 3 m. At the peak of their ascent the female turns slightly on her side and for about four seconds this stance is held as the fishes spawn. The ritual is repeated four times before the male departs to seek out other compliant females. Then, to my amazement, I see him revert in a flash to female coloration and resume feeding on the bottom, all sexual activity at an end for the day.

Later, I discovered I could elicit these surprising transitions with the aid of a mirror. When the transvestite male saw a lovely big female heading straight towards him, his colour changed like a neon sign. But in that instant he found himself tooth to tooth with this large alien male, one that he had never before encountered in his community, and he assaulted the aggressor with persistent displays of maleness until I withdrew the mirror.

Like so many sporadic colonisers, the combfishes gradually died out over the ensuing years, leaving no young to replace them. Then, 20 years later, in the winter of 1989, I found two tiny juveniles dancing about over rocks in deep water off South Harbour — history repeating itself! Combfishes grow to around 22 cm.

Courtship and Spawning
Combfish courtship dance: male circles female, fins tautly displayed.

Dorsal no longer erect, having been accepted, male straddles female. The pair ascend to spawn.

Crimson cleanerfish

The crimson spindle of his body emblazoned with a radiant white stripe, the male crimson cleaner is a most conspicuous fish, extremely abundant at all depths around the Poor Knights Islands. His violet chinstraps, elaborate scale flecks and fin markings, and his bright orange tail boldly proclaim male status. The white band advertises his parasite-picking role, attracting client fishes from afar and inhibiting potential predators, which prefer to recognise him as a groom rather than just another meal.

The female is a little less obvious, being orange with a white flash extending from the mouth and merging midway along the body into the general colour pattern. Her fins are translucent and she has a black distinguishing dot near the end of her dorsal.

The juvenile resembles the female, but being very small it is quite inconspicuous, even when present in great numbers just above or within the kelp forest. Life begins at the outset of the year when tiny juveniles just over a centimetre long settle out of the plankton. After about seven months, at 7 cm, they mature and, for the next one to two years, live as females, courted by harem-keeping males in small, heavily-guarded territories. Then, in February or March, a mass sex change occurs.

Biologist Dr Tony Ayling discovered this process of sex transition during an intensive series of observations in March 1972. At first, large numbers of very small males were noticed in groups of up to six, fighting with each other, raising their dorsals in threat display and circling pugnaciously. Nearby was a small male with a black dot on the rear of its dorsal — the distinctive marking of a female. Its body was just a pale red and still bore the faint vertical bands of a female — yet it also had the continuous white stripe of a male. This was a male fish in a state of transition from the female form. The complete sex reversal was surprisingly rapid: it took only one to two weeks for both the outward colour change and the internal conversion from ovary to gonad. The fighting, which Ayling observed among those newly transformed males, occurred while they were establishing territories. Within three days boundaries had been defined, each male patrolling a tiny patch and cleaning other fishes.

Several months of tempestuous warring followed during which many young males died, so that the stronger fishes gradually accumulated bigger and bigger territories and more and more females within their harems. By the time spawning commenced in June, everything had been sorted out and even many of the old-established males had died. The crimson cleaner has a lifespan of only four years, and reaches up to 15 cm in length.

To study the social lives of these fishes in detail, Tony Ayling first learnt to recognise each individual by noting differences in the basic colour patterns. He was then able to follow the history of each fish, give it a name, and learn the idiosyncrasies of its behaviour and the intimacies of its daily life. His study area was the Sand Garden, an expanse of brilliant white sand scattered with pebbles and kelp plants and surrounded by dense kelp forests and reefs at 10 m depth, where the two main islands almost meet. It is nourished by a steady current, but is well protected from violent weather.

On each dive, the biologist took down a detailed map of the Sand Garden, drawn on a sheet of plastic. Using a stopwatch for accurate timing, he would follow the path of a chosen fish for a 15-minute period, tracing its

Female crimson cleanerfish.

Transitional stage: male with female's black dot on dorsal rear.
Male crimson cleanerfish.

route on the map and making notes of its behaviour along the way. Comparing such observations, he soon found certain males remained consistently within the same well-defined areas, confronting others along the boundaries. Territories varied in size from the area of a small room (10 m^2) to that of a large house (150 m^2). Constant patrols were made, and there were frequent border disputes. If a fin display was not enough to repel an intruder, wild chases and fierce clashes ensued. Sometimes the combatants strayed into adjacent territories, bringing more and more males into battle. Up to six warriors would posture aggressively until harmony was restored and each returned to his own patch.

During the breeding season these territories become very important, because within them each male controls and dominates a harem of females, shepherding them back if they stray too close to the border. Some males have no harem and constantly attempt to court and control the females next door.

Others manage to retain more than ten females. Relentlessly, these females repel any intruding members of their sex, even while the male is frantically trying to court his new acquisition. In her adventurous wanderings across the Sand Garden, one errant female was seen to stray through six different territories. Each male ardently courted the stranger, showing far more vigour than he would towards one of his own. And in each territory one of the harem would chase the intruding 'Jezebel' into another territory, where the story was repeated.

Within its own territory a fish is relatively safe from predation, and has well-known refuges and resting areas to which it retires at night. If a male is ousted from his territory, he sets out on a journey that becomes increasingly erratic as he is continually harassed by the male in each territory he enters, and his life is brief. Neighbouring males quickly take over the vacant area and all the harem of the deceased.

On one occasion, when the young biologist was quivering with cold after a long dive, he was cheered by the sight of a male that made a gross mistake. It had been wandering around its territory, inspecting seaweed fronds for tiny crustaceans that make up its diet, when suddenly it veered aside and swam rapidly towards a juvenile Sandager's wrasse. Arching his brightly coloured fins and tail, the male crimson cleaner courted this yellow and white guild member, mistaking it for a female of his own kind. The young wrasse avoided his advances and swam off. Subsequently it was found that this particular male consistently made the same mistake. His neighbours never erred in this respect, but there were a few that would mistake this same yellow-striped fish for a rival male of their own kind and chase it away. The biologist was intrigued by these variations in the behaviour of individuals; such variations are not expected in fishes.

When approaching a fish to clean, the crimson cleaner raises its dorsal, perhaps to signal its intention. The host fish poses, all fins erect and mouth and gill plates expanded to provide access to parasite-infected areas, while the cleaner inspects its body minutely. Like the combfish, crimson cleanerfish are not obligate cleaners, but vary their diet by nipping minute organisms from rocks. Cleaning activity varies from day to day. At times it is intensive, everywhere one looks. At other times, in the whole of one bay where cleaners are so abundant we have named it Cleanerfish Bay, not a single cleaner will be working. This may be explained by variations in the

Sand Garden Map. Shows the male territories during February 1975. Sex change has recently taken place and 11 new males have established small territories around the larger territories of the four established males (M). The path followed by four of the males during the 15-minute observation period is marked by the thin arrowed lines.
(Courtesy of Dr A.M. Ayling)

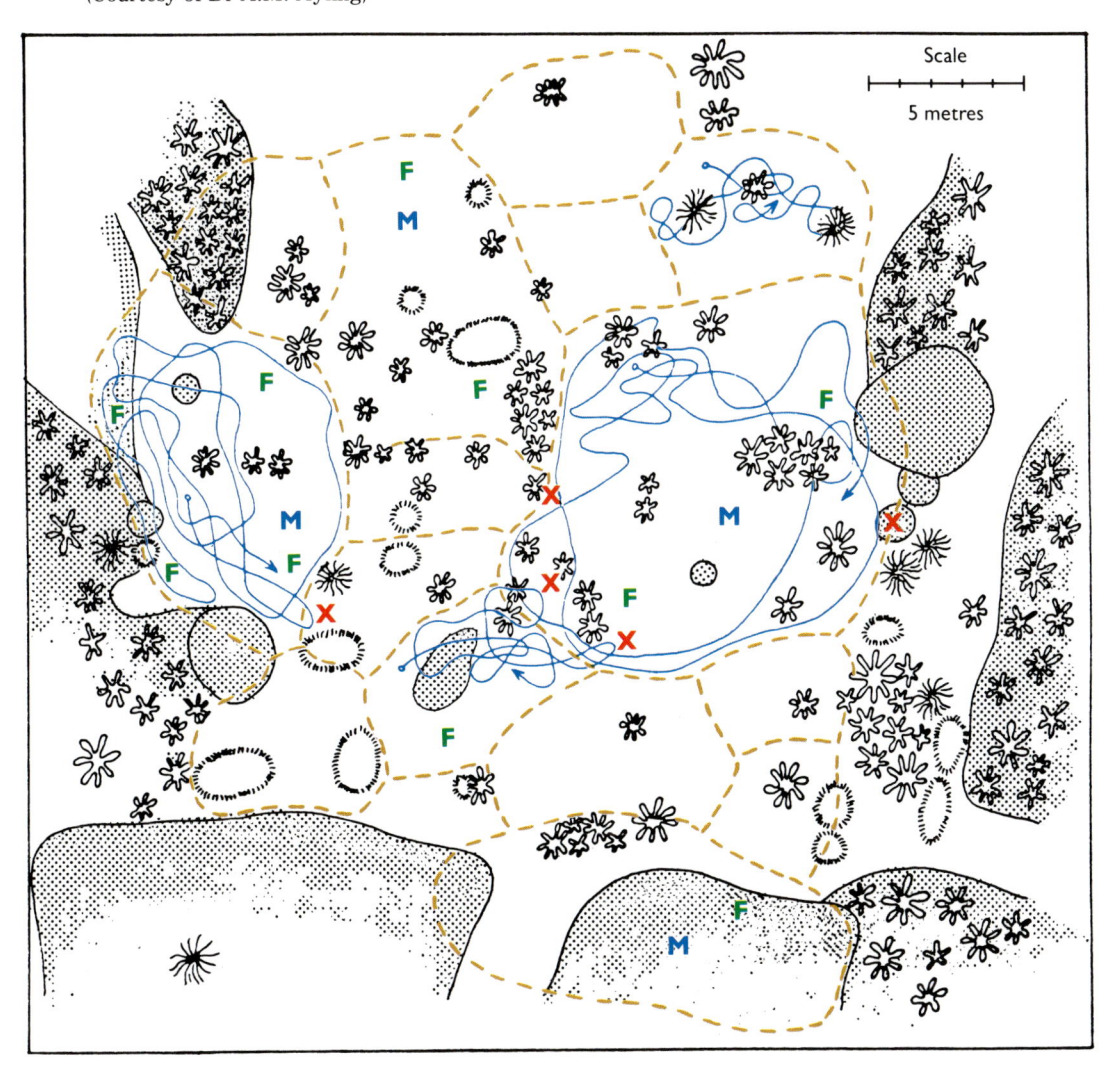

Key:

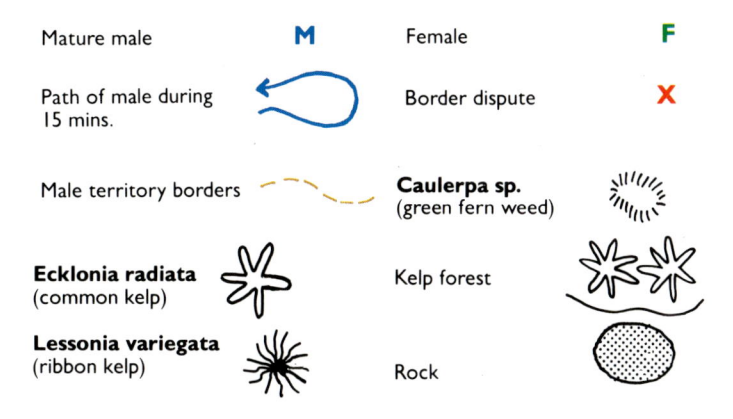

Mature male	M	Female	F
Path of male during 15 mins.		Border dispute	X
Male territory borders		Caulerpa sp. (green fern weed)	
Ecklonia radiata (common kelp)		Kelp forest	
Lessonia variegata (ribbon kelp)		Rock	

swarms of parasitic lice coming through with the plankton flow.

The biologist found that behaviour variations also extended to the cleaning activities of these fish. Some never cleaned at all, getting their food by foraging over the bottom; others would spend most of their time cleaning, continually surrounded by eager clients. However most fishes had a mixed approach.

Individuals also had clear preferences for certain species. 'Cross-tail' was a part-time cleaner and preferred the silvery blue bodies of koheru; another individual was always at the centre of a cluster of demoiselles; 'Violet' liked larger fishes, especially male Sandager's wrasses; and 'Goatie' specialised in goatfish so much he neglected his border patrols and the neighbouring males gradually whittled away his territory, claiming parts for themselves.

The reasons for such individual preferences are baffling and confute classical theories of animal behaviour, which stress the importance of 'releasing mechanisms' in determining an animal's response to any given situation. This means that behaviour is instinctive and everything that happens to an animal triggers the appropriate innate response. According to this theory, normal behaviour is made up of a predictable series of triggers and responses with which an animal is born.

For example, the beak-open feeding response of seagull chicks is triggered by the bright red spot on the parent's beak. A crude cardboard model of the gull will stimulate the chicks to open their beaks, provided the red spot is present on the bill. Even a pencil with a red spot will do the trick. But the most elaborate model of a seagull will fail if the 'releaser' spot is absent.

I wanted to test this theory with the crimson cleaner, so took down a flat plastic model of a male cleanerfish and anchored it in an area where cleaning was in progress. How would the host fish react to the sight of the cleaner's guild signal — the contrasting median stripe? Or was the characteristic swooping flight of the cleaner, which would be difficult to emulate with a model, essential to releasing a cleaning response? As my red and white model swayed gently on its tether just above the sand, several demoiselles and a red pigfish approached within a half metre and then veered off in seeming disgust.

As I shifted the model progressively towards the gloom of a cave, they would approach closer and closer; but I could not elicit a knee-jerk grooming posture with my model. They had been attracted by its colour and form, but at close range they could obviously discriminate and reject.

From his observations of cleanerfishes themselves Tony Ayling surmises that, whatever the reasons for the individual preferences of crimson cleanerfishes, parasite removal may be a learned behaviour, rather than an innate response, and that perhaps each individual concentrates on those fishes it learnt to clean earlier in its life. Certainly, it seems clear that reef fishes are much more complex than is commonly believed.

Courtship dance of crimson cleanerfishes: male encircles female.
Female above male, crimson cleanerfishes in their well-defined territory.

Guild of the bottom stalkers

Morays and congers

With jaws agape and staring eyes, a moray eel confronts me from a small cave. The needle-sharp, canine teeth, angled backwards, look ready to sink into my arm or leg and lock on to it. The jaws open and shut rhythmically as if the eel was already tasting its prey. Little wonder then that the moray has an evil reputation as a savage and aggressive animal. And yet, in many years of skindiving, very few divers have been injured by an eel. The threatening jaw movements are, in fact, linked with its breathing activity. In my own experience, morays are among the most approachable and placid of fish. Conger eels recoil timidly and river eels flee like shy kittens. The only times I have heard of eels causing injury are when someone has unwittingly thrust a hand right at an eel's head, usually when that person was hunting for shells or rock lobster.

Eels are a special group of fish which have become adapted to living in narrow crevices and holes, where they find both food and shelter. With such a habitat, many features of the normal fish anatomy were unnecessary or even a disadvantage. The eel's body has become long and slender, to enable it to insinuate itself into confined areas. This involves an exaggerated swimming action throwing the whole body into a series of elegant transverse waves, which increase in amplitude as they pass back along the body. There is also a reduction of tail fin, abandonment of pelvic fins and the development of one continuous dorsal/anal fin. While river eels and congers still have pectoral fins, the morays have lost these, too. Hydrodynamically, the eel's body shape is far from ideal. An eel 70 cm long measured 4.3 cm in diameter. For minimum friction and ideal body form, as in the tuna and other pelagic fishes, the body length should be about four and a half times the maximum diameter; our eel would then be only 20 cm long. Clearly the eel is not suited to prolonged fast swimming and has sacrificed a great deal to suit its special habitat.

For a fish to withdraw backwards into narrow fissures, bony gill covers would be an encumbrance. The eel has an arrow-like skull and its gill openings are reduced to small slits behind the pectoral fins or, with the morays, just a hole on either side of the head.

By having such tiny gills the eels are exceptions to the rule for bottom-dwelling fishes, which generally have large-capacity gill chambers working as suction pumps, to ensure adequate ventilation while resting inert for long periods. Lacking these large gill covers, to produce a bellows action the eel must keep its mouth open almost continuously. As the moray breathes, water is forced towards the gills by a swallowing action. Flow of water back out of the mouth is prevented by means of small, muscular ring-valves or sphincters at the internal gill slits. Pressure experiments with conger eels have shown that this type of pumping action is greatly superior to the gill-chamber suction method of most other fishes. It also explains the malevolent appearance of the gaping jaws.

For backward movement and sinuous swimming, scales would be a hindrance. River eels have only very tiny scales beneath a thick coating of mucus; congers and morays have no scales at all. Since these fishes must

Mottled moray. ▶

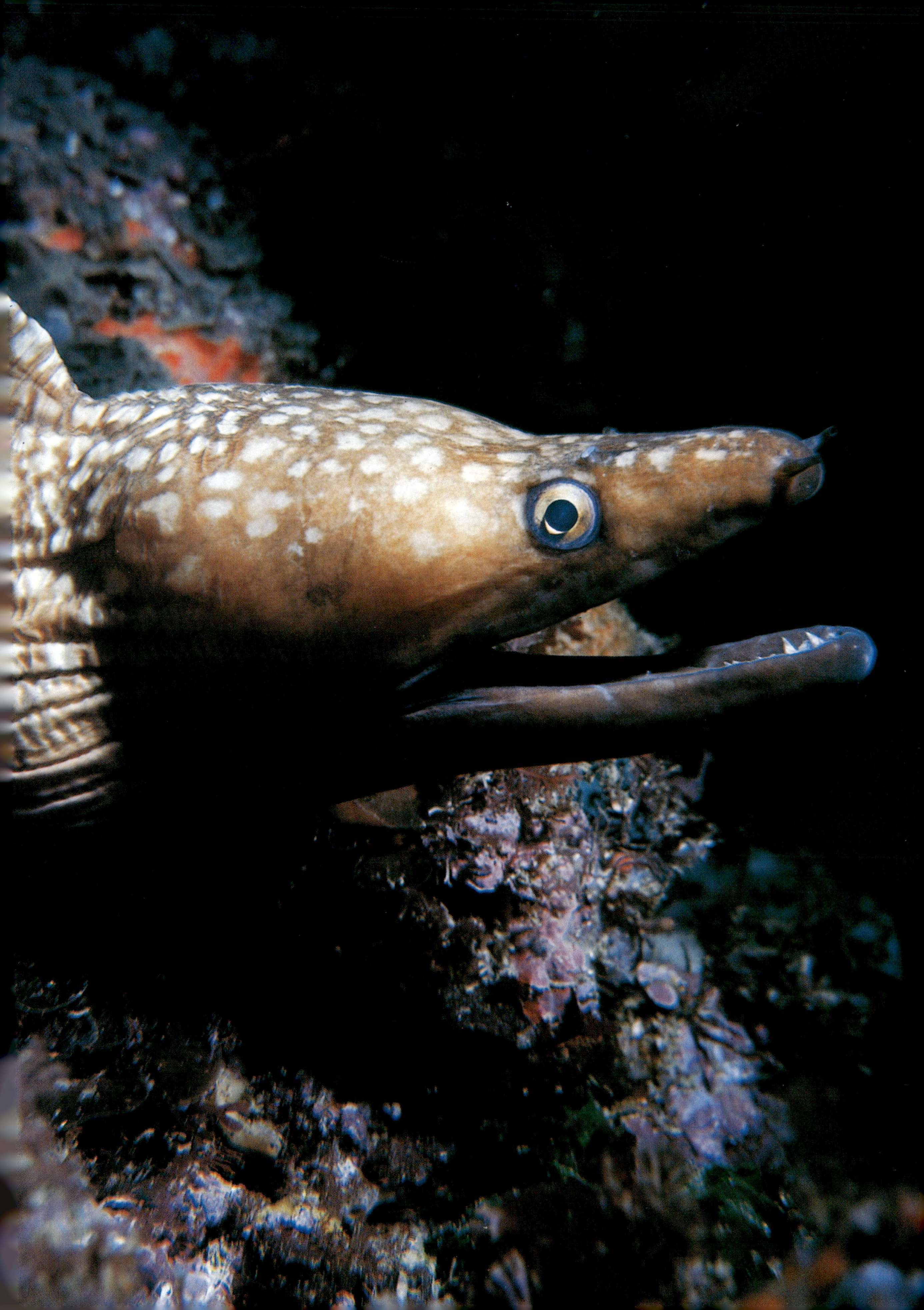

live near the bottom, a buoyant swim bladder would also be disadvantageous. In the eels the swim bladder retains its primitive condition and opens directly into the oesophagus; this explains why congers have been said to 'bark', releasing air from the swim bladder in explosive bursts.

For tracking their prey at night or in dark regions, eels have a highly developed sense of smell. The nostrils are spread well apart on the snout to provide accurate direction-finding as the head veers from side to side sampling the water currents. These nasal apertures are tubular, lined with tiny hair-like cilia which beat inwards to draw water into two large nasal cavities. As water flows over the olfactory organs, receptor organs in the delicately folded skin are able to sense the smallest odour traces. The water passes out through the rear part of the nostrils just in front and slightly above the eye.

The brain of an eel has an extremely large olfactory region, much larger than the optic centres. In contrast, the herring has only a small olfactory region, but a large part of its brain is concerned with vision. Experiments on morays showed they were unable to find food when their nostrils were plugged. Congers and river eels do not have such pronounced nasal tubes.

The eyes of eels differ from those of other fish. They are covered with a protective skin; and the iris is able to contract, controlling the amount of light reaching the retina. Most fish are unable to do this and are dazzled when we shine bright lights on them at night.

Grey moray

The grey moray is the most abundant and the smallest of the five morays at the Poor Knights Islands. It reaches 60 cm in length. Its snout is longer and more slender than that of the yellow moray, more suited to probing into narrow fissures and cracks for its prey of crabs, shrimps and small fishes. Its nasal tubes are longer and the dorsal fin is very high and fleshy, with a light blue fringe.

Although they are mostly seen in holes in the cliff, these morays frequently inhabit tube sponges or just entwine themselves among the fronds of kelp. One lived in the same sponge at Northern Archway for many months. Sometimes they share their refuge with another of their species, or with a yellow moray, the twin heads rearing from a hole like a nest of vipers. At dusk all morays become active hunters serpenting across the bottom, but the grey moray can often be seen stalking prey by day.

For some strange reason the grey moray is occasionally seen right alongside the scorpion fish, or even draped over its back. I now have reason to suspect it may strip the fish of eggs or milt, as river eels do to trout — a bizarre symbiosis, as the fish could easily withdraw.

Yellow moray

Although similar in diet and habits to the grey moray, I have never seen a pair of yellow morays in the same hole. I once watched two fighting viciously for several minutes until both were ripped and torn in many parts of their bodies, and eventually the most heavily lacerated one fled along the cliff face. This may well have been a territorial squabble.

Since crustaceans make up most of their diet, it is surprising to see yellow

Grey morays sometimes share the same refuge.
Yellow morays are aggressive and may inflict wounds.

morays at night with ruby red shrimps swarming over their skin, possibly removing parasites. By day these shrimps are seldom visible, as they hide in the deepest fissures. Yellow morays grow to a metre in length.

Mottled moray
The mottled and the mosaic morays have long, heavily armed jaws. They are far less abundant than the other three species — seldom is there more than one individual in any one area. While the other species are attracted to a bait in wriggling confusion, these morays are not easily tempted to leave their holes. Large specimens, up to a metre long, seem to prefer the greater depths. At times the ground colour of the skin can be so dark as to obscure the mottled pattern, but normally, where light levels are diminished, it is an effective camouflage. It must be remembered that flashlit photographs spoil this effect.

Mosaic moray
At times the mosaic moray looks ghostly white. It is a strange sight, with its slender, curving jaws swaying beneath a rocky ledge, for such lack of colour is rare among fishes. On other occasions the olive-green mosaic pattern is predominant and the moray is much better concealed. The jaws of this moray cannot close fully even when it snaps its mouth shut. The canine teeth are extremely fine, long and needle sharp.

Such jaws could inflict very painful wounds, yet the mosaic moray will let me approach within centimetres without the least sign of attack. Initially it just freezes and glowers at me, then it begins to withdraw, backing off very slowly at first, then with increasing rapidity, always keeping its eyes fixed on me. A body's length away (it grows to 1.8 m), it turns and flees. If I follow it, it will stop, draw into a rocky recess and repeat the performance. Most fishes would continue to flee and could easily evade a diver, but the mosaic moray prefers to face danger, perhaps because its fierce mien should be sufficient to discourage any aggressor — other than a diver with unexposed film in his camera.

Speckled moray
Found in similar areas to the grey, the speckled moray has an especially powerful and massive head. Its brown speckled camouflage conceals it from its quarry and its teeth are very well designed for seizing prey, for which there is no possibility of release. Like those of all morays, the teeth yield to backward pressure, but snap into a locked position when pushed forward towards the mouth opening. If damaged or dislodged, new teeth grow to replace them. I once watched a pair of these undersea pythons locked in furious combat. The largest of our morays, they can reach 2 m in length.

Very little is known of the biology of morays. It is likely that they spawn only once in a lifetime, like other eels, and that the morays at the Poor Knights may be derived from successful spawnings elsewhere (for example, Australia), and the larvae transported to New Zealand by ocean currents.

As nocturnal predators of juvenile fishes, morays would have an important role in regulating the populations of reef fishes.

Mosaic moray. ▶

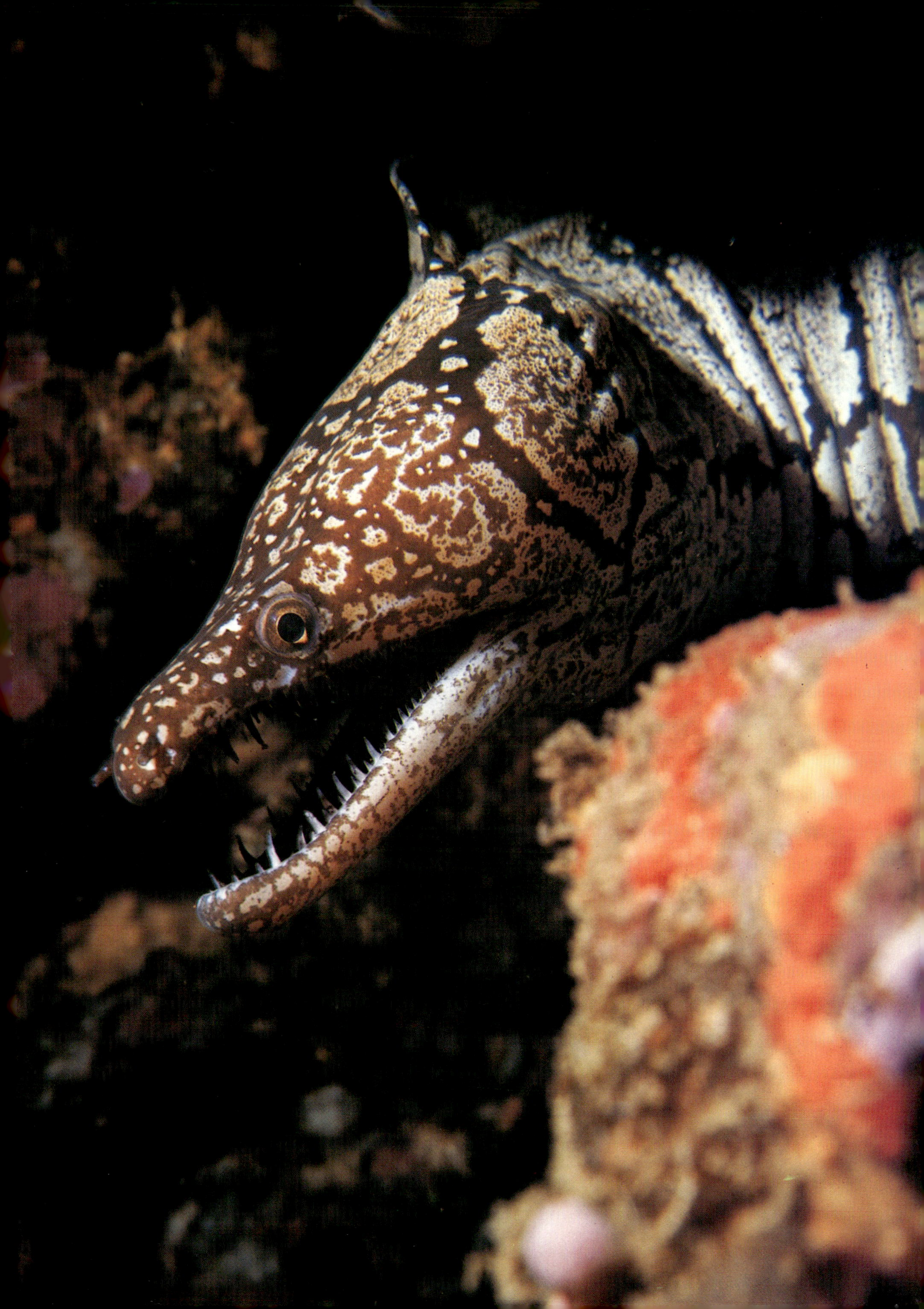

Speckled moray, the largest.
Strange symbiosis: morays sometimes entwine scorpionfishes.

Conger eel
The conger is distinguished from the moray by its more normal, fish-shaped head, slightly flattened, and the presence of pectoral fins. Whereas the dorsal fin of the moray begins near the head, raising its profile, that of the conger begins much further back, above the tip of the pectoral fin. The gills are small slits and the eyes are oval and much bigger. The teeth are all fine, the outer row forming a cutting edge in each jaw; the upper jaw projects slightly beyond the lower jaw, suiting it better to bottom feeding. At night it leaves its lair to prey on crustaceans and small fishes. Once congers reach their maximum length — around 180 cm — the body just continues to thicken. At the Poor Knights congers are not common, but certain huge individuals, like the one at the Middle Arch, have occupied the same area for more than a decade. Once, by mistake, I found myself tickling its glassy-smooth head!

Garden eel
A very rare and strange eel has been discovered at the Poor Knights. At 60 m in Landing Bay, a field of 100 slender heads may be seen nodding gently, like flowers, in the direction of a slight current.
   Garden eels are gregarious. With their tails in sandy burrows and their heads slightly bent, they feed upon plankton brought by the current. In a colony, each hole is about half a metre from its neighbour. As I approach, the whole meadow of eels begins to withdraw imperceptibly into the white sand. By the time I am above them they have all vanished. They are so sensitive to any disturbance that I have never been able to photograph them at a closer range than 6 m. They grow to 60 cm.

Conger eel has pectoral fins, which morays lack.

Lizard fish

At first nothing is discernible amidst the scraps of seaweed adrift on the white sand. Then a jewel eye appears, empty and silent, and a lizard-like nose tilts jauntily above the bottom. The lizard fish, counterpart of the ancient tuatara in the Poor Knights forest on the land above, uses the same strategy as the reptile to get a meal: obliterative camouflage and an attack stance, with retractable, double-hinged jaws well concealed by the general outline. While they are quite unrelated, it is no coincidence that both fish and reptile have assumed similar forms and behaviour. They have been tailored by convergent evolution to perform the same role — lurking carnivores each capable of hours of immobility, which end with a sudden, engulfing rush on their prey. Quite different animals may thus independently develop similar structures to perform the same task. Electric shock organs have been developed by six quite separate families of fishes. The octopus is a mollusc related to the oyster, but its eye functions much as our own. If such adaptations have survival value, they will be equally advantageous in the natural selection of several species.

Lizard fishes have a single dorsal fin; and the pelvic fins are sited on the abdomen, well back from the pectorals. In this position they serve the lizard fish as an undercarriage for resting on the bottom, steadied by the wing-like pectorals like a small fighter plane.

Lizard fishes are common on the Great Barrier Reef, but in New Zealand they were unknown until the spring of 1970, when they were discovered at the Poor Knights. At depths of 15–60 m they lurk in sandy areas and occasionally perch on rocky ledges or flat rocks adjacent to sand. I have also found them buried to the snout in the sand. Springing off their pelvic fins, these fierce little predators (up to 25 cm long) can dart forward faster than the eye can follow, driven by their tail and planing down onto the sand with their pectorals. They are often seen in pairs, but I have seen one attack a larger lizard fish and drive it from its territory.

Filtration of colour by the sea means the ruby-red coloration of the lizard fish is transformed into a dark, nondescript pattern, merging the fish perfectly into its surroundings. A sporadic invader of the Poor Knights, it does not appear to have spawned successfully there. Upon discovery it was named *Synodus doaki* — I do not know if it is an honour to be allied with a fish that has a big mouth and lies around doing nothing all day!

Paired lizard fishes, possibly male and female.

Lurking predator: lizard fish ready to launch an attack. ▶

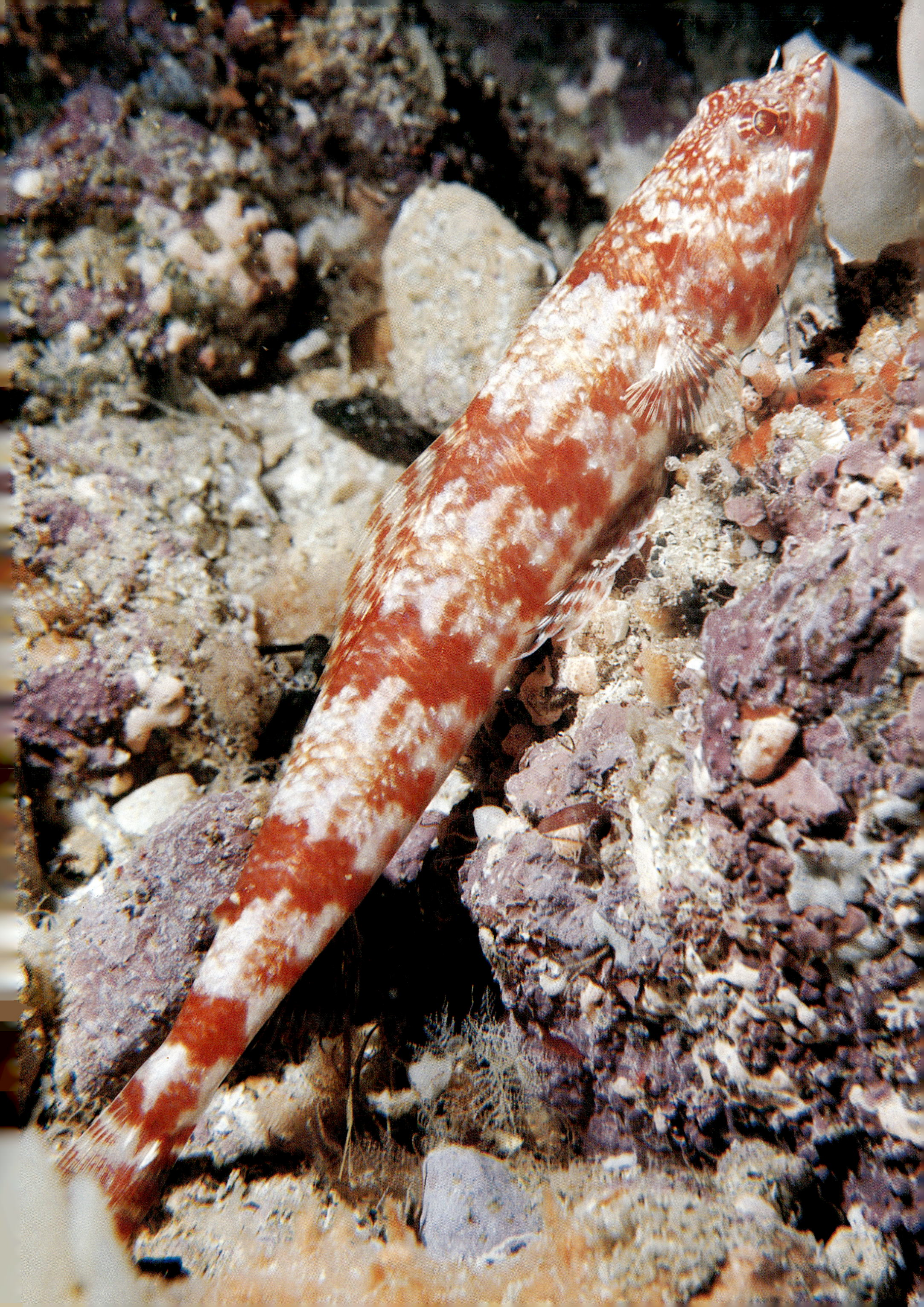

Scorpion fish

The only creature that has ever attacked me and caused pain is the scorpion fish. While I was photographing at close range the mottled moray shown in this book, my hand was suddenly wrenched away from the focus knob. Already tensed for a possible moray attack, I whipped around to find my hand engulfed by a very angry red fish. Fortunately, scorpion fishes have feeble dentition, just sufficient to grasp their prey firmly in the course of swallowing it whole. I saved my hand with a flick but it was roughly lacerated on both sides and stinging with the salt water. Unwittingly, in approaching the moray grotto I had encroached on the territory of a scorpion fish and it did not hesitate to drive me out. On other occasions they have charged my face and bitten furiously at my flash reflector. Many other divers have suffered similar harassment.

For aggressiveness I thought it took the prize, until one day I saw a small halfbanded perch repeatedly drive off a scorpion fish four times its size, which I had unsettled and sent over to the perch's territory. This shows the boldness of a fish on home ground — the halfbanded perch is a food species of the scorpion fish. Large specimens of scorpion fish eat mainly fish: blennies, demoiselles and blue maomao have been found in them, along with crabs, shrimps and small octopus. They are nocturnal feeders and range out over the bottom and up and down the cliff faces at night, when many fishes seek rest among the holes and crevices. Although the scorpion fish often attacks divers without warning, it will allow us to approach within inches, and sometimes even handle it. Poisonous, well-armoured fishes, being so well protected, are often permissive in this way.

The scorpion fish's body is a remarkable example of cryptic camouflage. Its numerous dermal flaps and filaments closely resemble the encrusting sponges and bryozoans among which it lurks. The rags and tatters on its head and body may become pale green or white when it lies among kelp or in the open, and so aptly can it match the background that one may gaze almost directly at a scorpion fish without noticing it.

Like many bottom-living fishes, the scorpion fish has no swim bladder for hovering; its greatly developed pectoral fins are used as props for resting. When it approaches a small fish at night, the scorpion fish makes a short, swift rush, propelled by these fan-like pectorals and the broad tail. The huge mouth yawns open to engulf the prey with a combined sucking and grasping action, and the victim is swallowed whole. There is another reason for the large head. Inactive for long periods, like many bottom-lurkers it requires capacious gill chambers to irrigate its gills. With a gentle bellows action the greatly extended gill flaps can pump a steady flow across the gills without disturbing the immobile posture of the fish.

For all its aggressiveness, the scorpion fish has a peculiar relationship with the morays. I have seen a yellow moray draped over a scorpion fish's back and, on another occasion, a grey moray lying right alongside — a formidable line-up of nocturnal fish eaters, perhaps happy to rest together during the day when there is no competition.

Scorpion fish grow to 60 cm in length.

Scorpionfish on the deep reef. ▶

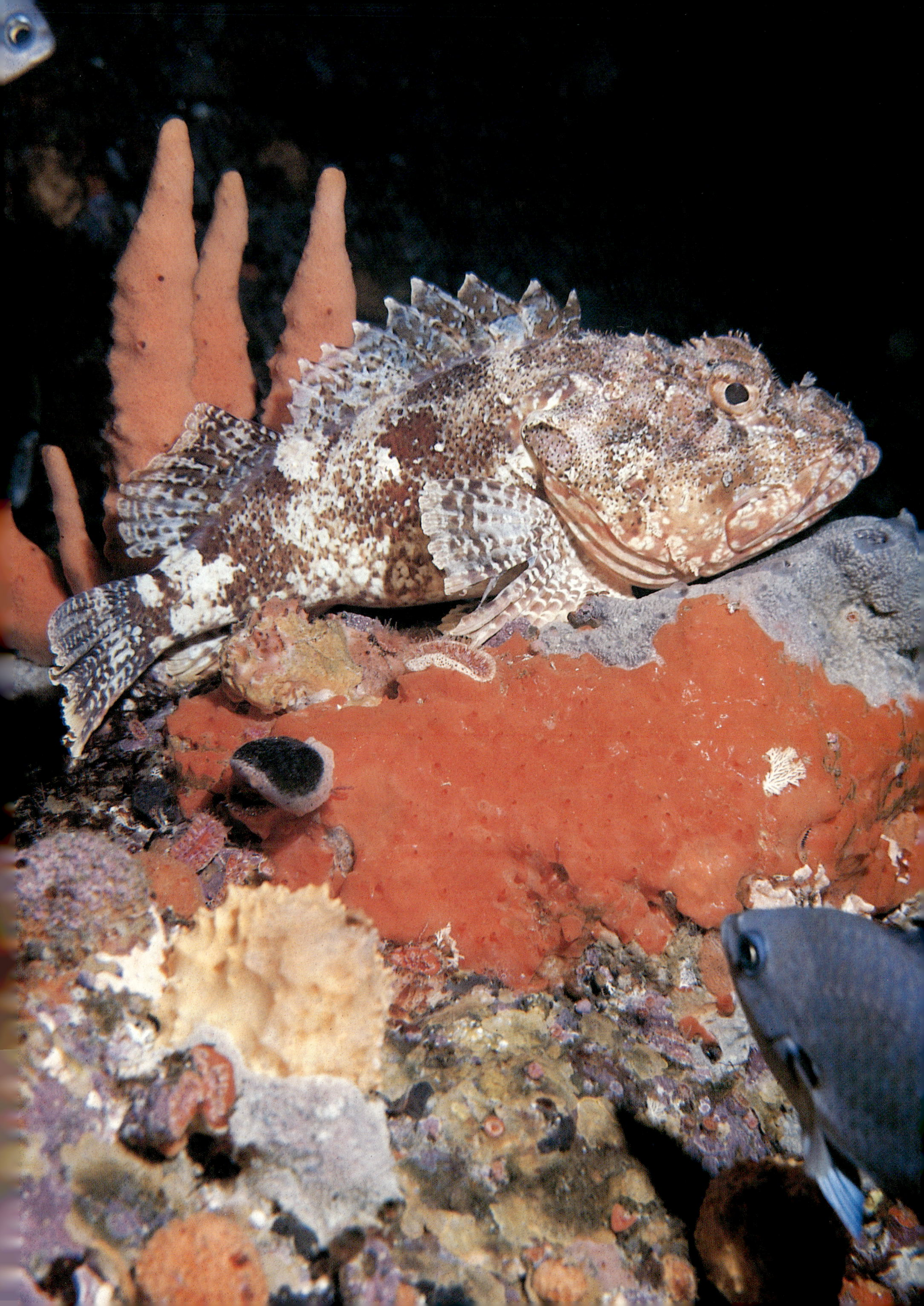

Rock cod
Hovering by day beneath a deep overhang, a shy, bearded fish peers out at the diver. Its small, sinuous tail flexes and the pectorals beat gently, for it seldom rests on the bottom. In a flash it disappears into a dark fissure. At night, ranging over the rocky bottom and across the sand, these cods are everywhere, feeding on crabs and small, sleepy fishes.

The rock cod is a bottom-dwelling carnivore equipped with a large mouth and a single sensory barbel beneath its chin. Each jaw has an outer band of strong, conical teeth, followed by a narrow band of small, velvety ones. Its scales are small and its pelvic fins are in front of the pectorals — an unusual arrangement.

Rock cod live in rock crevices and holes during the day. A pair have been seen in the same crevice for two years. Often solitary, they occasionally form groups of three or more. They grow to around 40 cm.

Rock cod.

Giant stargazer, emergent from its sub-sand ambush.

Giant stargazer
Near the mouth of Rikoriko Cave, 50 m down on the white sand, I saw something odd amongst the coral rubble. A gentle prod and hey presto! A weird, fat fish emerged in a flurry and settled on the sand nearby. In 20-odd years of exploring the area, this was my only opportunity to see and photograph the highly secretive giant stargazer. Its huge, armour-plated head, bristling with sharp spines, houses an upward-gaping, cavernous mouth. Right on top of the flattened skull, its eyes command an all-round view. With pectoral fins like small wings it can rapidly fan its way down into the sand until only the eyes and a faint suggestion of jaws remain visible. Should a fish or crab wander by, the trapdoor opens and the grotesque monster surges up to engulf its prey. Giant stargazers can reach almost a metre in length and their capacious jaws can accommodate fishes almost half their own size. They are most abundant in southern waters to depths of 500 m. A smaller species, sometimes called a 'toe-biter', inhabits coastal estuaries and tidal rivers.

Triplefins and blennies

Propped on slender pelvic fins, alertly scanning their surroundings with prominent eyes, the triplefins and blennies form a miniature society within the reef fish community. Smallness enables them to adapt to a very wide range of habitats, there being many more food niches available to small animals. They have complex social and breeding behaviour. Many have camouflage colours to blend with drab environments, or to merge with the richly variegated colours of the rock face, while others are brightly coloured, territorial fishes, with advertising coloration that enables the population to space out to best advantage.

Triplefins and blennies are a key link in the marine food chain. Eaten by a variety of predatory reef fish, they themselves browse on invertebrates too small for larger fishes. In turn, the prey of the blenny feed on microscopic plants. The only living things capable of using the sun's energy to synthesise carbohydrates, plants provide the basic food of all animals.

Each species of triplefin and blenny has its special diet, from the tentacles of hydroids to shellfish eggs, barnacle cirri, tiny worms, minute shellfish, and all manner of small crustaceans. Several species remove parasitic lice from larger fishes, and nip off white fungal growths from fins and infected areas.

The triplefins of offshore islands are generally brightly coloured, while those of tide pools and coastal waters are camouflaged to suit their particular habitat. As with most of the brightly coloured species, the males put on courtship colours during the spawning season, with changes in body pattern and gaily adorned fins.

Around the Poor Knights there are seven different kinds. The yellow-black triplefin has a black, striped body, with a yellow rear half. At winter spawning time the male's head becomes black. The blue-eyed triplefin has a red and white barred body and iridescent eye rings. It stands out boldly among the red sponges, emerald-green bryozoans and pink corals of the cliff face. During spawning, in early spring, the hind part of the body takes on a sooty colour and the head becomes yellow. With yaldwyn's triplefin, males change from pale brown, speckled with black, to a gorgeous yellow-orange. The male spectacled triplefin changes from an orange red fish, with distinctive black spectacles, to near black. With other species, there are no significant changes.

Tiniest of all is the blue-dot triplefin, which has bright blue dots on its body and red speckled cheeks. The scalyheaded triplefin resembles a miniature scorpion fish, with rough, bony armour on its head. A nocturnal species, its camouflage makes it very hard to see, as it rests in cracks and crevices by day. The large, mottled triplefin is very like a coastal species, the variable triplefin, with its six irregular brown bars.

From a vacant barnacle shell the crested blenny peers, each eye adorned with a feathery crest. Blennies make their home in disused barnacle shells, adhering to the cliff. During winter, males entice females to deposit eggs in these shells, which the males guard fiercely until they hatch.

The spawning activity of most triplefins begins in mid winter. In late June I once watched a pair of variable triplefins (on the adjacent coast) on the side of a sloping rock. The male wore his nuptial colours: his body a smooth satin black, the three dorsal fins made more conspicuous with a fringe of sky blue. All his fins were held erect to magnify his size. When I

Crested blenny and mimic blenny — see page 179 (top) for oblique triplefins that it mimics.

first saw the couple, the male was making aggressive rushes at a large red moki. As I approached I became the object of his rage. Deciding to give him the satisfaction of working off his aggressive drive, I backed off a few metres. The tiny fish was placated and returned to his female. Both began to quiver, side by side. The female's belly rippled like a belly-dancer's, until the tip of her tail began to quiver. The movement increased until her whole body was shaking. This excited the male. He approached, dashed away and darted back to the nest. Then he put his pelvic fins on her, erected all other fins and began to quiver all over. Such bouts of courting may continue for two weeks or more before spawning takes place. This contrasts with the demoiselle and black angelfish, where courtship is immediately followed by egg-laying and fertilisation.

During spawning, the female's ovipositor strokes the rock, depositing a single layer of tiny eggs and the male fertilises them as they are stuck in place. Nuptial colours now fade. For a few days the couple remain together on the nest, but eventually the male remains alone, savagely repelling intruders until the eggs hatch. A male usually mates with several females and may establish as many as nine nests over the breeding season. Other triplefins have similar spawning patterns, but are much more secretive and difficult to observe.

Found above the crests of the kelp forest, alongside cliff walls and swarming in small rocky alcoves, the oblique-swimmer is the most unusual triplefin of all. The only triplefins known to swim in schools, oblique-swimmers truly belong in the plankton-feeding guild. Their yellow and black bodies are constantly darting and undulating almost like a swarm of bees, as they snatch minute plankton animals from the current. Unlike the bottom-dwelling blennies, their eyes are at the sides of the head instead of on top. The lips are not protruberant and the head is more rounded. Except when spawning in winter, they seldom rest on the rock face. During spawning they darken in tone. If alarmed, they dart en masse into crevices or hover beneath seaweed fronds.

One day at the Poor Knights we noticed something odd amongst a swarm of oblique-swimmers: a stranger in their midst. We had discovered the mimic blenny. In tropical seas, similar blennies imitate the swimming movements, fin patterns and markings of the cleaner wrasse *Labroides*. By this subterfuge the mimic is able to approach fishes that are anxious to be cleaned. It dances up in the fashion of the true cleaner, but instead uses the fish's trust to make a vicious attack, nipping off a small portion of the host's fins.

Similarly, this species mimics the harmless little oblique-swimming triplefin to his own advantage. Once in clear focus, the mimic gives himself away by his longer body and more sinuous swimming movements. While he seeks acceptance in the school, he is not fully in tune with his models. His predatory mouth is not at the front of his head, but, like a shark's, is concealed on the underside, and, unlike his plankton-feeding model, the mimic has needle-sharp teeth.

By swimming with these harmless triplefins, the mimic blenny is able to get close to larger fishes. A lightning attack on the unsuspecting victim's fins puts it to flight with startled rapidity. At times mimic blennies retreat into a tube worm shell or barnacle, wriggling in backwards until just the head is visible.

In nature, mimicry achieves a variety of purposes. Butterflies mimic wasps to gain protection; orchids mimic wasps for pollination; and a harmless snake eel imitates a poisonous sea snake so perfectly that only an expert can tell the difference.

Male yellow-black triplefin in summer.
Male yellow-black triplefin during winter in sexual coloration.

Blue-eyed triplefin and Yaldwyn's triplefin.

Spectacled triplefin and blue-dot triplefin, the tiniest.

Scalyheaded triplefin and mottled triplefin.

Oblique-swimming triplefins: plankton feeders.
Triplefin nest site.

Halfbanded perch

For three years I observed the same small grouper resting passively in a crevice at the Poor Knights. The only time I have seen halfbanded perch foraging in the open was at dusk; when darkness fell they all returned to their ledges. Sometimes they rest upside down beneath an overhang.

These tiny groupers (up to 15 cm long) are intensely territorial and live at all depths down to 60 m, wherever they find a suitable recess. Studies by Dr Geoff Jones at the Poor Knights show they have a home range of about 3 m^2. Along the reef edge at 18 m in Nursery Cove he found a density of eight fishes per 50 m^2.

Like many groupers, halfbanded perch begin life as females and reverse sex to become males, usually after their second year. Naturally the males are bigger and there is a ratio of 2.7 males to each female. Geoff Jones found that solitary perch are usually males and it seems they may form breeding pairs, one large and one small.

Spawning takes place in spring (September–December). I have seen the juveniles, miniature replicas of the adult, during January. They grow rapidly, reaching maturity in a year. On the adjacent coast another species, the slightly larger redbanded perch, is abundant; it seems strange that we never see it at the Poor Knights, just 24 km offshore. For some time we believed it was the adult form of the halfbanded perch. It has seven complete, chocolate-brown vertical bands on its body and lacks the ruby-red head markings and eye-concealing stripes of the halfbanded perch. Whereas the former has a diet of crabs and small fishes, the halfbanded perch has been observed fossicking among kelp fronds for tiny mysid shrimps and other small crustaceans. In summer it steals eggs from the nests of demoiselles.

Halfbanded perch.

Yellowbanded perch.

Yellowbanded perch
First discovered at the Poor Knights in January 1969, this solitary, tropical grouper is another sporadic coloniser from Australian waters that can reach 60 cm in length on its home ground.

Like its relatives, it is a lurking predator and spends the day within a small cave, probably ranging out at dawn and dusk to feed on small fishes and crustaceans. For a fish that lives in dimly lit waters, the pattern of markings on its body and head is an excellent example of disruptive coloration.

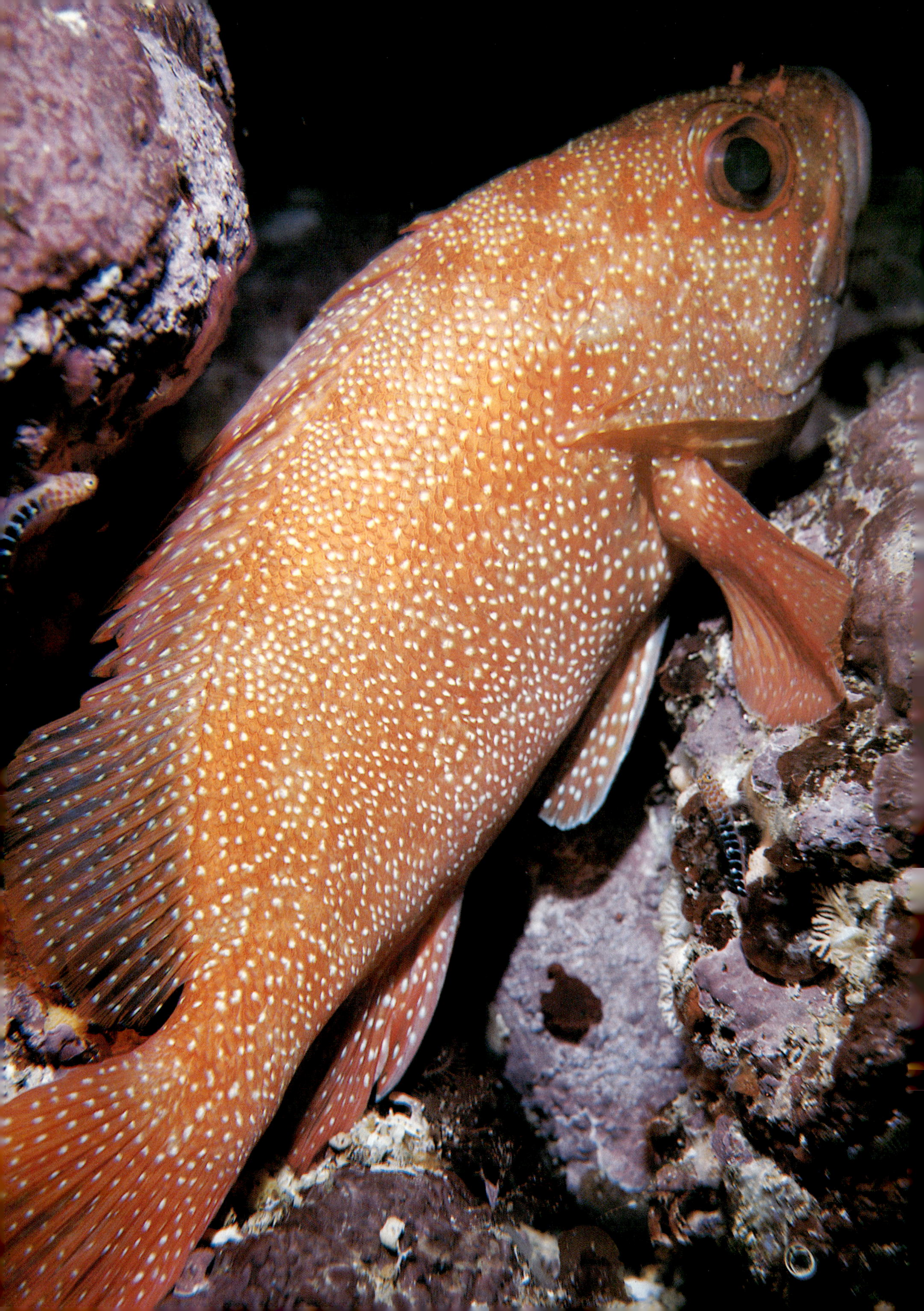

Toadstool grouper

Another small solitary species, up to 40 cm in length, the toadstool grouper was first discovered at the Poor Knights in 1969. As it stares from a crevice in the shallows during daylight hours, its brilliant, orange-red, polka-dot pattern has an obliterative effect in the dim light. At night its white spots change to dark blue, concentrated in vertical bands, and it prowls over the bottom in quick spurts, preying on small fishes and crustaceans with its fine, sharp teeth.

I once watched a pair of tiny, blue-dot triplefins moving over the skin of a resting toadstool grouper, probably removing parasites — yet such fishes are normally part of the toadstool grouper's diet.

When I was night diving in the Lord Howe Island lagoon, I found these grouper very abundant everywhere, even beneath ledges just under the surface at the sea's edge.

Goldribbon grouper

The goldribbon grouper was first reported at the Poor Knights in May 1968. Unlike the others, this small slender grouper, which grows to 40 cm, does not rest on the floor of a cave but hovers near the roof and beneath vaulting overhangs, usually at depths beyond 30 m.

Its coloration is well suited to this habitat: the gold band on its back is a reversal of the usual obliterative countershading strategy used by most fishes, with the back much darker than the belly. Since this fish swims near the roof, most light reaching it comes from below, bouncing up from the entrance. Accordingly, its underside is dark, so as to reflect less light. The yellow band running through its eye has a disruptive effect, breaking the outline of the body and drawing attention away from its telescopic jaws.

The goldribbon grouper is only marginal at the Poor Knights and probably originates from the Kermadec Islands. It belongs to a separate family of fishes from the other groupers — the soapfishes, so named because their skin can exude a toxic mucus to discourage predators. An eminent ichthyologist on a fish-collecting expedition once stored a small soapfish in his swim shorts. He had to be admitted to hospital, and it took considerable effort to convince the staff his strange complaint was caused by a fish!

◄ *Toadstool grouper.*

Cave-dwelling goldribbon grouper has reverse countershading.
(Roger Kempthorne)

Spotted black grouper.

Kermadecs spotted black grouper relaxes with diver. ▶
(Jaan Voot)

Spotted black grouper
At the Poor Knights Islands, spotted black grouper only reach about 60 cm, but in tropical waters they grow to more than 2 m: massive, man-size bottom-dwellers. Whereas those at the Poor Knights are small and solitary, in home waters they form small groups of varying sizes. I have seen individuals living in the same cave, month after month. The lair usually has several alternative exits and the grouper hovers just off the bottom at the entrance, often just the snout and goggly eyes protruding. On seeing a diver it ducks back, then peers out for a second glance before disappearing into another chamber in its lair. Its diet is small fishes and crabs. It has a formidable array of sharp, conical teeth, and older specimens will prey on much larger fishes.

As this grouper stalks across the bottom, its camouflage pattern can be seen to alter rapidly from white dots to vertical dark bars to match the areas it is passing through. Over stones and sand, dots prevail; among weed and rocks the bars stand out. Within its lair the skin becomes so dark, the patterns are obscure.

While young grouper are rather shy and timid, adults show great curiosity towards divers. At Lord Howe Island a photographer thought somebody was touching her leg as she concentrated on a picture. When she turned around she found to her dismay that a grouper had sucked part of her leg gently into its mouth. Since these grouper begin life as females, and later reverse sex, the large fishes are all males.

At the remote Kermadec Islands a population of large spotted grouper, ranging from 16 to 80 kg, has become quite famous for its peculiar response to divers, and special protection has been accorded to the area. In 1984 Jaan Voot and companions discovered they could play with these huge creatures. If a diver swam towards one, it would flee. But if ignored, the big fishes would approach, even thrusting their heads between two divers, touching both. The divers soon discovered that if they tickled a grouper under the gill plates and stomach, it relaxed totally, all colour draining away to near white. In this entranced state they could turn it upside down, rotate it end for end and pass it to and fro. If a fish disapproved of any action it would darken slightly. The divers came away dazed at the situation and convinced that creatures with such a strong affinity towards humans should be protected from mindless slaughter.

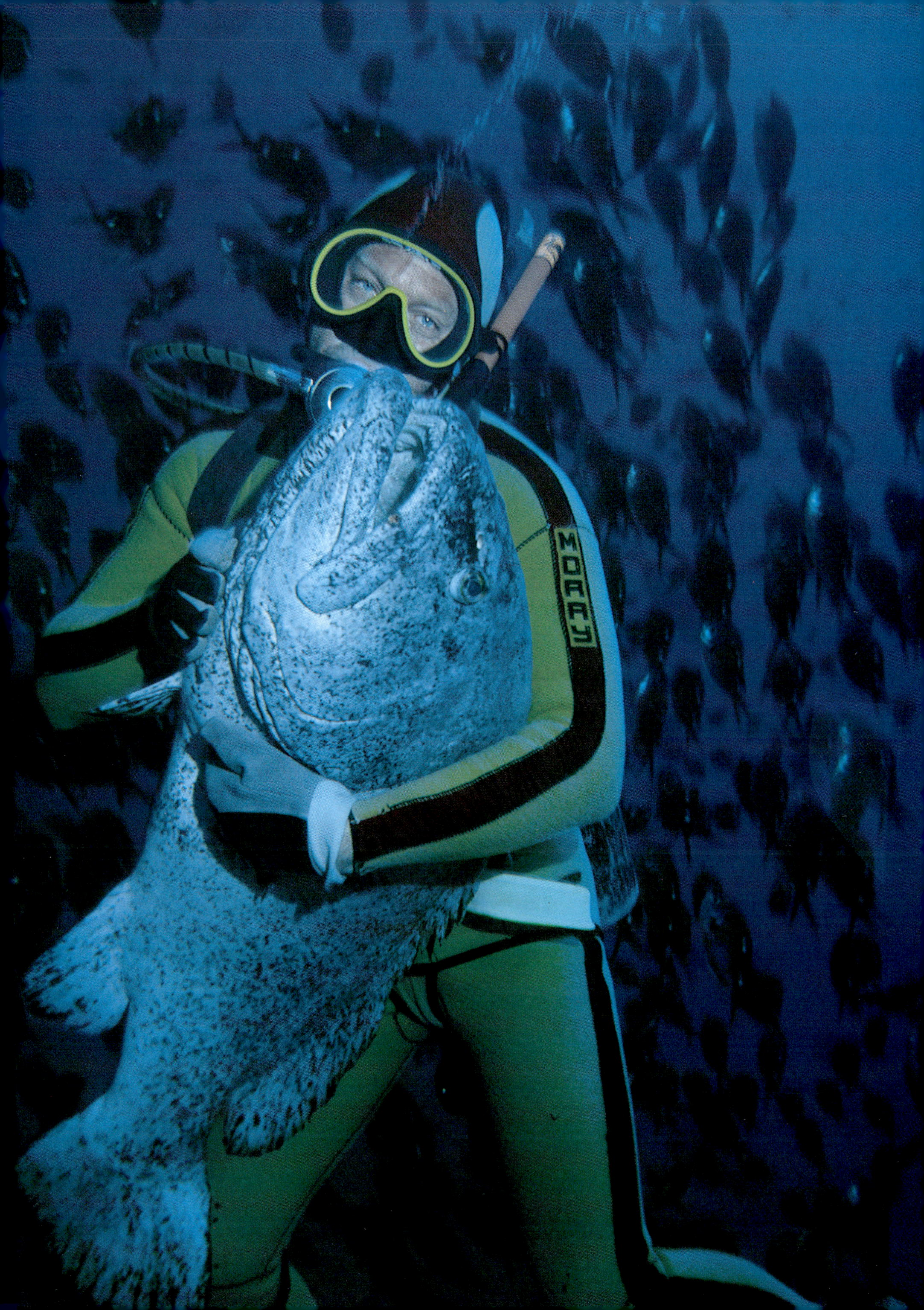
MORAY

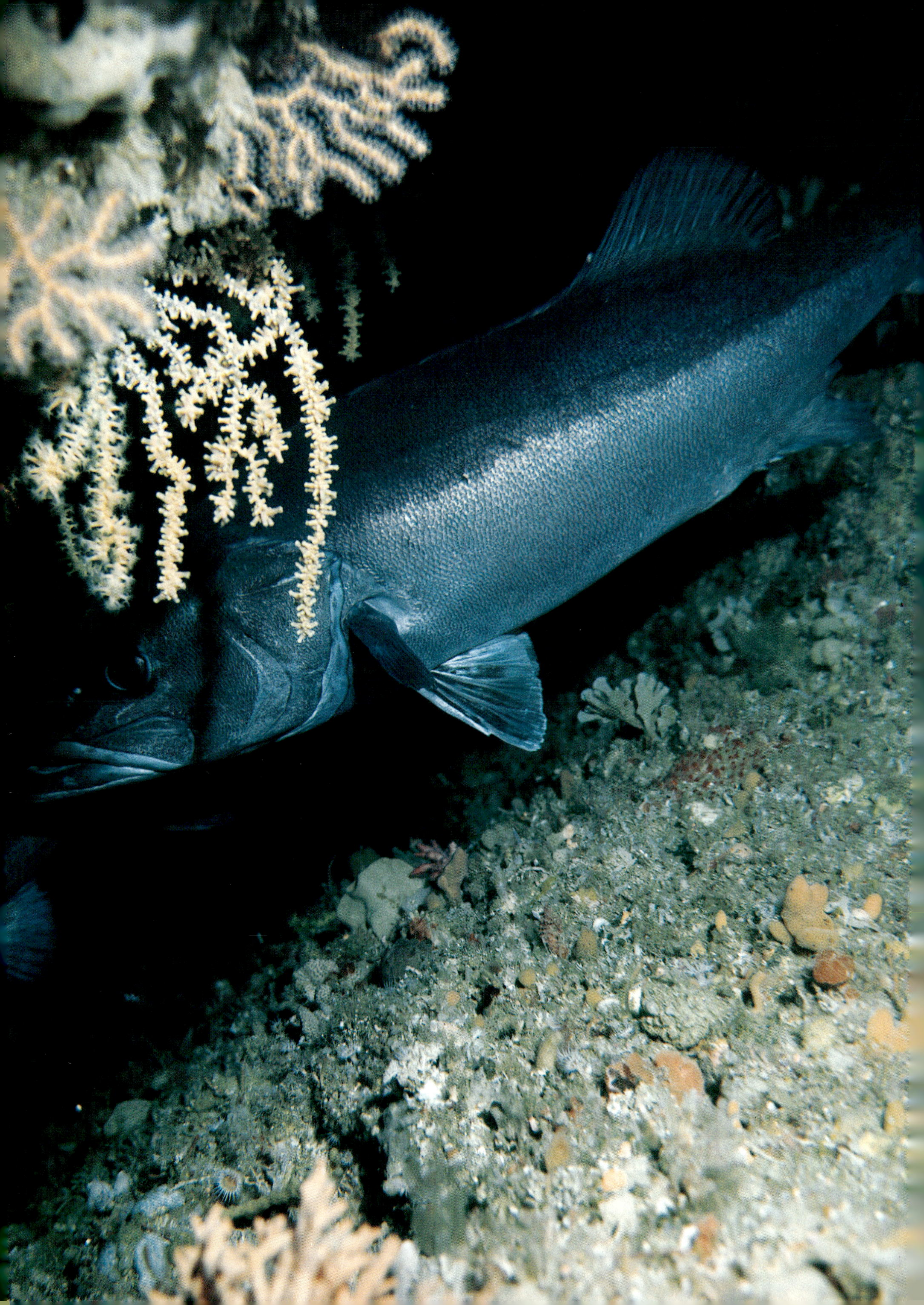

Hapuku

An impressive sight, with its huge goggly eyes and great undershot jaws, jagged dorsal fin and powerful, thwacking tail, the hapuku is one of New Zealand's largest fishes. It can reach over 1.8 m in length. Found also in East Australia, it inhabits our entire continental shelf, aggregating around undersea pinnacles where preyfish such as orange roughy school.

At the Three Kings Islands I was once surrounded by a huge herd of hapuku, which came whirling up from the deeps like a maelstrom and caromed around me for 10 minutes before vanishing again into the dark blue. Unexploited populations like this are very rare nowadays and have long since vanished from the Poor Knights. Although the latter has been a marine reserve since 1981, hapuku will need a much larger protection zone before their populations can recover.

They used to show such naive curiosity. One came up to a diver in South Harbour, circling him so close he could run his hand along its side. On another occasion I watched a large hapuku pose for a photographer; like a big dog it lay with the diver's flipper draped over its dorsal fin while he juggled with his recalcitrant gear.

When its numbers have not been reduced by over-fishing, the hapuku is a gregarious animal and seldom swims alone. Herds used to be from 30 to 100 individuals of all sizes. Each year the hapuku herds would return from deeper waters to the same caves and clefts for their winter spawning season. In late June a large grotto at the Poor Knights Islands, called the Slot, used to harbour up to 30 hapuku, ranging in size from 10 to 60 kg. The biggest would have measured 1.8 m. All have now been caught.

I last saw them in this grotto in 1971 when I desperately needed a dramatic hapuku photo for the cover of my first book on New Zealand fishes. At 60 m I held my breath. A huge hapuku was hurtling towards my camera. Closer and closer came the great pointed jaws, the jagged dorsal spines and the saucer-shaped eyes. I preset the focus at 2 m, adjusted the flashgun angle and watched through the lens. For a split second it was in focus. As I fired it veered aside, offering a more dynamic angle. Knowing how much I needed that photo, my companions watched from behind. They had seen the big fish emerge from the Slot and head straight towards me; within the Slot the rest of the herd was huddled, a seething mass of 'chumbling' jaws and silhouetted dorsals. At that depth we could spend only a few minutes before heading up.

The tragedy for the lost hapuku population lies in their biology: once hauled to the surface, their swimbladder expands irreversibly. Wise fishermen always release undersized fish, but hapuku cannot return to the bottom and must soon die. Line fishing is one of the more conservative fishing methods, but the set-line spells doom for the hapuku.

Recently I was privileged to join in the exploration of a sunken ship that lies beyond diver range near the Poor Knights. Using a robotic submarine, we found the wreck was sheltering a herd of hapuku. The davits, rails and rigging were festooned with lost trawl nets. As the band of survivors milled around our diving machine, our 'eyeball on a cable', I wished fervently that they could be spared to restock their old haunts.

◀ *Hapuku in winter quarters, 'the Slot'.*

Reef fish ecology through time and space

Reef fish communities in tropical and temperate waters show certain resemblances and certain differences. In both regions, communities are in a constant state of change through time and space. Variations in sea temperature and weather can produce changes through time. On any one reef, variations in reef structure, and hence available habitats, cause changes in the spatial distribution of populations. Getting to grips with these changes, by visiting a number of different reefs and developing a long familiarity with one particular reef, provides the diver with a constant source of interest and curiosity throughout a lifetime.

At the Poor Knights Islands, Drs Tony Ayling and Howard Choat have made a detailed study of certain fish populations over a period of 12 years — from 1972 to 1984. In a paper entitled 'Temporal and Spatial Variation in an Island Fish Fauna' they reported that there was a major influx of subtropical species in the early seventies, followed by a marked decline; and then a modest increase in the early eighties. (As I write, in 1990, a dramatic resurgence of these subtropical fishes is taking place, along with species hitherto unknown in the area, such as lionfish, and on the adjacent coast, surgeonfishes.)

The combfish was found in modest numbers in 1974, but by 1978 it had become locally extinct. The crimson cleaner, which appears to originate from the Three Kings Islands to the north, went through a 15-fold decrease in population over that same period. The pattern of these changes correlates with variations in sea temperature and severe storms. Climate records kept at the nearby Goat Island Marine Laboratory from 1966 to 1988 show annual variations in sea surface temperatures which support their study.

With the crimson cleaner there were two peak settlement periods in 1972 and 1974 when sea temperatures were high. From then their populations declined to very low levels between 1980 and 1982. There was another modest increase from 1984 to 1986, related to temperature.

A severe storm hit the Sand Garden area in September 1978, and rocks were shifted and kelp plants swept away. It must be remembered that reef fishes cannot shift readily to another territory when disaster strikes. The crimson cleaners, orange wrasses and other wrasses in shallow areas suffered a marked decline.

Wrasses which derive from coastal waters and southern locations, such as the spotty, banded wrasse and scarlet wrasse, have relatively low population densities at the Poor Knights, and these species did not show any major fluctuations during the study period.

Ayling and Choat also found there were major variations in the distribution of certain species around the Poor Knights, due to habitat selection at the stage when young larval fishes settle out of the plankton. Many of the wrasses and the black angelfish showed major variations in population density around the islands. Sandager's wrasses were most abundant in relatively sheltered areas with shallow, sandy reefs, such as at Nursery Cove and Labrid Channel. On the other hand, the black angel preferred exposed shores amongst shallow, weed-covered reef 'benches', such as in Bartles Bay, where peak densities occur. By contrast, the leatherjackets showed a very even pattern of distribution, but were more abundant in deeper water.

Such long-term studies show trends of which the casual visitor to a reef could not be aware. A community of fishes is not a static thing and needs to be viewed through time as well as space. Similar patterns of change have been found by scientists on temperate reefs in the Northern Hemisphere, such as California, and on tropical reefs, such as in Queensland and Hawaii. Their studies parallel those at the Poor Knights Islands.

In summation, on all reefs of the world there will be yearly variations in the recruitment of species where larvae have to make long ocean voyages. These larval fishes are subject to unpredictable events that may enhance or decrease their survival as they drift with the plankton: differences in temperature, nutrients, available food, currents, etc. Such variations apply to all species but have a more noticeable effect on uncommon species, or those at the limits of their distribution range.

Recruits are usually very habitat selective. For example, young leather-jackets make for dense kelp thickets. Any change in such habitats may also influence populations through time. If sea urchins graze through an *Ecklonia* kelp bed the fish populations may change as well. And all shallow water reef fishes are subject to the effects of major storms and cyclones.

Viewed through space, there will be large scale changes in reef fish ecology due to geographic factors such as temperature, and small scale changes such as differences in water mass produced by inshore and offshore currents (a major factor at the Poor Knights Islands in relation to the adjacent coast). Around any island or indented coastline there will be habitat differences: kelp forests, rock flats, deep reefs, caused by exposure variations and geology; and variations in microhabitats: seahorses and pipefish are found only amongst the large erect seaweeds.

In considering the ecology of islands such as the Poor Knights, the role of the plankton-feeding fishes is also important. Long-term studies in the area by Michael Kingsford and others showed that plankton feeders such as pink maomao, blue maomao and demoiselles favour the upcurrent side of archways and tunnels such as the Northern Arch. Since such currents are determined by moon and tide, population surveys at regular intervals can produce erratic results. On any one day, a particular archway may be seething with fishes, or may be almost deserted.

Significantly the scientists' work shows that plankton feeders are the most abundant fishes around offshore islands and greatly outnumber bottom feeders and weed eaters. The prevailing current at the Poor Knights flows from the north, bathing the island cliffs in a rich soup of plant and animal plankton. This energises the entire ecosystem, from the encrusting animals to the mobile invertebrates and the fishes; then to the sea birds and, from their droppings, to the forest above and all its inhabitants. By using special nets to sample plankton at the northern and southern ends of the island group, the scientists were able to show that the daytime plankton feeders greatly reduce the density of plankton animals as they pass the islands. Samples taken a kilometre out to sea provided a dramatic demonstration of the effect of these nimble banqueteers. Since these plankton feeders intercept the flow of nutrients and transmit their body wastes to the local community, they, like the seabirds roosting in the forest above, support and enhance the food web, boosting the diversity and richness of the 'wall of mouths': the mobile invertebrates and the reef fishes that depend on these food sources.

Unfortunately, as I write there are indications that certain plankton feeders that use the islands as a dormitory, especially pink maomao and golden snapper, are suffering from recreational fishing pressure. Metal jigs are being used to evade the ban on sinkers. The marine reserve status of the Poor Knights Islands is being severely compromised by the ingenuity of sports fishermen who don't yet understand the drastic effect of their efforts. They assume the fishes they haul up come from some inexhaustible, pelagic 'mother lode'. The reduction in plankton-feeding fishes can only diminish the richness of the whole ecosystem, which most New Zealanders want to protect.

Leigh Marine Reserve surface temperatures: major monthly differences, based on averages over ten years.

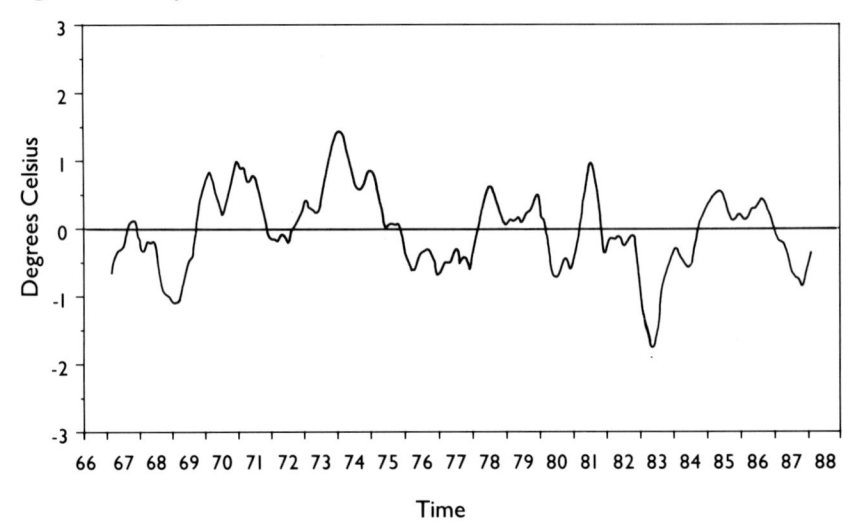

Changes in density of crimson cleaners in Nursery Cove. Note effect of major storm.

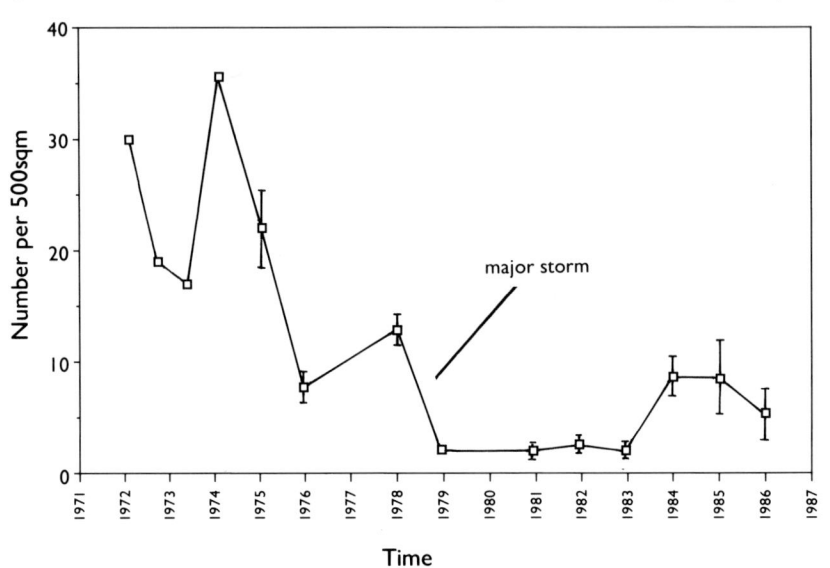

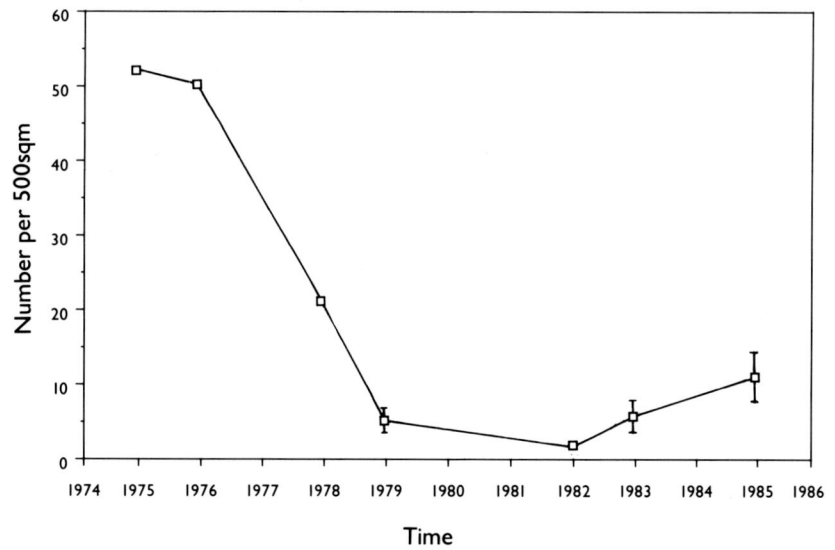

Changes in density of crimson cleaners from a deep-water site (20 m) at Nursery Cove.

Changes in density of orange wrasses at Nursery Cove.

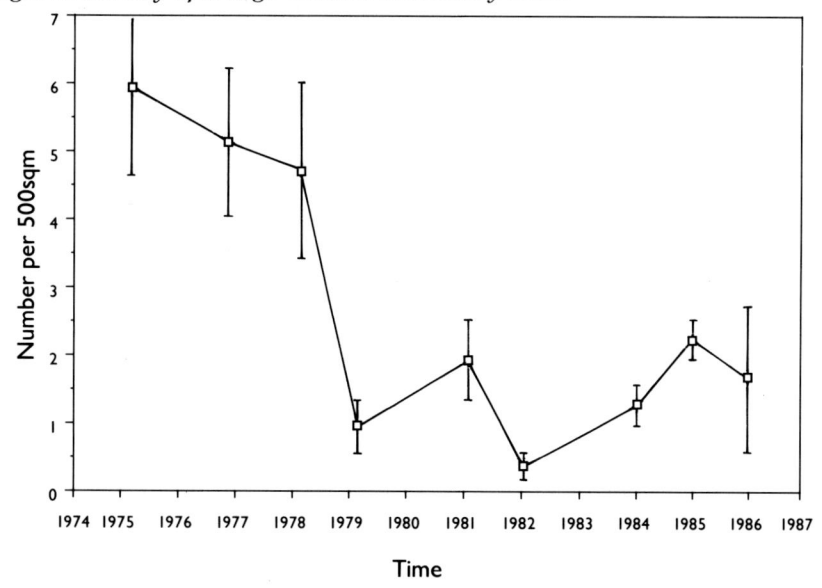

Changes in density of Sandager's wrasses at Nursery Cove. Includes estimates of juveniles.
(Courtesy of Dr A.M. Ayling. Journal Exp. Mar. Biol. Ecol. 1988, Vol. 121: 91–111)

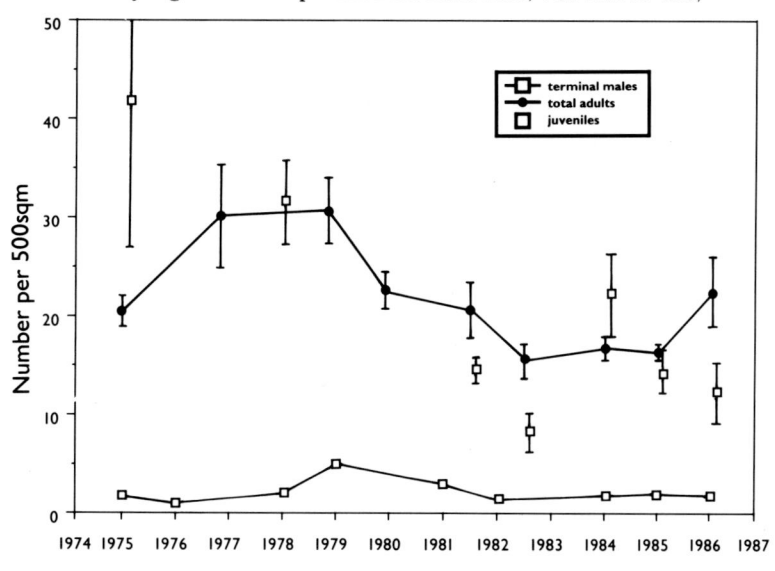

Squirrelfish, tropical relative of New Zealand slender roughy.

Part Three

Reef fishes of tropical waters

Tropical relatives

Clearly it would be impossible to produce a book like this, with detailed descriptions of all the inhabitants of a tropical reef fish community, without running to several volumes. But I hope to show how knowledge of a relatively simple community, such as that of the Poor Knights, can be extended to provide a framework for understanding one of the most complex and ancient societies on our planet.

The key lies in tracing the origin of the fishes I have described so far: almost every one of them has tropical relatives. For me this became clear as I photographed more and more species hitherto unrecorded in the area, and discovered some new to science.

New Zealand is one of the most isolated land masses on earth, and has been for a very long time. As a result, on land there evolved peculiar animals such as the flightless birds — the kiwi and the moa. But in the sea there was much more opportunity for species to arrive from other regions. Only a handful of the fishes of New Zealand waters are endemic — all the rest are expatriates, like *Homo sapiens* himself. Gradually I came to realise I was witnessing the evolutionary process of species radiation and colonisation in action: the way in which tropical fishes have spread into all oceans, either adapting to new habitats or dying off.

During the ice-ages, tropical life forms withdrew to the warmest regions of the earth. Then, as the world warmed again, from the Philippines-Indonesia region, fish species radiated west, across the Indian Ocean to Africa and up into the Red Sea; and east across the Pacific to the coast of the Americas. Before the Central American land-bridge formed, they passed into the Caribbean and the Atlantic. This theory is borne out by the scientists' fish collections. The greatest abundance of species is found in the

Radiating from the Indo-Malayan region, pomacentrid species diminish. Each contour represents a decrease of 20 species (except the last which marks the limit for Indo-West Pacific pomacentrids).

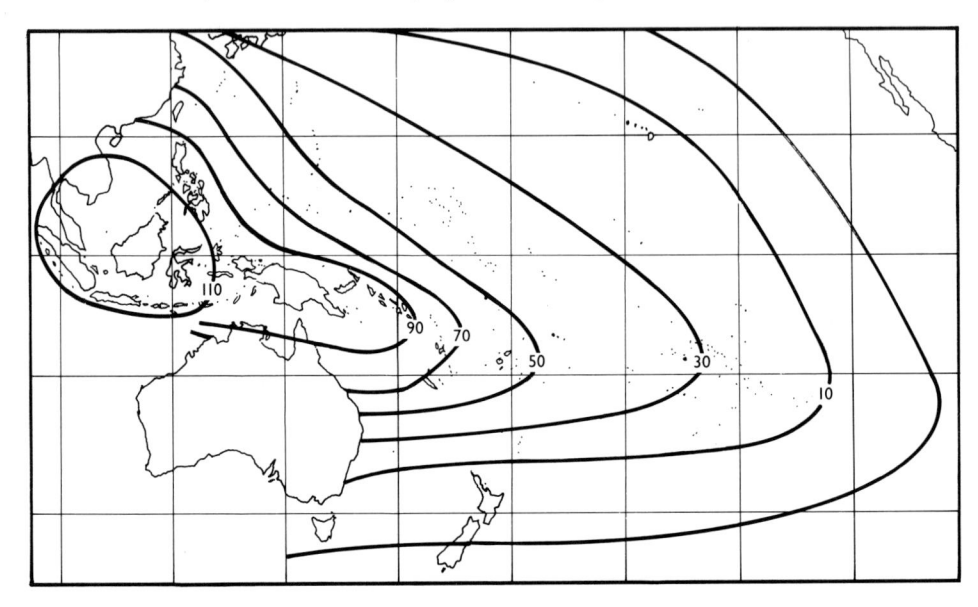

Indo-Malayan archipelago. The farther one travels from there in any direction, the more a progressive fall-off in species diversity occurs.

For one well-studied family, the pomacentrids (damsel fishes, anemone fishes and sergeant majors), Dr Gerald Allen has published, in *Damsel Fishes of the South Seas*, detailed charts of distribution that clearly explain the zoogeography of reef fishes. He has kindly permitted their use here.

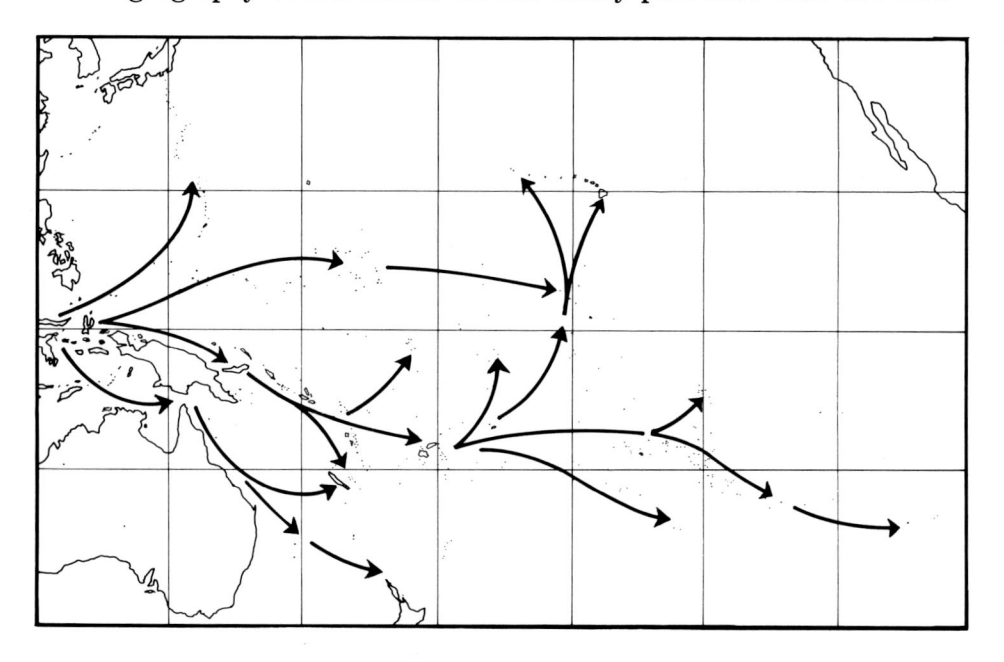

Probable routes of colonisation by pomacentrids in the Western Pacific.

Distribution of pomacentrid species and genera in the South Pacific.
Genera indicated by smaller numbers.
(Courtesy of Dr G.R. Allen, 'Damselfishes of the South Seas', T.F.H. 1975)

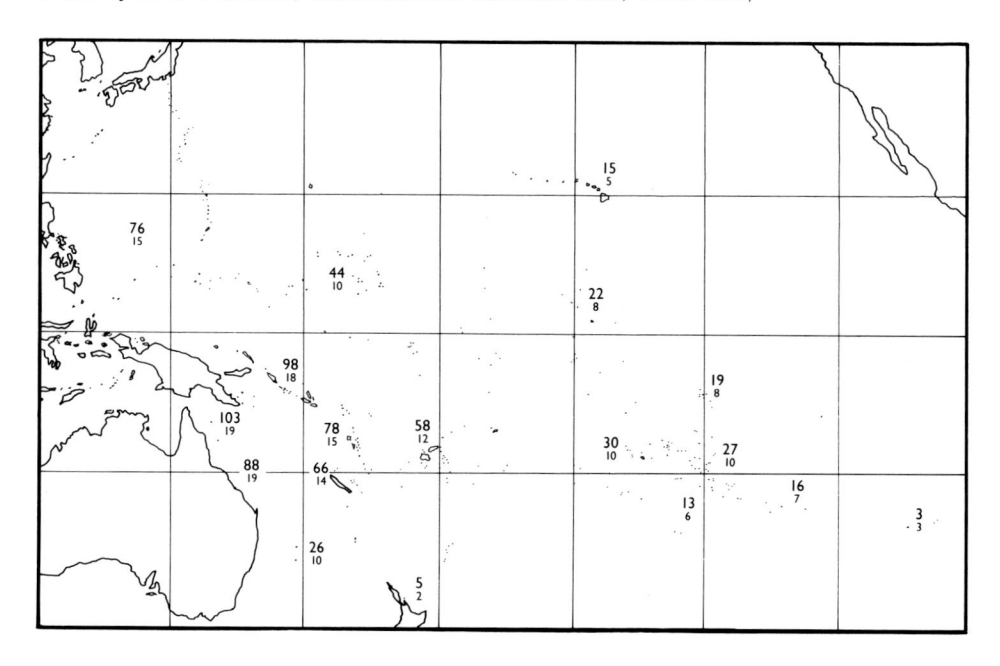

Each time a new fish swam in front of my lens in New Zealand I would first see it as a juvenile. Reef fishes make their random ocean voyages drifting with the plankton in a transparent larval form. Some have a larval life of only a few weeks, while others have extended larval stages and can make long crossings. If within the larval period they should reach a suitable habitat, they settle to the bottom, develop pigmentation, and begin living as a new colony of tiny juveniles.

I was keen to learn more about this process and to establish the possible origins of New Zealand fishes as a component of the world picture now emerging from zoogeographical studies. I also suspected that, with quite a few of our marginal species, the scattered populations are not maintained from local spawnings but are supported from overseas recruitment. I yearned to see the 'mother lode'.

Since the distances from points of origin are very great, there would be a series of stepping stones, such as ocean islands or seamounts, where intermediate colonies are established, spawning and releasing a second or third batch of larval space travellers on their ocean voyage to New Zealand.

In 1972 the opportunity arose for me to join a scientific fish-collecting expedition, funded by the National Geographic Society, to Lord Howe Island. I was overjoyed as Lord Howe was where I suspected so many of our new fishes were originating; 640 km off the New South Wales coast, it is directly up-current from the Poor Knights and has the southernmost coral reef in the world, together with extensive kelp forests — a rare combination.

I had begun diving on coral reefs at the age of 19, when the seething diversity of fishes in the New Caledonian lagoon completely overloaded my senses. There seemed to be no way I could begin to understand them. It was an alien, hostile world of stinging corals, sharks and multiple hidden dangers. At that age and in tune with the times, all my companions and I could think to do was to spear the larger fishes for dinner. Fittingly we all ended up with a severe dose of 'la gratte' — fish poisoning or ciguaterra!

But 13 years later, after serving my apprenticeship learning about all the fishes at the Poor Knights, as well as all the invertebrate world, diving at Lord Howe Island was like entering a library with whose literature I was already familiar. I found I had a mental framework on which to attach new knowledge, much as a child extends its vocabulary. Despite the absolute newness of the location, I felt surprisingly at ease, as appears from this account of my first dive at the Admiralty Rocks: 'To avoid being carried away on the current we went sliding to the seabed down the anchor rope. The underwater scene was among the most beautiful I have ever experienced. The prevailing current produced a luxurious development of exquisite deep-water alcyonarians or soft corals: lobular, water-inflated animal trees like alien triffids, and huge, yellow elephant's ear sponges, waving in the ocean wind. The bottom consisted of masses of rock split with trenches, valleys and caves, everywhere encrusted with plate corals, forests of multi-hued feather stars, tall, black coral trees, swaying gorgonian fans, ruby-red and mauve stylaster corals and a whirlwind of fishes of every size, shape and colour. So many of them already were familiar to me from the scattered individuals that reach the Poor Knights.

'Schools of pelagic fishes and big kingfishes swarmed over the bottom, along with groups of large sweetlip, clusters of yellow-striped boarfishes, and a few reef sharks. Closer to the reef multitudes of small coral fishes darted to and fro nipping at the encrusting life. The unusual richness of this area would be due to the steady, plankton-bearing current. These nourish all the filter-feeding animals encrusting the rocks and support the dense fish population which feeds either directly on the plankton or grazes the filter feeders.'

After my first week diving at Lord Howe I had a good grasp of the reef fishes there. I could assign most species new to me to their appropriate families and guilds, which made it easy to grasp their lifestyles and understand what they were doing. I could see that this was probably one of the most important migrant stations for New Zealand fishes from both the warm temperate New South Wales coasts and the coral reefs of Queensland and New Caledonia. The fishes that kept turning up in New Zealand were, in almost every case, among the most abundant in the Lord Howe lagoon. It seems likely that their spawn provides the recruitment

Striped catfishes in Lord Howe Island lagoon.

Tropical relatives of the Lord Howe coralfish: vagabond butterfly fish and blue-girdled angelfish.

On the crowded coral reef brilliant coloration spaces species apart: semicircle angelfish and blue-spot butterfly fish.

larvae that reach New Zealand in greater or lesser numbers each year, depending on the vagaries of currents and annual fluctuations in water temperatures.

As they establish themselves and become isolated from the parent stock, there may be a tendency for some species to drift genetically from the type of fishes they were in their tropical homes, adapting to a new environment and hence evolving into new species. I saw some evidence of this, too.

The Lord Howe lagoon, intersected with several passes, provides a wide range of habitats that suit quite a diversity of fishes. Being the southernmost coral reef in the world, there is an unusual mixture of both tropical and temperate water species.

In the richest diving area in New Zealand, the Poor Knights Islands, there are about 120 different species. At Lord Howe the list of species known before our expedition was 225, based on a paper published in 1904. Since our efforts and subsequent research, the list now extends to 399 (M. Francis, unpublished paper, 1990). But that is a long way short of the total for a truly tropical reef, where the list would extend to at least 2000!

The following year, I had the opportunity to explore a sequence of tropical reefs extending westward to the Solomons: Fiji, New Caledonia, the Vanuatu group and beyond. The first was Cook Reef, a young atoll in Vanuatu, where I learned an important lesson.

Our vessel was anchored on a pinnacle in clear oceanic water, and I leapt in and swam down the side of a six-storey coral palace. I flew around one flank through a fairground of multi-hued reef fishes and came into a narrow defile which sloped down into deep, dark blue ocean. With perfect weightlessness and no feeling of cold, I just glided like a thought pattern past walls of much richer decor than the most elaborate eastern temple; gorgonian fans of ochre and crimson red, feather stars waving their spiralling plumes and the most delicate and varied array of corals and fishes I have ever seen. Down I glided to where a blue, shadowless world offered a new range of sights. As I flattened out my glide path over the white, sandy bottom at the reef foot, a forest of waving heads withdrew into the sand, a colony of slender, plankton-feeding garden eels. The most timorous and evasive of animals.

Just then a huge Napoleon fish or Maori wrasse glided past, attracted to the carcass of a tuna dropped from our ship. Suddenly a grey shark whipped over the sand and seized the middle of the tuna. The predator's whole body convulsed with waves of energy. It thrashed and twisted, knocking off chunks of coral in showers. The sea went green with blood. A huge armada of dogtooth tuna hovered around, baring their fierce teeth like Alsatian dogs, but not daring to challenge the shark. Some bullet-shaped tropical snappers, called job fishes, whisked through them as close to the carcass as they dared, raising their dorsal fins to reveal a black dot, as a threat gesture. Red snapper gnashed their teeth and several species of grouper moved ponderously around, close to the rocks, gulping with greed. The shark made three violent attacks. A few job fishes zoomed in to snap up scattered morsels as they passed by, then I could see nothing for blood — a dense green fog.

Further down the reef another fight had developed; three grey sharks and a blacktip shark were scrapping over the tuna's severed head and gills. Like seagulls they fought over it, dropped it and snapped it up repeatedly until it was entirely devoured. Near me, only the tattered tail remained. From beneath a coral head a moray eel of enormous girth emerged, fastened its speckled jaws on the tuna tail and began to suck and chew and twist. Within a few minutes an animal with one third my body weight had been demolished, only metres from my camera lens.

The efficiency of all those big predators impressed me deeply. They constitute a major difference between the relatively benign community of fishes at the Poor Knights and the teeming multitudes in the tropics. With the increase in diversity comes a leap in the numbers of fish-eating predators. For me this was a valuable key to understanding the difference between the Poor Knights community and the fishes of a coral reef. I came to see that avoidance of all these predators exerts special pressure on tropical reef fishes, a factor much less apparent in temperate waters. Survival in the coral jungle demands new strategies of defence and concealment.

Eventually our expedition reached the Solomon Islands, and when I dived on an atoll close to the equator I found that the basic pattern of guilds and habitats still exists there. The plankton feeders in the Solomons are mostly tiny fishes, hovering close to the corals on the reef crest. With the abundance of open-water hunters, feeding on plankton becomes a risky business. Scarcely bigger than tropical butterflies, swarms of orange and mauve anthias (barbers — pygmy relatives of the pink maomao) and azure damselfishes (minute replicas of the demoiselle) are all ready to swoop down and hide in the branches of stagshorn coral at the least threat.

Here smallness is a great advantage. So effective are their disruptive black and white stripes that sergeant majors, some as big as demoiselles, are one of the few tropical species brave enough to school in the open. Another is the fast-moving, sardine-shaped fusilier, which feeds in dense schools, mostly at first light.

But most plankton feeding is done under cover of darkness. By day the bright red, huge-eyed soldierfishes and iridescent, twin-dorsal cardinalfishes hover beneath coral heads and within grottoes, as do compact schools of lanternfishes and crimson bullseyes. (Male cardinalfishes incubate fertilised eggs in their mouths, aerating them constantly until they hatch.)

One night-feeder of plankton has solved the problem of prey location in the dark in an amazing and unique way; in fact, it *only* feeds when there is no moon. It relies on surprise tactics to take its prey. On a moonless night in the Solomon Islands, I thought there must be a diver down in the lagoon, as a patchy glare of light darted about in the gloom — but all our crew were on board. Local people told us it was *Bulbulu*, the light-making devilfish. We discovered it was the supposedly rare *Anomalops kaptoptron*, a small, snub-nosed, jet-black fish about 8 cm in length, which moves about in a school. Each fish has a pair of light organs beneath its eyes; they consist of flaps hinged at the base so they can fold upwards, exposing an inner array of luminous, symbiotic bacteria. Used intermittently, these organs provide ample light to surprise tiny planktonic creatures in pitch-black water. To our delight we found that four of them in an aquarium tank emitted enough to illuminate the large print in a newspaper. On moonlit nights the devilfish remains within recesses in the reef: opportunities to feed are surprisingly limited.

By day, the leopard-spotted sweetlips shelter under clumps of coral in compact cohorts, resting until nightfall when they disperse over sandy

Gold-lined sea-bream and blue-banded hussars, Solomon Islands: mixed school of invertebrate browsers' guild that, in the tropics, must await nightfall to feed.

Harlequin sweetlip, Solomon Islands: lips like New Zealand porae.

Anthia, Solomon Islands: tiny, plankton-feeding relative of the New Zealand pink maomao.

Diana's wrasse, Solomon Islands: tropical relative of the New Zealand red pigfish.

areas to glean the bottom, using the 'kiss' technique of the porae to extract food. Tropical snappers are nocturnal, too. By day, bright yellow and blue striped hussars and sea-bream hover in vertically stacked schools, often mingling with the sweetlips at 10–20 m; red snapper in small groups or on their own laze around near the bottom. All are awaiting nightfall to forage out over the reef browsing on invertebrates with their powerful jaws and dog-like teeth. Here and there I see the bottom stalkers. Relatives of the scorpion fish now have much more elaborate defences. Best armed of all is the lionfish; bristling with long, venom-loaded spines it drifts slowly in the open, in wait for small fishes. It has no fear of predators.

Sharp spines and deep incompressible bodies confer equal immunity to all the myriad forms of butterfly fishes, angelfishes and moorish idols. With brilliant advertising colours, false eye spots and eye stripes, they weave amongst their coral garden territories, nipping at polyps and sucking up shrimps with long tube mouths or grazing thin, filmy seaweeds.

Here, camouflage is mainly used for predation. The champion must be the virtually invisible, highly venomous stonefish. The first one I ever sighted was so indistinguishable from the surrounding coral rubble that if I shifted my gaze for a moment, it required a major effort to rediscover its outline. The crocodile fish is another bottom stalker, flattened and patterned to near invisibility. Using the branches of a broad gorgonian fan as a plankton net, the exquisitely camouflaged longnose hawkfish sucks in tiny crustaceans with its pipette-like beak.

Up to a metre long, the tube-like trumpetfish or flute mouth uses the john dory technique to hunt in mid-water, drifting vertically, head down, over the corals. Sometimes it rides over the back of a harmless herbivore, such as a parrotfish, adapting its colour to its mount, so it can get close enough to small, unsuspecting preyfish to vacuum-clean them in.

Clownfishes have a very special defence. These small, plankton-feeding relatives of the New Zealand black angelfish (all are members of the big pomacentrid family), usually in a male/female pair, spend their entire lives amidst the stinging tentacles of sea anemones. The giant polyps can reach more than a metre across, and any fish touching the tentacles is stung to death and thrust into the central maw. No clownfish has ever been found without its symbiotic fortress. A thick, inert coating of mucus on its skin gives protection to the clownfish from the deadly tentacles. In return for such shelter it protects the host from parasites and helps it obtain food.

Often, within the anemone's writhing coils a group of miniature clownfishes may be seen. These timid little fishes were long assumed to be juveniles, but researchers have discovered they are just as old as the 'adults'. Their growth has been suppressed by the dominant fishes, who intervene whenever they attempt to feed, just as the female spotty does to her 'little' sisters in New Zealand. On removal of the dominant fishes, some of the runts will develop rapidly to replace them.

Everywhere over the corals multi-hued wrasses weave in enormous variety, able to hide in a flash if threatened. The largest wrasse of all, the giant, lofty-browed Napoleon fish, can reach 100 kg. Somewhere on the reef it has a favourite hole or tunnel, where it wedges its body so that nothing can extract it.

The tiniest of wrasses are the parasite pickers, such as the blue cleaner wrasse *Labroides dimidiatus*. Very like the combfish in appearance, but much smaller, this cleanerfish is a full-time surgeon. Above its cleaning station it performs a distinctive dance, inviting customers to partake of its services by spreading its tail and seesawing up and down. It seems to be torn between the desire to swim forward and the desire to dive down into the coral. But the cleaner is very rarely attacked and needs no defence other than its guild signal. Fishes queue up for its services.

At Heron Island, on the Great Barrier Reef, Dr Ross Robertson has made a study of this cleanerfish. He found that male *Labroides* control the process of sex change within their social groups. Each harem consists of a male with up to nine females. The death of a male has a startling effect on the dominant female in the harem. Within two hours of liberation from his influence, she starts performing male aggressive displays to other females. She patrols the borders of his territory and shapes up to the rival males next door. Within four days her behaviour is totally male and after 18 days she has become a fully functional male, capable of spawning and releasing sperm. The whole sex change process is under social control, with the harem boss regularly bullying the strongest female, who in turn dominates those beneath her. As long as she remains under his domination her body does not produce the sex change hormone. Once the stress is removed, hormone production is uninhibited and a rapid transition occurs.

Ross Robertson believes that this social system would have genetic advantages. As individuals enter the group and move up the ranks, only the best adapted female reverses sex. The new harem boss, derived from the strongest female, is the best adapted to local conditions and he alone gets to spawn with all the other females, passing on the best genes.

This cleanerfish has a devious mimic, the sabre-toothed blenny, which uses its benign disguise to approach trusting customers and bite off a morsel of skin, much as I have described with the mimic of the oblique-swimming triplefin.

Another group of reef fishes with excellent defences and little need to hide are the triggerfishes, puffers and boxfishes. Many of these have brilliant colour patterns to warn predators they are so deadly. The boxfish can secrete such a virulent toxin, that, when placed in an aquarium tank, all the other fishes turn belly up and die within seconds. As at the Poor Knights, these fishes are mostly invertebrate grazers, but the clown triggerfish is able to snap off the long spines of the tropical urchin with its powerful jaws, until it can smash the shell and devour the contents.

Solitary, night-stalking groupers or 'coral cod' of many kinds hover by day at the entrances to caves and tunnels, with brilliant disruptive patterns of spangled dots, brindled patches, stripes and bars, which they can change with lightning speed to blend with varying backgrounds. The greatest grouper of all, the mighty *Promicrops*, can reach 400 kg and may live for around 100 years. Such a fish has no fear of anything, and is often very curious towards divers.

Out over the coralline sand I see familiar schools of goatfishes of many species: ghostly white and dazzle-patterned or chrome-yellow, some moving in tight formation for safety, some solitary, all dabbling in the sand with their barbels for tasty morsels. Lizard fishes lurk in attack stances, sometimes only the eyes and tip of the snout visible above sand level. At the least threat, pallid, wafer-thin sand wrasses dive into the sand. Amidst the spines of urchins, strange, vertical swimming columns of razorfishes

Devilfish, Solomon Islands: night-time plankton feeder with its own flashlight.

Trumpetfish, Solomon Islands: tropical mid-water hunter, same guild as New Zealand john dory.

Batfish, Solomon Islands: vertical compression taken to the extreme.

Crocodile fish, Solomon Islands: example of horizontal compression, like rays and flounder.

hover, snout down; the fearsome spines offer a secure refuge. If I shift an urchin over the bottom, all its refugees maintain position perfectly.

Above their sand burrows, gobies and gudgeons hover, ready to retreat in a flash. One goby has a very special defence system: it shares its burrow with a shrimp. While the crustacean works tirelessly like a tiny bulldozer, maintaining the burrow, the goby rests on the sand mound by the entrance. The shrimp keeps one long antenna in contact with the fish so that, at any sign of danger, it receives an early warning and both animals dive for cover.

To the visitor from temperate seas, one of the major paradoxes of the coral reef is the prevalence of weed-eating fishes or herbivores. On the coral reef, seaweed hardly seems very significant. Heavily calcified for protection, erect plants grow on the wave-swept reef crest; but otherwise, little plant life is apparent. What we may fail to see is that every non-living surface is constantly sprouting plant material. All the dead coral supports a thin fuzz of fast-growing algae, which herbivores graze before it attains any size. Within the cells of each coral polyp a plant exists. The plant production or algal biomass of a coral reef is very high, so it is understandable that the biggest single group of fishes on a coral reef are the herbivorous parrotfishes. Like the wrasses in form, but with powerful beaks for crushing coral to extract plant material or scrape the algal fuzz from dead coral, brightly coloured territorial parrotfishes usually dominate any reef scene in the sunlit shallows. The biggest, the bumphead, can reach 7 kg. The wastes of parrotfishes contribute in a major way to the production of coral sand.

Up in the surf zone are big schools of fast-moving, herbivorous surgeon fishes (tangs) and unicorn fishes, well defended with retractable, scalpel-like blades which flick out at right angles on either side of the tail, like the knives of Boadicea's chariot. Schools of rabbit fishes of several kinds, all with toxic spines, are also important algal grazers, along with certain damselfishes and butterfly fishes.

When I first contemplate the scene on a coral reef it seems utterly confusing. But with an understanding of the basic guilds a broad pattern soon emerges, which becomes increasingly detailed day by day. First I see the microfauna of anthias and damselfishes dancing around the coral heads; then the metropolis of wrasses and parrotfishes, and the schools of surgeon fishes and rabbit fishes, helter-skeltering over every surface, grazing and nipping at invertebrates and sea plants, along with all the poster-colour butterfly fishes, triggerfishes and puffers.

And then there are all the night-feeding guilds, resting in tight schools near the coral wall or under ledges, in caves and tunnels. These guilds await the cover of darkness to emerge and browse on invertebrates, and to stalk resting fishes or prey on the plankton.

Of course, with the immense variety of fishes on the coral reef, there are endless, oddball surprises. Certain species favour unusual habitats. There is always the unexpected reward for exploring the least likely places. In the rain forest I find a warm tropical stream bejewelled with dainty damselfishes, adapted to living in fresh water. In a turbid harbour a host of exotic, vertical-plan bat fishes (spade fishes) enfold me in their eager, curious midst. Out over the mud I meet a whimsical, most unfish-like cowfish with its rigid, triangular body and weird horns. Over a vast, featureless sandbank in the Bahamas I encounter the most peculiar fish of all — an extraterrestrial invader, the impossibly ugly frog fish.

Boxfish, Solomon Islands: tropical relative of the triggerfish and puffer, exudes toxic substance that can kill attackers.

Clown anemonefish, Solomon Islands: relative of the black angelfish, spends its entire life in the same refuge.

Hawkfish, Solomon Islands: adapted to living on a gorgonian fan which it uses as a fishing net.

Part Four

The learning capacities of reef fishes

How smart are reef fishes?

When considering the ecology of reef fishes it is important not to underestimate their capacity for learning. Not everyone has killed a cow or a sheep for food, but many of us are accustomed to hooking a fish, hauling it from its element, and splitting it open while it is still alive. Science can inform us, but there is no scientific basis for ethics: culturally, we inherit an attitude to the fish which equates it with the worm. We would consider it very cruel to tear a live bird apart, yet in many ways birds and fishes are comparable. If warm blood is our emotional criterion, we might remember that the blood of a tuna is commonly 10°C higher than the water in which it swims. The common attitude towards the fish is a barrier to a true understanding of its mode of life and the complex community in which it lives. (Perhaps things are changing: in 1989 a West German court brought in a successful prosecution, for cruelty to fishes, against commercial operators.)

What do we know about the abilities of fishes from formal research? The relative capacity of different animals for learning is part of the study of ethology or behavioural science. Present-day evidence indicates that learning ability need not be commensurate with an animal's position in the scale of organisation. A hedgehog is not necessarily much more capable of learning than an octopus, yet the octopus is a mollusc, like an oyster. The lobster, a crustacean, belongs to the same phylum as a flea, but obviously far outmatches it in complexity of behaviour, as most divers will attest!

To evaluate its learning achievements, researchers may present an animal with two stimuli side by side, such as a circle and a cross. One object is associated with food, the other with no reward or an electric shock. The positions of the circle and cross are switched at random and the animal learns to choose the reward stimulus. An octopus mastered three tasks and was able to discriminate between six different stimuli. Trout mastered up to six tasks, iguana five, large chickens up to seven and an Indian elephant and a horse, up to 20 tasks (B. Rensch 1962).

It is not just the evolutionary level of a phylum to which an animal belongs which determines its ability to learn, but the demands of its way of life, for which learning may have greater or lesser advantage for natural selection. Grazing and browsing animals, including fishes, are often less versatile than predators, which show more varied behaviour and capacity to learn in accordance with their special needs. The grazing and browsing species are most easily caught in fish traps; whereas some carnivorous species learn to enter and leave a trap at will. Thus there will be some species of fishes for which learning capacity is selectively much more important than for others.

The ability to understand spatial relationships is more easily demonstrated in higher animals, but it has been successfully shown in a species of goby and may exist in many other fishes. The frill fin goby, *Bathygobius soporator*, of California, swims above submerged tide pools at high tide. As the tide recedes, it leaps from pool to pool, always finding the biggest ones to land in. It cannot see where it will land before leaping, yet it does not miss its target and land on the rocks. 'Control' fishes, on the other hand, which have never swum over the area of tide pools at high water, do not know where to jump. This goby can retain its orientation for 40 days.

Memory retention has been tested in many animals: a carp was able to distinguish a circle from a cross after 18½ months; a trout still retained its mastery of a task after 150 days, and a rat after 15 months; an elephant retained 12 or 13 visual discriminations after a year, and a horse retained 19 out of 20. It is 'memory' of stream odours that guides the salmon home to its native stream to spawn after five years at sea.

Blennies, being easily maintained in aquarium conditions, have been the subject of much behavioural research. Blennies and gobies would probably surpass many a reptile in their learning abilities; but fishes do not, in comparison with mammals, easily learn habit reversal. (Habit reversal means mastering a task in which, after learning that one of two stimuli is positive, a previously learnt negative stimulus is reversed to positive and then, when relearned, is reversed once more.) Rats, monkeys and pigeons learn such reversals. After considerable training, the goldfish has been able to transfer a response learned on the basis of olfactory signals to visual clues, and from auditory to thermal clues.

Fishes are easily conditioned — that is, they can learn simple tasks and remember how to attain a reward, such as food — but this ability varies greatly according to the individual and some fishes seem quite unteachable. From comparative tests with rats and fishes, researchers have concluded that the fish tends to perform in a more stereotyped and rigid manner than the mammal. The fishes approached their maze experiments in a plodding, straightforward way; the rat 'gambled' and won. However, there still remains a huge amount to be studied about the intelligence of the more flexible and adaptable reef fishes, those that would be at some disadvantage in a laboratory situation. Knowledge of such creatures can best be obtained from underwater observation and experiment.

One of the most devoted field marine biologists I have met is Dr Tony Ayling. He has spent many hundreds of hours observing the relationship between encrusting communities and reef fishes. Slowly he became aware that many scientists, during their objective studies of fishes and their behaviour, neglect to consider these fishes as other than items to be categorised or patterns to be analysed according to a series of conditioned reflexes. From his intensive underwater observations he was able to build up a picture of a fish's perception of its world, and how an individual's responses increase its chances of survival and reproductive success.

When we dive in the same area consistently we soon notice that certain fishes are always 'at home'. Most reef fishes live in territories which vary in area according to their size. Within its home range it is an advantage for the fish to build up a mental map of all the bottom features. Ayling calls this 'terrain memory' and claims that a fish knows exactly where it is all the time. Should danger threaten, it instantly seeks the best escape route. Each fish knows all the best feeding places within its home range and has a safe dormitory area where it spends the hours of darkness. Memory of all these factors increases its chances of survival. As a fish grows, its terrain memory develops and it ranges over a wider area. But if it is forced to leave its home range it becomes nervous and confused.

This is borne out by two experiments that I assisted in documenting at the Poor Knights, in the days before it became a marine reserve. In the first, a scientist captured and tagged a male Sandager's wrasse; we called it 'Sammy'. It was then transported in a totally enclosed drum from South Harbour to the Sand Garden, a distance of 3 km around the steep flanks of Aorangi. Upon release into a community of fishes similar to its own, all hell broke loose! Naturally a male of his own species chased Sammy. But then, every nest-guarding demoiselle attacked him. Everywhere that Sammy went he was harassed. He even suffered the indignity of being chased away by females of his own kind.

A week later Sammy had disappeared. We assumed that he had died, perhaps over-stressed from constant harassment. To our amazement, when we returned to South Harbour, there was Sammy beside Blue Maomao Archway, exactly where he had been captured. Even more surprising, he came up and rubbed against my hand as a cat would. Somehow, within those seven days Sammy had found his way around the cliff faces, through hundreds of rival territories, to the only place in the sea where he was accepted.

In the second experiment, a large group of wrasses of several kinds was moved from home territory to an area several hundred metres away. To do this, they were enticed into the cockpit of a small wet-submarine. Before releasing them, a bait was placed nearby. In no time all the local wrasses were feasting themselves on this bounty. Now was the time to release the captive strangers and film the locals' response when a host of invaders descended on their feast. To our amazement, when the cockpit canopy was raised, *nothing* happened. The captives hovered on the verge of freedom, then slunk back into the submarine. Not one dared to leave. Repeatedly they came to the exit and paused. Then, one by one, each fish made a helter-skelter dash — but not to join in the alien feeding frenzy. Every one of the prisoners vanished from sight, heading for home ground.

From these experiments it was clear that, besides its terrain memory, each fish could instantly recognise individuals of every species he was likely to encounter during his daily life. From an early age Sammy had to distinguish the harmless goatfish, dabbling in the sand, from the scorpion fish lurking on a nearby rock. A john dory has to learn which fishes are edible and which have stomach-rending spines like the leatherjacket.

Such knowledge has to be learned. Most reef fishes arrive on their home ground after a long journey in larval form amidst the plankton. Rather than inheriting a set of instinctive responses, the young fish inherits a card index mind, capable of storing data about all the features and inhabitants of its world. Tony Ayling's study of the crimson cleanerfish, described earlier, illustrates just how important individual recognition is for reef fishes.

First the biologist learnt to recognise the bar code-type ID system that reef fishes have developed to provide instant identification: he learnt to read their language. Each species displays a special pattern on its side, which varies with individuals — the spots on the spotty, the wedges of colour on the saddle of the Sandager's male, and the complex array of bars and spots around the eye of the goatfish. Just as the human face has variable features which we learn to recognise at a very early age, so it is with the reef fish. Its mind must also store individual behaviour differences. It must know that there is a certain cleanerfish specialising in goatfishes, that lives by a certain rock. Females need to know all the distinctive marks of males, since they have the choice in accepting a mate. And within a society of females there may be a hierarchy or 'pecking order': a social system that relies on instant recognition.

With all the features of its terrain memory and the stored IDs of some 50 to 200 individuals within its daily range, the reef fish needs an accurate, long-term memory. In its mind it carries an awareness of itself and the surrounding world. As Ayling wrote in the foreword of my first fish book: 'If a normal reef fish is intimately familiar with his surroundings and recognises most other individual fishes he comes in contact with, altering his behaviour accordingly, then his day-to-day existence will be a far cry from the tooth and claw struggle that is generally envisioned in nature. Obtaining sufficient food for normal needs is a relatively easy process, occupying only a small proportion of each day for most adult reef fishes. As long as he keeps his distance from the few known predators, the remainder of his time can be spent resting, grooming or in various activities such as territory maintenance and courting that are associated with reproduction.' Over the years a number of anecdotes have come to me from reliable sources, which offer further insights into the capacities of reef fishes and indicate that we have a great deal to learn by entering their world and gaining acceptance.

Two married Floridian scientists kept a coralfish in a home aquarium. The wife always fed it with a sprinkle of fish food on the surface of its tank. When the time came for them to take an extended holiday in New Zealand, they decided to return their fish to the nearby coral reef where it had been captured. Soon it was swimming amidst its kin. Several months later they dived on this reef again. To their astonishment, the coralfish swam over to them. The husband was ignored; but it came right up to his wife and investigated her fingers.

On the Great Barrier Reef a marine scientist had to collect specimens of a certain reef fish for special study. On this stretch of reef the fishes had never been speared and were unafraid of divers. Following the spearing of a number of fish in one small area, the scientist was amazed to find that all along several kilometres of reef, this particular species avoided divers.

A prominent ichthyologist kept an archerfish in an aquarium tank near his breakfast table. Each morning he was accustomed to give it a pinch of fish food. The archerfish is a remarkable species that inhabits tropical mangroves. It is able to knock a fly from an overhanging branch with a jet of water ejected from its mouth. Once the scientist forgot to feed his fish. As he ate breakfast he was surprised to receive a jet of water in his face.

Ever since skindiving began, divers have yearned to soar like eagles, clinging to the back of a huge and harmless manta ray. Consistently the graceful creatures have eluded us — until one day a very special situation arose that provides a unique insight into the capacities of fishes.

In 1981 a film crew of seven was working with Peter Benchley on the majestic El Bajo sea mount in the Sea of Cortez, Mexico. A manta ray was sighted with heavy rope tangled around its head. Gordy Waterman followed it around for an entire dive, trying to remove it. The rope was deeply embedded in the manta's flesh but eventually Gordy managed to get rid of most of it. Later that day Michele Binder was allowed a ride on the manta's back and she removed the rest of the rope.

Perhaps this manta regarded humans as care-givers like cleanerfishes, (which they are known to visit), but thereafter every member of the crew was given a ride. Often they would hang on to a pair of remora fishes that were attached to its back like hand straps. The manta would approach and slow down until a diver grasped its shoulders. It would accelerate, giving the diver a high-speed tour of the sea mount. If a diver released the ray, its wings stopped beating and it would glide slowly as if waiting for him to catch up. Excellent film and photos documented the entire episode.

On this sea mount there were several other manta rays. Within a year a further three of them were giving rides, according to expert cameraman, the late Jack McKenney. But his nine-person team found the one with the two remoras on its back was the easiest. When divers scratched its back it would often stop and flutter its wings. It was decided to attempt removal of the remoras, assuming that they were a nuisance to the host. During the operation the manta stayed perfectly still. When one remora came off, after a struggle, the ray did a U-turn and stopped in front of the divers, as if inviting them to remove the other. Patiently it waited until this was accomplished. During a later ride Jack found he could guide the manta by tugging at its upper jaw when he wanted to ascend. In 25 years of diving, this widely travelled cameraman had never managed to get closer than 10 m to a manta — which would be the usual experience. (Jack's film is called *The Rays of El Bajo*.)

What does the future hold for the creatures in this book and all their relatives along the coasts of our planet? Reef fishes are closely allied with humans in that they share that portion of the continental shelf most affected by the destructiveness of civilisation: pollution, over-exploitation and reclamation. These fishes are vital indicators of the state of health of our oceans, as they are the first to vanish when we desecrate coastal waters.

Major cities are usually located near harbour and river systems, where large areas of water are confined and tidal action is reduced. In such areas industrial wastes, sewage (treated or raw) and heavy run-off from human habitation combine to reduce light penetration drastically. Marine life is then inhibited. Near many cities in the past 20 years, clear oceanic water has been replaced by a turbid, often poisonous brew. Such waters have a low oxygen content because of the presence of dead organic wastes with a high oxygen uptake. Near Tokyo, New York and Los Angeles, such defilement spreads along the coastline, keeping pace with urban sprawl. The first signs can be seen in the harbour areas of Auckland and Sydney. We must heed the lessons learnt from square kilometres of barren sea and lifeless, polluted beaches which may herald the death of the oceans. The diversity and beauty of the reef fishes presented here should be sufficient to recommend their conservation globally and to encourage government-funded research into them. But even for those with a materialistic outlook it is absurdly shortsighted to value only those fishes which support commercial exploitation. All fishes are involved in a complex web of life and none is independent of the others in the quest for food and living space, as competitors or as prey. Aspects of the biology of a commercial species may defy scientific investigation; but another more easily studied species may provide essential clues. The conservation and appreciation of reef fishes should be for both aesthetic and materialistic reasons.

Where else on earth can humans be accepted into such a diverse and complex society of animals, approaching them to within an arm's length? There are certain species which should be registered as living works of art; on a recent trip to the tropics I saw them being collected for home aquarium enthusiasts — a price of 50 cents on their exquisite heads.

Appendix A
The families

About 370 million years ago the first animals with backbones developed in the sea. Today, 48 per cent of all vertebrates are fishes and only 7 per cent are mammals. Six per cent are amphibians, 16 per cent are reptiles, and 23 per cent are birds. Clearly the sea has provided an immense range of ecological niches. The guilds presented in this book are groupings of fishes according to their habitats, but they also have another kind of relationship that goes right back to their ancestors.

If all the early fishes had remained carnivores, they would have been competing with each other for the available food supply. Instead, they met competition by adapting to untapped energy sources and new environments. This tendency of animals to spread into every available niche is called 'adaptive radiation'. (In much the same way, the manufacturer of a successful car design seeks to produce vehicles for every possible road use, from sedans to utilities, vans, trucks and buses.)

But as the members of a new family of fishes adapt to a variety of ecological niches on the reefs, their family resemblances may become obscure. A plankton-feeding fish, such as the blue maomao, needs a different body form from its weed-eating relatives, the drummer and the parore. This often leads to outward resemblances between members of entirely different families. These have evolved from quite separate ancestors, but because they share the same lifestyle, their fins, swimming patterns, head and teeth gradually come to look alike. This is the principle of convergent evolution.

Convergences can be puzzling, because the diver sees a fish like the pink maomao and thinks it must be a relative of the blue maomao. In this case both fishes are plankton feeders. It is hard to believe that the pink maomao is actually a member of the bottom-stalking grouper family that has adapted to a new, open-water lifestyle. Popular names often reflect the layperson's perception of these convergences: so many bottom-stalking fishes are called 'cod'.

Scientists prefer to group fish species according to their ancestral origins, or families. Since this classification system is well understood internationally, it is a valuable method for categorising the vast numbers of fishes on our planet. But I feel the guild groupings offer a more meaningful set of relationships to the non-scientist, as they do to the ecologists who developed them, and so I have chosen to look at the Poor Knights reef fish community in this way. At the same time, the family origins of these fishes deserve attention.

The fishes of our New Zealand-Australian region are part of the Indo-Pacific fish fauna, by far the richest in the world. Extending more than half-way round the globe, from the Red Sea to the Hawaiian and Polynesian islands, and California, the Indo-Pacific region contains representatives of almost all known families of marine fishes. Its many islands and continents provide a great diversity of habitats and it is probable that from this great basin most of the fishes of the world radiated. As new species developed, they extended their ranges far around the world, giving rise to populations that split again and again.

Of the 37 families of fishes represented in this book, 29 have representatives in the Mediterranean, the Atlantic and the Caribbean. The remaining seven (distinguished by an asterisk) are peculiar to the Indo-Pacific region.

For the benefit of readers in other countries, here are the families represented in this book from the Poor Knights Islands, with several of their common names:

Dasitidae: rays
Myliobatidae: mantas
Muraenidae: morays
Congridae: congers
Synodontidae: lizard fishes
Gadidae: cods, beardies
Berycidae: red snappers, alfonsinos
Trachichthyidae: roughies, squirrel-fishes
Zeidae: dories
Scorpaenidae: scorpion fishes, rock cod
Serranidae: sea bass, groupers and perch groupers
Polyprionidae: wreck-fishes, hapuku
Callanthidae: goldies
Gramistidae: soap-fishes
Carangidae: jacks, trevally, pompano, yellow tails, amberjacks
Arripidae*: sea salmon, ruffs
Sparidae: snapper, porgies, dentex, bream
Mullidae: surmullet, goatfishes
Pempheridae: bullseyes, sweepers
Kyphosidae: drummers, rudderfishes, chubs
Chaetodontidae: butterfly fishes, coralfishes
Pentacerotidae*: boarfishes
Pomacentridae: damselfishes, pullers
Chironemidae*: kelpfishes
Aplodactylidae*: marblefishes, sea carp
Cheilodactylidae*: morwongs, hawkfishes
Latridae*: trumpeters
Labridae: wrasses, rainbow-fishes, tuskfishes
Odacidae*: rock whiting, herring cale
Uranoscopidae: stargazers
Blenniidae: blennies
Tripterygiidae: triplefins
Balistidae: triggerfishes, file fishes
Tetraodontidae: pufferfishes, clown toados
Diodontidae: porcupine-fishes
Molidae: sunfishes

A few species from these families have global distribution. On the other hand, a few are endemic to New Zealand waters: an odacid, *Odax pullus*; the mugiloid, *Parapercis colias*; the pomacentrid, *Chromis dispilus*; the tetraodontid, *Parika scaber*, and some triplefins and wrasses.

Appendix B
Dayshift and nightshift guilds

The common belief that fishes are always hungry and seeking to eat is not true. The times when feeding takes place are generally related to the availability at specific times of any one of four types of food supply: encrusting marine life, plankton, mobile invertebrates, or other fishes.

Since the seaweeds, encrusting invertebrates and larger, fixed animals form a source of food which cannot hide, and which can easily be harvested by day, the fishes which feed on this food are largely diurnal. Plankton constantly passes over reef communities, and some fishes are adapted to feeding on this by day; other species replace these fishes at night.

Mobile species of invertebrates, such as crabs, lobsters and shrimps, mostly hide by day and feed by night. They form a rich food supply exploited by many night predators that remain inactive by day. Many small fishes are quiescent at night, seeking refuge in cracks and crevices, and they also provide a valuable food source for the nocturnal predators. Those fish-eating predators that attack plankton-feeding school fish — the kingfish, kahawai and other pelagic fishes — are inactive at night and withdraw to open water.

As soon as the sun gets low on the horizon, there is frenetic activity among the fishes. This is the time for a changeover in shifts and many big predators seem to take advantage of the confusion that then occurs. Diurnal-feeding species, such as the wrasses, butterfish, parore and drummer, leave off feeding and begin to mill about in a general mêlée, which gradually quietens down as the darkness deepens.

With the last rays of light, the Sandager's wrasse dives into the sand, where it buries itself until dawn; spotties hide under ledges and secrete a protective envelope of mucus over their bodies; red pigfish withdraw into the narrowest rocky confines they can find; small snapper shelter quietly in scooped-out sand hollows, their bodies taking on dark vertical stripes. A pufferfish roosts in the branches of a candelabra sponge. Larger snapper may continue to feed on moonlit nights, and it is often possible to approach one resting in a kelp forest and touch it; by day, this sensitive fish is one of the most unapproachable in the sea.

Just before dusk, the marblefish feeds intensively for the second time in the day: at first light and dusk it fills its capacious stomach with seaweed and digests it over the intervening hours. For some time it was hard to discover when the kelpfish fed on its diet of crabs, brittle stars, marine worms and blennies. By day it rests beneath rock ledges, often in groups of varying sizes, and is quite inactive; at night it retreats further under the rocks. By diving at dusk and dawn, it was eventually discovered that the kelpfish takes advantage of the undersea twilight to see and feed on the first crabs and worms that respond to the diminishing light levels and leave their daytime refuges. Once day arrives, its prey withdraws, and at night the kelpfish gives way to the nocturnal fishes which seek the same prey.

At dusk, the plankton-feeding demoiselles, pink maomao and blue maomao descend to the reef. During twilight, they hover in dense swarms beneath ledges and in caves, and as darkness closes in they settle down among the rocks. Their bodies then undergo colour changes: the pink maomao's skin is blotched with white; the demoiselle's twin white dots fade, its colour becomes a midnight blue and its dorsal fin is held erect to maximise its size, just as it does when the fish is acting aggressively. The goatfish nestles beneath the rocks, its skin suffused with a brilliant rosy-coloured pattern. The leatherjacket hovers just above the rocks, its dorsal trigger erect as a protective device.

From beneath ledges and in caves, where they shelter during the day, come the nocturnal predators — the big eyes, roughies and golden snapper — which take over plankton feeding where the other species have left off. In mid-water, roughies, golden snapper and big eye hang motionless, their huge eyes focusing on planktonic prey in the undersea starlight. The morays, congers, scorpion fish and the toadstool grouper stalk the bottom, snapping up crabs and small blennies. Most nocturnal fishes are red in colour and have larger eyes than others. The eels are exceptions, as they rely more on their keen sense of smell to track down prey.

Throughout the night, the daytime plankton feeders rest in every nook and cranny of the reef. While fishes have no eyelids and do not appear to 'sleep', many species become completely inert. I can reach out and stroke a pink maomao, which would be impossible by day; it seems they are in such a state of rest that they do not respond to the vibrations of the diver striking their sensitive lateral line. Other species, such as the blue maomao, the mado and the parore, are inactive at night but remain alert and respond with startled flight at a diver's approach.

Further reading

Marine Reserves for New Zealand, Bill Ballantine. Leigh Laboratory, Leigh, 1991.
Collins Guide to the Sea Fishes of New Zealand, Tony Ayling & Geoff Cox. Collins, Auckland, 1982.
Coastal Fishes of New Zealand, Malcolm Francis. Heinemann Reed, Auckland, 1988.
New Zealand Fishes, Larry Paul. Reed Methuen, Auckland, 1986.

Index of common and scientific names
Poor Knights Islands Fishes

Banded wrasse, *Notolabrus fucicola* 124
Bar-tailed goatfish, *Upeneus* sp. 47, 116
Big eye, *Pempheris adspersus* 72
Black angelfish, *Parma alboscapularis* 78
Black-spot goatfish, *Parupeneus spilurus* 116
Blue-dot triplefin, (undescribed) 177
Blue-eyed triplefin, *Notoclinops segmentatus* 176
Bluefish, *Girella cyanea* 101
Blue-headed wrasse, *Pseudojuloides elongatus* 137
Blue maomao, *Scorpis violaceus* 64
Blue moki, *Latridopsis ciliaris* 92
Butterfish, *Odax pullus* 86
Butterfly perch, *Caesioperca lepidoptera* 56
Combfish, *Coris picta* 146
Conger eel (common), *Conger verreauxi* 165
Crested blenny, *Parablennius laticlavius* 173
Crimson cleanerfish, *Suezichthys aylingi* 152
Elegant wrasse, *Anampses elegans* 135
Demoiselle, *Chromis dispilus* 58
Eagle ray, *Myliobatis tenuicaudatus* 112
Flounder, *Rhombosolea* 110
Flyingfish, *Cypselurus lineatus* 34
Fox fish, *Bodianus* sp. 134
Garden eel, (undescribed) 165
Giant stargazer, *Kathetostoma giganteum* 171
Green wrasse, *Notolabrus inscriptus* 130
Grey moray, *Gymnothorax nubilus* 160
Goatfish, *Upeneichthys lineatus* 114
Golden snapper, *Centroberyx affinis* 70
Goldribbon grouper, *Aulacocephalus temnincki* 183
Halfbanded perch, *Hypoplectrodes* sp. 180
Hapuku, *Polyprion oxygeneios* 187
Jack mackerel, *Trachurus novaezelandiae* 67
John dory, *Zeus faber* 76
Kahawai, *Arripis trutta* 75
Kelpfish, *Chironemus marmoratus* 110
Kingfish, *Seriola lalandi* 74
Koheru, *Decapterus koheru* 67
Leatherjacket, *Parika scaber* 94
Lizard fish (red), *Synodus doaki* 166
Long-finned boarfish, *Zanclistius elevatus* 108
Lord Howe coralfish, *Amphichaetodon howensis* 106
Mado, *Atypichthys latus* 100
Marblefish, *Aplodactylus arctidens* 84
Mimic blenny, *Plagiotremus tapeinosoma* 173
Mosaic moray, *Enchelycore ramosa* 162
Mottled moray, *Gymnothorax prionodon* 159, 162
Mottled triplefin, *Forsterygion malcolmi* 178
Oblique-swimming triplefin, *Obliquichthys maryannae* 179
Orange wrasse, *Pseudolabrus luculentus* 128
Painted moki, *Cheilodactylus ephippium* 91
Parore, *Girella tricuspidata* 84

Pink maomao, *Caprodon longimanus* 50
Porae, *Nemadactylus douglasii* 92
Rainbow fish, *Suezichthys arquatus* 136
Redbanded weaver, *Parapercis binivirgata* 47
Red moki, *Cheilodactylus spectabilis* 88
Red mullet (goatfish), *Upeneichthys lineatus* 114
Red pigfish, *Bodianus vulpinus* 132
Rock cod, *Lotella rhacinus* 170
Sandager's wrasse, *Coris sandageri* 138
Scarlet wrasse, *Pseudolabrus miles* 126
Scorpion fish (northern), *Scorpaena cardinalis* 168
Sharpnosed pufferfish, *Canthigaster callisterna* 98
Silver drummer, *Kyphosus sydneyanus* 85
Single-spot demoiselle, *Chromis hypsilepis* 36
Scalyheaded triplefin, *Karalepis stewarti* 178
Slender roughy, *Optivus elongatus* 71
Snapper, *Chrysophrys auratus* 102
Speckled moray, *Gymnothorax obesus* 162, 164
Spectacled triplefin, *Ruanoho whero* 177
Splendid perch, *Callanthias australis* 55
Spotted black grouper, *Epinephelus daemelii* 184
Spotty, *Notolabrus celidotus* 121
Sting ray (short-tailed), *Dasyatis brevicaudatus* 112
Striped boarfish, *Evistias acutirostris* 35
Sunfish, *Mola mola* 68
Tarakihi, *Nemadactylus macropterus* 104
Trevally, *Pseudocaranx dentex* 66
Toadstool grouper, *Trachypoma macracanthus* 183
Yaldwyn's triplefin, *Notoclinops yaldwyni* 176
Yellowbanded perch, *Acanthistius cinctus* 181
Yellow-black triplefin, *Forsterygion* sp. 175
Yellow moray, *Gymnothorax prasinus* 160

Tropical Reef Fishes

Anthia, *Pseudoanthus* n.sp. 203
Batfish, *Platax pinnatus* 207
Blue-banded hussar, *Lutjanus kasimira* 202
Blue girdled angelfish, *Euxiphipops navarchus* 198
Blue-spot butterfly fish, *Chaetodon plebeius* 199
Boxfish, *Ostracion* 209
Clown anemonefish, *Amphiprion percula* 209
Crocodile fish, *Platycephalus* sp. 207
Devilfish, *Anomalops kaptoptron* 206
Diana's wrasse, *Bodianus diana* 203
Gold-lined sea-bream, *Gnathodentex aurolineatus* 202
Harlequin sweetlip, *Plectorhynchus chaetodontoides* 202
Hawkfish, *Oxycirrhites typus* 210
Semicircle angelfish, *Pomacanthus semicirculatus* 199
Squirrelfish, *Holocentrus spinifer* 192
Striped catfish, *Plotosus* 197
Trumpetfish, *Aulostoma chinensis* 206
Vagabond butterfly fish, *Chaetodon vagabundus* 198

Index of scientific names
Poor Knights Islands Fishes

Acanthistius cinctus 181
Amphichaetodon howensis 106
Anampses elegans 135
Aplodactylus arctidens 84
Arripis trutta 75
Atypichthys latus 100
Aulacocephalus temnincki 183
Bodianus sp. 134
Bodianus vulpinus 132
Caesioperca lepidoptera 56
Callanthias australis 55
Canthigaster callisterna 98
Caprodon longimanus 50
Centroberyx affinis 70
Cheilodactylus ephippium 91
Cheilodactylus spectabilis 88
Chironemus marmoratus 110
Chromis dispilus 58
Chromis hypsilepis 36
Conger verreauxi 165
Coris picta 146
Coris sandageri 138
Chrysophrys auratus 102
Cypselurus lineatus 34
Dasyatis brevicaudatus 112
Decapterus koheru 67
Enchelycore ramosa 162
Epinephelus daemelii 184
Evistias acutirostris 35
Forsterygion malcolmi 178
Forsterygion sp. 175
Girella cyanea 101
Girella tricuspidata 84
Gymnothorax nubilus 160
Gymnothorax obesus 162, 164
Gymnothorax prasinus 160
Gymnothorax prionodon 159, 162
Hypoplectrodes sp. 180
Karalepis stewarti 178
Kathetostoma giganteum 171
Kyphosus sydneyanus 85
Latridopsis ciliaris 92
Lotella rhacinus 170
Mola mola 68
Myliobatis tenuicaudatus 112
Nemadactylus douglasii 92
Nemadactylus macropterus 104
Notoclinops segmentatus 176
Notoclinops yaldwyni 176
Notolabrus celidotus 121
Notolabrus fucicola 124
Notolabrus inscriptus 130
Obliquichthys maryannae 179
Odax pullus 86
Optivus elongatus 71
Parablennius laticlavius 173
Parapercis binivirgata 47
Parika scaber 94
Parma alboscapularis 78
Parupeneus spilurus 116
Pempheris adspersus 72
Plagiotremus tapeinosoma 173
Polyprion oxygeneios 187
Pseudocaranx dentex 66
Pseudojuloides elongatus 137
Pseudolabrus luculentus 128
Pseudolabrus miles 126
Rhombosolea 110
Ruanoho whero 177
Scorpaena cardinalis 168
Scorpis lineolatus 64
Scorpis violaceus 64
Seriola lalandi 74
Suezichthys arquatus 136
Suezichthys aylingi 152
Synodus doaki 166
Trachurus novaezelandiae 67
Trachypoma macracanthus 183
Upeneichthys lineatus 114
Upeneus sp. 47, 116
Zanclistius elevatus 108
Zeus faber 76

Tropical Reef Fishes

Amphriprion percula 209
Anomalops kaptoptron 206
Aulostoma chinensis 206
Bodianus diana 203
Chaetodon plebeius 199
Chaetodon vagabundus 198
Euxiphipops navarchus 198
Gnathodentex aurolineatus 202
Holocentrus spinifer 192
Lutjanus kasimira 202
Ostracion 209
Oxycirrhites typus 210
Platax pinnatus 207
Platycephalus sp. 207
Plectorhynchus chaetodontoides 202
Plotosus 197
Pomacanthus semicirculatus 199
Pseudanthus n. sp. 203